MORE'S HISTORY OF KING RICHARD III

MORE'S HISTORY OF KING RICHARD III

Thomas More

General Books

www.General-Books.net

Publication Data:

Title: More's History of King Richard Iii
Author: More, Thomas, Sir, Saint, 1478-1535
Publisher: Cambridge [Cambridgeshire] : University Press
Publication date: 1883

MORE'S HISTORY OF KING RICHARD III

PREFACE.

The text here printed, from p. i to p. 91, is from the foho edition of Sir Thomas More's Works, London, 1557. The continuation is from the edition of Hardyng's CJironicle, printed by Richard Grafton, 1543, while the additions given in the notes, from Halle's Chronicle, are taken from ' The Unyon of the twoo noble and illustre famelies of Lancastre and Yorke," printed also by Grafton in 15 50. Thus the language of the volume is all of one period.

Sir Thomas More's work was evidently left incomplete. This is shewn by its abrupt termination (see p. 91), and by the many omissions of names and dates which occur in the text, and which in the notes have been supplied from Halle. To this unfinished character of the work we owe many roughnesses of language which on revision and preparation by the author would have disappeared. But this cannot be counted a disadvantage. For we have here many colloquial expressions and some probably provincial usages, of which we should not have had any illustration in the m. ore completed work. The notes it is hoped will be found sufficient for the explanation of all that is peculiar in the language. The narrative is plain enough in itself, though Bacon's History of Henry VII. (Pitt Press Series), especially the early portion, may be read with profit in conjunction with the history and notes of the present volume.

Cambridge, Feb. 1883.

rbarir tl) tljivt t (unfims ftetj) luntm bg i las ter fiomas Jilore tjban oiu of tl) untrcrsfiexifks of Honljon: a= bout the yeare of our Lorde. 1513. Which worke hath htm before tjis tgme printed, m arljj)ng s ronicle, anb in l allps (JTronide: but bery mucbe cortupte m mang places, sometime fiaugng lesse, anti sometime Ja- uing mote, antr alteieb in b crties anti tobole sentences: mucbe barging fro tbe co- pie of im oton banu, bp b3bic tjbgs IS prinlelj.

KYNG RYCHARDE THE THIRDE.

lyNG Edwarde of that name the fowrth, after that I hee hadde lyued fiftie and three yeares, seuen monethes, and sixe dayes, and thereof reygned two and twentye yeres, one moneth, and eighte dayes, dyed at Westmynster the nynth daye of Aprill, the 5 yere of oure redempcion a thowsande foure houndred foure score and three, leauinge muche fayre yssue, that is to witte, Edwarde the Prynce, a thirtene yeare of age: Richarde duke of Yorke, two yeare younger: EHzabeth, whose fortune and grace was after to bee Quene, wife unto kinge Henrie 10 the seuenth, and mother unto the eighth: Cecily not so fortunate as fayre: Brigette, whiche representynge the vertue of her whose name she bare, professed and obserued a rehgious Hfe in Dertforde, an house of close Nunnes: Anne, that was after honourablye maryed unto Thomas, 15 than Lorde Hawarde, and after Earle of Surrey. And Ka-theryne whiche longe tyme tossed in either fortune, somme-time in wealth, ofte in aduersitye, at the laste, if this bee the laste, for yet she lyueth, is by the benignitye of her Ne-phewe, Kinge Henrye the eighte, in verye prosperous estate, 20 and woorthye her birth and vertue.

This noble Prince deceased at his palice of Westminster, and with greate funerall honoure and heauynesse of his people from thence conueyde, was entered at Windesor.

A Kinge of suche gouernaunce and behauioure in time of peace (for in war eche parte muste needes bee others ene-Theioueofthe 1 7) that there was neuer anye Prince of this people. lande, attaynynge the Crowne by battayle, so 5 heartely beloued with the substaunce of the people; nor he hymselfe so speciallye in anye parte of his Hfe, as at the time of his death. VVhiche fauour and affeccion yet after his decease, by the crueltie, mischiefe, and trouble of the tempestious worlde that folowed, highelye towarde hym 10 more increased. At suche time as he died, the displeasure of those that bare him grudge, for kinge Henries sake the sixte, whome he deposed, was well asswaged, and in effecte quenched, in that that man ye of them were dead in more then twentie yeares of his raigne, a great parte of a longe 15 lyfe. And many of them in the meane season growen into his fauoure, of whiche he was neuer straunge.

Descripcion of j-n 1

Edwarde the He was a goodly parsonage, and very Prmcely to behold, of hearte couragious, politique in counsaile, in aduersitie nothynge abashed, in prosperitie 20 rather joyfull then prowde, in peace juste and mercifull, in warre sharpe and fyerce, in the fielde bolde and hardye, and nathelesse no farther then wysedome woulde aduen-turouse. Whose warres who so well consyder, hee shall no lesse commende hys wysedome where hee voyded, than 25 hys mannehoode where he vainquisshed. He was of visage louelye, of bodye myghtie, stronge, and cleane made: howe bee it in his latter dayes, wyth ouer liberall dyet, sommewhat corpulente and boorelye, and nathelesse not vncomelye; hee was of youthe greatlye geuen to fleshlye wantonnesse, from 30 whiche healthe of bodye, in great prosperitye and fortune, wythoute a specyall grace hardelye refrayneth. Thys faute not greatlye gryeued the people: for neyther could any one mans pleasure stretch and extende to the dyspleasure of verye manye, and was wythoute violence, and ouer that in hys latter dayes lessyd and wel lefte. In whych tyme of hys latter daies thys Realm was in quyet and prosperous estate: no feare of outewarde enemyes, no warre in hande, nor none towarde, but such as no manne looked for; the 5 people towarde the Prince, not in a constrayned feare, but in a wyllynge and louynge obedyence: amonge them selfe, the commons in good peace. The Lordes whome he knewe at varyaunce, hymselfe in hys deathe bedde appeased. He hadde lefte all gatherynge of money (which is the onelye 10 thynge that withdraweth the heartes of Englyshmenne fro the Prynce) nor anye thynge entended hee to take in hande, by which hee shoulde bee dryeuen theretoo, for hys trybute oute of Fraunce hee hadde before ob-tayned. And the yere foregoynge hys deathe ' 15 hee hadde obtayned Barwycke. And al bee it that all the tyme of hys raygne hee was wyth hys people soo benygne, courteyse, and so familyer, that no parte of hys vertues was more estemed; yet that condicyon in the ende of hys dayes (in which many princes, by a long continued souerainty, 20 decline in to a prowde porte from debonayre behauioure of theyr beginning) meruaylouslye in him grewe and increased; so farrefoorthe that in the sommer the laste that euer he savve, hys hyghenesse beeyng at Wyndesore in huntynge, sente for the Mayre and Aldermenne of London to hym. 25 For none other eraunde, but too haue them hunte and bee mery with hym, where hee made them not so statelye, but so frendely and so familier chere, and sente venson from thence so frelye into the Citye, that no one thing, in many dayes before, gate hym eyther moe heartes or more heartie 30 fauoure amonge the common people, whiche oftentymes more esteme and take for greatter kindenesse a lyttle cour-tesye, then a greate benefyte.

So deceased (as I haue said) this noble Kynge, in that tyme in whiche hys life was moste desyred. Whose loue of hys people, and theyr entiere affeccion towarde him, hadde bene to hys noble children (hauynge in themselfe 5 also as manye gyftes of nature, as manie Princely vertues, as muche goodlye tovvardenesse as theire age coulde receiue) a meruailouse forteresse and sure armoure, if deuision and discencion of their frendes hadde not vnarmed them, and lefte them destitu t e, and the execrable desire of souerayntee 10 prouoked him to theire destruccion, which yf either kinde or kindenesse hadde holden place, muste needes haue bene theire chiefe defence. For Richarde the Duke of Gloucester, by nature theyr vncle, by office theire protectoure, to theire father beholden, to them selfe by othe and allegy- 15 aunce bownden, al the bandes broken that binden manne and manne together, withoute anye respecte of Godde or the worlde, vnnaturallye contriued to bereue them, not onelye their dignitie, but also their lines. But forasmuche as this Dukes demeanoure ministreth in efifecte all the 20 whole matter whereof this booke shall entreate, it is therefore conueniente, sommewhat to shewe you ere we farther goe, what maner of manne this was, that coulde fynde in his hearte so muche mischiefe totfconceiue.

Richarde Duke of Yorke, a noble manne and a mightie,

"S Richard Duke beganuc uot by warre, but by lawe, to challenge of Yorke. crown, puttyug his claime into the parlia- mente. Where hys cause was eyther for right or fauour so farrefoorth auaunced, that kinge Henrye his bloode (all bee it he hadde a goodlye Prince) vtterlye rejected, the crowne 30 was by authoritye of parliament entaylled vnto the Duke of York and his issue male in remainder immediatelye after the deathe of Kinge Henrye. But the Duke not endurynge so longe to tarye, but entending vnder pretexte of discencion and debate arisynge in the realme, to preuente his time, and to take vppon hym the rule in Kinge Harry his Hfe, was with manye nobles of the realme at Wakefielde slaine, leauinge three sonnes, Edwarde, George and Rycharde. Al three as they wer great states of birthe, soo were they 5 greate and statelye of stomacke, gredye and ambicious of authoritie, and impacient of parteners. Ed- .,.!-,-,,1. T 1. Edwarde.

ward, reuengmg his fathers death, deprmed knig Henrie, and attained the crown. George Duke of Clarence was a goodly noble Prince, and at all pointes George Duke fortunate, if either his owne ambicion had not of ' ence. set him against his brother, or the enuie of his enemies his brother agaynste hym. For were it by the Queene and the Lordes of her bloode whiche highlye maligned the kynges kinred (as women commonly not of malice but of nature 15 hate them whome theire housebandes loue) or were it a prowde appetite of the Duke himself entendinge to be king, at the lest wise heinous Treason was there layde to his charge, and finallye, wer hee fautye were hee faultlesse, attainted was hee by parliament and judged to the death, 20 and therupon hastely drouned in a Butte of Malmesey, whose death kyng Edwarde (albeit he commaunded it) when he wist it was done, pitiously bewailed and sorow-fully repented.

Richarde the third sonne, of whom we nowe entreate, 25 was in witte and courage egall with either of them, in bodye and prowesse farre vnder them cionofrich-bothe, little of stature, ill fetured of limmes, croke backed, his left shoulder much higher then his right, hard fauoured of visage, and suche as is in states called 30 warlye, in other menne otherwise, he was malicious, wrath-full, enuious and, from afore his birth, euer frowarde. It is for trouth reported, that the Duches his mother had muche adoe in her trauaile, and that hee came into the worlde with the feete forwarde, as menne bee borne out-warde, and (as the fame runneth) also not vntothed, whither menne of hatred reporte aboue the trouthe, or 5 elles that nature chaunged her course in hys beginninge, whiche in the course of his lyfe many thinges vnnaturallye committed. None euill captaine was hee in the warre, as to whiche his disposicion was more metely then for peace. Sundrye victories hadde hee, and sommetime ouerthrowes, 10 but neuer in defaulte, as for his owne parsone, either of har-dinesse or poly tike order; free was hee called of dyspence, and sommewhat aboue hys power liberall, with large giftes hee get him vnstedfaste frendeshippe, for whiche hee was fain to pil and spoyle in other places, and get him stedfast ir hatred. He was close and secrete, a deepe dissimuler, lowlye of counteynaunce, arrogant of heart, outwardly coumpinable where he inwardely hated, not letting to kisse whome hee thoughte to kyll; dispitious and cruell, not for euill will alway, but ofter for ambicion, and either for the 20 suretie or encrease of his estate. Frende and foo was muche what indifferent, where his aduauntage grew, he spared no mans deathe, whose life withstoode his purpose.

He slewe with his owne handes king Henry

The death of., rr king Henry the sixt, bcmg prisoncr m the 1 ower, as menne constantly saye, and that without commaunde- mente or knoweledge of the king, whiche woulde vndoubt- ' edly, yf he had entended that thinge, haue appointed that boocherly office, to some other then his owne borne brother.

Somme wise menne also weene, that his drifte couertly

Q conuayde, lacked not in helping furth his brother Clarence to his death: whiche hee resisted openly, howbeit somwhat (as menne demed). more faintly then he that wer hartely minded to his welth. And they that thus deme, think that he long time in king Edwardes life forethought to be king in case that the king his brother (whose life hee looked that euil dyete shoulde shorten) shoulde happen to decease (as in dede he did) while his children wer yonge. And thei deme, that for thys intente he was gladde of his brothers 5 death the Duke of Clarence, whose life must needes haue hindered hym so entendynge, whither the same Duke of Clarence hadde kepte him true to his nephew the yonge king, or enterprised to be kyng himselfe. But of al this pointe is there no certaintie, and whoso diuineth vppon lo conjectures maye as wel shote to farre as to short. How-beit this haue I by credible informacion learned, that the selfe nighte in whiche kynge Edwarde died, one Mystle-brooke longe ere mornynge came in greate haste to the house of one Pottyer dwellyng in Reddecrosse strete without 15 Crepulgate; and when he was with hastye rappyng quickly letten in, hee shewed vnto Pottyer that kynge Edwarde was departed. By my trouthe, manne, quod Pettier, then wyll my mayster the Duke of Gloucester bee kynge. What cause hee hadde soo to thynke harde it is to saye, 20 whyther hee, being toward him, anye thynge knewe that hee suche thynge purposed, or otherwyse had anye inke-lynge thereof: for hee was not likelye to speake it of noughte.

But nowe to returne to the course of this hystorye, were 25 it that the duke of Gloucester hadde of olde foreminded this conclusion, or was nowe at erste thereunto moued, and putte in hope by the occasion of the tender age of the younge Princes his Nephues (as opportunitye and lykely-hoode of spede putteth a manne in courage of that hee 30 neuer entended) certayn is it that hee contriued theyr destruccion, with the vsurpacion of the regal dignitye vppon hymselfe. And for as muche as hee well wiste and holpe to mayntayn a long continued grudge and hearte bren-nynge betwene the Quenes kinred and the kinges blood, eyther partye enuying others authoritye, he nowe thought that their deuision shoulde bee (as it was in dede) a for-5 therlye begynnynge to the pursuite of his intente, and a sure ground for the foundacion of al his building yf he might firste, vnder the pretext of reuengynge of olde displeasure, abuse the anger and ygnoraunce of the tone partie, to the destruccion of the tother: and then wynne to lo his purpose as manye as he coulde: and those that coulde not bee wonne, myght be loste ere they looked therefore. For of one thynge was hee certayne, that if his entente were perceiued, he shold soone haue made peace beetwene the bothe parties, with his owne bloude.

15 Kynge Edwarde in his life, albeit that this discencion beetwene hys frendes sommewhat yrked hym, yet in his good health he sommewhat the lesse regarded it, because hee thought whatsoeuer busines shoulde falle betwene them, hymselfe should alwaye bee hable to rule bothe the partyes.

20 But in his laste sickenesse, when hee perceiued his naturall strengthe soo sore enfebled, that hee dyspayred all recouerye, then hee consyderynge the youthe of his chyldren, albeit hee nothynge lesse mistrusted then that that happened, yet well foreseynge that manye harmes myghte growe by theyr de- 25 bate, whyle the youth of hys children shoulde lacke discrecion of themself and good counsayle of their frendes, of whiche either party shold counsayle for their owne commodity and rather by pleasaunte aduyse too wynne themselfe fauour, then by profitable aduertisemente to do the children good, 30 he called some of them before him that were at variaunce, and in especyall the Lorde Marques Dorsette, the Quenes Sonne by her fyrste housebande, and Richarde the Lorde Hastynges, a noble man, than lorde chaumberlayne, agayne whome the Quene specially grudged, for the great fauoure the kyng bare hym, and also for that shee thoughte hym secretelye familyer with the kynge in wanton coumpanye. Her kynred also bare hym sore, as well for that the kynge hadde made hym captayne of Calyce (whiche office the 5 Lorde Ryuers, brother to the Quene, claimed of the kinges former promyse) as for diuerse other greate giftes whiche hee receyued, that they loked for. When these lordes with diuerse other of bothe the parties were comme in presence, the kynge liftinge vppe himselfe and vndersette 10 with pillowes, as it is reported on this wyse sayd vnto them. My Lordes, my dere kinsmenne and alies,, ', The oracion of in what pliarhte I lye you see, and I feele. By the kynge in ,, T ', 1., his death bed.

whiche the lesse whyle I look to lyue with you, the more depelye am I moued to care in what case I 15 leaue you, for such as I leaue you, suche bee my children lyke to fynde you. Whiche if they shoulde (that Godde forbydde) fynde you at varyaunce, myght happe to fall themselfe at warre ere their discrecion woulde serue to sette you at peace. Ye se their youthe, of whiche I recken the onely suretie to 20 reste in youre concord. For it suffiseth not that al you loue them, yf eche of you hate other. If they wer menne, your faithfulnesse happelye woulde suffise. But childehood must bee maintained by mens authoritye, and slipper youth vnderpropped with elder counsayle, which neither they can 25 haue, but ye geue it, nor ye geue it, yf ye gree not. For wher eche laboureth to breake that the other maketh and, for hatred of ech of others parson, impugneth eche others counsayle, there must it nedes bee long ere anye good conclusion goe forwarde. And also while either partye 30 laboureth to bee chiefe, flattery shall haue more place then plaine and faithfull aduyse, of whyche muste needes ensue the euyll bringing vppe of the Prynce, whose mynd, in lo THE HISTORIE OF tender youth infect, shal redily fal to mischief and riot, and drawe down with this noble realme to ruine, but if grace turn him to wisdom: which if God send, then thei that by euill menes before pleased him best, shal after 5 fall farthest out of fauour, so that euer at length euil driftes dreue to nought, and good plain wayes prosper. Great variaunce hath ther long bene betwene you, not alway for great causes. Some time a thing right wel intended our misconstruccion turneth vnto worse, or a smal displeasure lo done vs, eyther our owne affeccion or euil tongues a-greueth. But this wote I well ye neuer had so great cause of hatred, as ye haue of loue. That we be al men, that we be christen men, this shall I leaue for prechers to tel you (and yet I wote nere whither any preachers woordes 15 ought more to moue you, then his that is by and by gooyng to the place that thei all preache of). But this shal I desire you to remember, that the one parte of you is of my bloode, the other of myne alies, and eche of yow with other, eyther of kinred or affinitie, whiche spirytuall kynred 20 of affynyty, if the sacramentes of Christes Churche beare that weyghte with vs that woulde Godde thei did, shoulde no lesse moue vs to charitye, then the respecte of fleshlye consanguinitye. Oure Lorde forbydde that you loue together the worse, for the selfe cause that you ought to 25 loue the better. And yet that happeneth. And no where fynde wee so deadlye debate, as amonge them whyche by nature and lawe moste oughte to agree together. Suche a pestilente serpente is ambicion and desyre of

Ambicion. 1 i vameglorye and soueramtye, whicne amonge 30 states where he once entreth crepeth foorth so farre, tyll with deuision and variaunce hee turneth all to mischiefe. Firste longing to be nexte the best, afterwarde egall with the beste, and at laste chiefe and aboue the beste. Of which immode- rate appetite of woorship, and thereby of debate and dissen-cion what losse, what sorowe, what trouble hathe within these i(t Nt yeares growen in this reahne, I praye Godde as well forgeate as wee well remember. Whiche thinges yf I collide as well haue foresene, as I haue with my more payne 5 then pleasure proued, by Goddes blessed Ladie (that was euer his othe) I woulde neuer haue won the courtesye of mennes knees, with the losse of soo many heades. But sithen thynges passed cannot be gaine-called, muche oughte wee the more beware, by what occasion we haue 10 taken soo greate hurte afore, that we eftesoones fall not ' in that occasion agayne. Nowe be those griefes passed, and all; s (Godde bee thanked) quiete, and likelie righte wel to prosper in wealthfuu peace vnder youre coseyns my children, if Godde sende them life and you loue. 15 Of whyche twoo thinges the lesse losse wer they, by whome thoughe Godde dydde hys pleasure, yet shoulde the Realme alway finde kinges and paraduenture as good kinges. But yf you among youre selfe in a childes reygne fall at debate, many a good man shal perish and happely 20 he to, and ye to, ere thys land finde peace again. Wher-fore in these last wordes that euer I looke to speake with you, I exhort you and require you all, for the loue that you haue euer borne to me, for the loue that I haue euer born to you, for the loue that our Lord 35 beareth to vs all, from this time forwarde, all grieues forgotten, eche of you loue other. Whiche I verelye truste you will, if ye any thing earthly regard, either Godde or your king, affi. nitie or kinred, this realme, your owne countrey, or your owne surety.

And therewithal the king no longer enduring to sitte vp, 30 laide him down on his right side, his face towarde them: and none was there present that coulde refraine from weping.

But the lordes recomforting him with as good wordes as they could, and answering for the time as thei thought to stand with his pleasure, there in his presence (as by their wordes appered) ech forgaue other, and joyned their hands 5 together, when (as it after appeared by their dedes) their herts wer far asonder. As sone as the king was departed, the noble prince his sonne drew toward London, which at the time of his decease, kept his houshold at Ludlow in Wales. Which countrey being far of from the law 10 and recourse to justice, was begon to be farre oute of good wyll and waxen wild, robbers and riuers walking at libertie vncorrected. And for this encheason the prince was in the life of his father sente thither, to the end that the authoritie of his presence should refraine euil dis- 15 posed parsons fro the boldnes of their formar outerages.

To the gouernaunce and ordering of this yong prince at his sending thyther, was there appointed sir Antony Woduile

Lord Riuers and brother vnto the Queue, a right honourable man, as valiaunte of hande as poli- 20 tike in counsayle. Adjoyned wer there vnto him other of the same partie, and in effect euery one as he was nerest of kin vnto the Queue, so was planted next about the prince. That drifte by the Queue not vnwisely deuised, whereby her bloode mighte of youth be rooted in the princes fauor, the 25 Duke of Gloucester turned vnto their destruccion, and vpon that grounde set the foundacion of all his vnhappy building. For whom soeuer he perceiued either at variance with them, or bearing himself their fauor, hee brake vnto them, some by mouth, som by writing and secret messengers, 30 that it neyther was reason nor in any wise to be suffered, that the yong king, their master and kinsmanne, shoold bee in the handes and custodye of his mothers kinred, sequestred in maner from theyr compani and attendance, of which eueri one ought him as faithful semice as they, and manye of them far more honorable part of kin then his mothers side; whose blood (quod he) sauing the kinges pleasure, was ful vnmetely to be matched with his; whiche nowe to be as who say remoued from the kyng, and the 5 lesse noble to be left aboute him, is (quod he) neither honorable to hys magestie, nor vnto vs, and also to his grace no surety, to haue the mightiest of his frendes from him, and vnto vs no litle jeopardy, to suffer our wel proued euil willers to grow in ouer gret authoritie with the prince 10 in youth, namely which is lighte of beliefe and sone per-swaded. Ye remember, I trow, king Edward himself, albeit he was a manne of age and of discrecion, yet was he in manye thynges ruled by the bende, more then stode either with his honour, or our profite, or with the commo- 15 ditie of any manne els, except onely the immoderate aduauncement of them selfe. Whiche whither they sorer thirsted after their own weale, or our woe, it wer hard I wene to gesse. And if some folkes frendship had not holden better place with the king, then any respect of 20 kinred, thei might peraduenture easily haue betrapped and brought to confusion somme of vs ere this. Why not as easily as they haue done some other alreadye, as neere of his royal bloode as we? But our Lord hath wrought his wil, and thanke be to his grace that peril is paste. Howe 25 be it as great is growing, yf wee suffer this yonge kyng in oure enemyes hande, whiche without his wyttyng, might abuse the name of his commaundement, to ani of our vndoing, which thyng God and good prouision forbyd. Of which good prouision none of vs hath any thing the lesse 30 nede, for the late made attonemente, in whyche the kinges pleasure hadde more place then the parties willes. Nor none of vs I beleue is so vnwyse, ouersone to truste a newe frende made of an olde foe, or to think that an houerly kindnes, sodainely contract in one houre, continued yet scant a fortnight, shold be deper setled in their stomackes then a long accustomed malice many yeres 5 rooted.

With these wordes and vvritynges and suche other, the Duke of Gloucester sone set afyre them that were of them-self ethe to kindle, and in especiall twayne, Edwarde Duke of Buckingham, and Richarde Lorde Hastinges and chaum- 10 berlayn, both men of honour and of great power. The tone by longe succession from his ancestrie, the tother by his office and the kinges fauor. These two, not bearing eche to other so muche loue, as hatred bothe vnto the Quenes parte, in this poynte accorded together wyth the Duke of Glou- 15 cester, that they wolde vtterlye amoue fro the kynges com-panye all his mothers frendes, vnder the name of their enemyes. Upon this concluded, the Duke of Gloucester vnderstandyng that the Lordes whiche at that tyme were aboute the kyng entended to bryng him vppe to his Coro- 20 nacion, accoumpanied with suche power of theyr frendes, that it shoulde bee harde for him to brynge his purpose to passe, without the gathering and great assemble of people and in maner of open warre, wherof the ende he wiste was doubtuous, and in which the kyng being on their side, his 25 part should haue the face and name of a rebellion; he secretly therefore, by diners meanes, caused the Quene to be perswaded and brought in the mynd, that it neither wer nede, and also shold be jeopardous, the king to come vp strong. For where as nowe euery lorde loued other, and 30 none other thing studyed vppon, but aboute the Coronacion and honoure of the king; if the lordes of her kinred shold assemble in the kinges name muche people, thei should geue the lordes, atwixte whome and them hadde bene sommetyme debate, to feare and suspecte, leste they shoulde gather thys people, not for the kynges sauegarde,-whome no manne enpugned, but for theyr destruccion, hauyng more regarde to their olde variaimce, then their newe attonement. For whiche cause thei shoulde assemble 5 on the other partie muche people agayne for their defence, whose power she wyste wel farre stretched. And thus should all the realme fall on a rore. And of al the hurte that therof should ensue, which was likely not to be litle, and the most harme there like to fal wher she lest would, 10 all the worlde woulde put her and her kinred in the wyght, and say that thei had vnwyselye, and vntrewlye also, broken the amitie and peace that the kyng her husband so pru-dentelye made bet wen e hys kinne and hers in his deathbed, and whiche the other party faithfully obserued. 15

The Quene being in this wise perswaded, suche woorde sente unto her sonne, and vnto her brother being aboute the kynge, and ouer that the Duke of Gloucester hym-selfe, and other Lordes the chiefe of hys bende, wrote vnto the kynge soo reuerentelye, and to the Queenes frendes there 20 soo louyngelye, that they nothynge earthelye mys-trustynge, broughte the Kynge vppe in greate haste, not in good speede, with a sober coumpanye. Nowe was the king in his waye to London gone from Northampton, when these Dukes of Gloucester and Buckyngham came thither. 25 Where remained behynd, the Lorde Ryuers, the Kynges vncle, entendyng on the morowe to folow the Kynge, and bee with hym at Stonye Stratford miles thence, earely or hee departed. So was there made that nyghte muche frendely chere betwene these Dukes and the Lorde Riuers 30 a greate while. But incontinente after that they were oppenlye with greate courtesye departed, and the Lorde Riuers lodged, the Dukes secretelye, with a fewe of their moste priuye frendes, sette them downe in counsayle, wherin they spent a great parte of the nyght. And at their risinge in the dawnyng of the day, thei sent about priuily to their seruantes in their Innes and lodgynges about, 5 geuinge them commaundemente to make them selfe shortely readye, for their Lordes wer to horsebackward. Uppon whiche messages, many of their folke were attendaunt, when manye of the lorde Riuers seruantes were vnreadye. Nowe hadde these Dukes taken also into their custodye the 10 kayes of the Inne, that none shoulde passe foorth without theyr Hcence. And ouer this in the hyghe way towarde Stonye Stratforde where the Kynge laye, they hadde bee-stowed certayne of theyr folke, that shoulde sende backe agayne, and compell to retourne, anye manne that were 15 gotten oute of Northampton toward Stonye Stratforde, tyll they should geue other lycence. For as muche as the Dukes themselfe entended, for the shewe of theire dyly-gence, to bee the fyrste that shoulde that daye attende vppon the Kynges highnesse oute of that towne; thus bare 20 they folke in hande. But w hen the Lorde Ryuers vnder-stode the gates closed, and the wayes on euerye side besette, neyther hys seruauntes nor hymself suffered to gone oute, parceiuyng well so greate a thyng without his knowledge not begun for noughte, comparyng this maner present with 25 this last nightes chere, in so few houres so gret a chaunge marueylouslye misliked. How be it sithe hee coulde not geat awaye, and keepe himselfe close hee woulde not, leste hee shoulde seeme to hyde him selfe for some secret feare of hys owne faulte, whereof he saw no such cause 30 in hym self; he determined vppon the suretie of his own conscience, to goe boldelye to them, and inquire what thys matter myghte meane. Whome as soone as they sawe, they beganne to quarell with hym, and saye that hee intended to sette distaunce beetwene the Kynge and them, and to brynge them to confusion, but it shoulde not lye in hys power. And when hee beganne (as bee was a very well spoken manne,) in goodly wise to excuse himself, they taryed not the ende of his aunswere, but shortely tooke him 5 and putte him in warde, and that done, foorth-

The Lorde wyth wente to horsebacke, and tooke the waye Riuers putte to Stonye Stratforde. Where they founde the kinge with his companie readye to leape on horsebacke and departe forwarde, to leaue that lodging for them, because it ro was to streighte for bothe coumpanies. And as sone as they came in his presence, they lighte adowne with all their companie aboute them. To whome the Duke of Buckingham saide, goe afore, Gentlemenne and yomen, kepe youre rowmes. And thus in a goodly arraye thei came to the kinge, 15 and on theire knees in very humble wise salued his grace; whiche receyued them in very joyous and amiable maner, nothinge earthlye knowing nor mistrustinge as yet. But euen by and by in his presence they piked a quarrell to the Lorde Richard Graye, the kinges other brother-p e Lord 20 by his mother, sayinge that hee, with the lorde ' ' Marques his brother and the Lorde Riuers his vncle, hadde coumpassed to rule the kinge and the realme, and to sette variaunce among the states, and to subdewe and destroye the noble blood of the realm. Toward the accoumplishinge 25 whereof, they sayde that the Lorde Marques hadde entered into the Tower of London, and thence taken out the kinges Treasor, and sent menne to the sea. All whiche thinge these Dukes wiste well were done for good purposes and necessari by the whole counsaile at London, sauing that sommewhat 30 thei must sai. Unto whiche woordes the king aunswered, what my brother Marques hath done I cannot saie. But in good faith I dare well aunswere for myne vncle Riuers and

RICH.

my brother here, that thei be innocent of any such matters. Ye, my liege, quod the Duke of Buckingham, thei haue kepte theire deahng in these matters farre fro the knowledge of your good grace. And foorthwith thei arrested the Lord 5 Richarde and sir Thomas Vaughan knighte, in the kinges presence, and broughte the king and all backe vnto Northampton, where they tooke againe further counsaile. And there they sente awaie from the kinge whom it pleased them, and sette newe seruauntes aboute him, suche as lo lyked better them than him. At whiche dealinge hee wepte and was nothing contente, but it booted not. And at dyner the Duke of Gloucester sente a dishe from his owne table to the lord Riuers, prayinge him to bee of good chere, all should be well inough. And he thanked the 15 Duke and prayed the messenger to beare it to his nephewe the lorde Richard with the same message for his comfort, who he thought had more nede of coumfort, as one to whom such aduersitie was straunge. But himself had bene al his dayes in ure therwith, and therfore coulde beare it the 20 better. But for al this coumfortable courtesye of the Duke of Gloucester he sent the lord Riuers and the Lorde The death of Richardc with sir Thomas Vaughan into the Riul rsnd Northe countrey into diuers places to prison, others. afterward al to Pomfrait, where they were -5 in conclusion beheaded.

In this wise the Duke of Gloucester tooke upon himself the order and gouernance of the young king, whom with much honor and humble reuerence he conuayed vppewarde towarde the citye. But anone the tidinges of this mater 30 came hastely to the quene, a litle before the midnight folowing, and that in the sorest wise, that the king her Sonne was taken, her brother, her sonne and her other frendes arested, and sent no man wist whither, to be done with God wot what. With which tidinges the quene in gret fright and heuines, bewaihng her childes rain, her frendes mischance, and her own infortune, damning the time that euer shee diswaded the gatheryng of power aboute the kinge, gate her selfe in all the haste possible with her yonger sonne 5 and her doughters oute of the Palyce of West- 1-11 1 1 1 " Quene mmster m whiche shee then iaye, mto the takethsain-Sainctuarye, lodginge her selfe and her coum-panye there in the abbottes place.

Nowe came there one, in likewise not longe after mydde- 10 nighte, fro the Lorde Chaumberlayn vnto the archbishoppe of Yorke then Chaunceller of Englande, to his place not farre from Westminster. And for that he shewed his ser-uauntes that hee hadde tidinges of soo greate importaunce, that his maister gaue him in charge not to forbeare his reste, 15 they letted not to wake hym, nor hee to admitte this messenger in to his bedde syde. Of w iome hee hard that these Dukes were gone backe with the Kynges grace from Stonye Stratforde vnto Northampton. Notwithstanding, sir, quod hee, my Lorde sendeth youre Lordeshippe woorde 20 that there is no feare. For hee assureth you that all shall bee well. I assure him, quod the Archebishoppe, bee it as well as it will, it will neuer bee soo well as wee haue scene it. And thereuppon by and by after the messenger departed, hee caused in all the haste al his seruauntes to bee 25 called vppe, and so with his owne householde aboute hym, and euerie manne weaponed, hee tooke the greate Seale with him, and came yet beefore daye vnto the Queene. Aboute whome he found muche heauinesse, rumble, haste and businesse, carriage and conueyaunce of her stuffe into 30 Sainctuary, chestes, coffers, packes, fardelles, trusses, all on mennes backes, no manne vnoccupyed, somme lading, somme goynge, somme descharging, somme commynge for more, somme breakinge downe the walles to bring in the nexte waye, and somme yet drewe to them that holpe to carrye a wronge waye. The Quene her self satte alone alowe on the rishes all desolate and dismayde, whome the 5 Archebishoppe coumforted in the best manner hee coulde, shewinge her that hee trusted the matter was nothynge soo sore as shee tooke it for. And that he was putte in good hope and oute of feare by the message sente him from the Lorde Chamberlaine. Ah, woo worthe him, quod she, for lo hee is one of them that laboureth to destroye me and my bloode. Madame, quod he, be ye of good chere. For I assure you if thei crowne any other kinge then your sonne, whome they nowe haue with them, we shal on the morowe crowne his brother whome you haue here with you. And I- here is the greate Seale, whiche in likewise as that noble prince your housebande deliuered it vnto me, so here I deliuer it vnto you, to the use and behoofe of youre sonne, and therewith hee betooke her the greate Seale, and departed home agayne, yet in the dauninge of the daye. By 2 0 which tyme hee might in his chaumber window see all the Temmes full of bootes of the Duke of Gloucesters seruantes, watchinge that no manne shouldego to Sainctuary, nor none coulde passe vnserched. Then was there greate commocion and murmure as well in other places about, as specially in : i5 the city, the people diuerselye diuiningevppon this dealinge. And somme Lordes, Knightes, and Gentlemenne either for fauou; of the Quene, or for feare of themselfe, assembled in sundry coumpanies, and went flockmele in harneis; and manye also, for that they reckened this demeanoure at- 30 tempted, not so specially againste the other Lordes, as agaynste the kinge hymselfe in the disturbaunce of hys coronacion. But then by and by the Lordes assembled together at. Towarde which meting, the Arche- bishoppe of Yorke fearing that it wold be ascribed (as it was in dede) to his ouermuch lightnesse, that he so sodainly had yelded vp the great seale to the Quene, to whome the custodye thereof nothing partained, without especial com- maundement of the kynge, secretely sent for the seale 5 againe, and brought it with him after the customable maner. And at this meting the lord Hasting, whose trouth towarde the king no manne doubted nor neded to doubte, per-swaded the Lordes to bclieue, that the Duke of Gloucester j was sure and fastlye faithfall to hys prince, and that the 10 lorde Riuers and lord Richard with the other knightes wer, for maters attempted by them against the dukes of Gloucester and Buckingham, putte vnder arreste for theire surety, not for the Kynges jeopardye; and that thei were also in sauegarde, and there no lenger shoulde remayn, then tyll 15 the matter wer, not by the dukes onelye, but also by all the other Lordes of the Kynges counsayle indifferentelye examyned, and by other discrecions ordered, and eyther judged or appeased. But one thynge hee aduised them beware, that they judged not the matter to farrefoorth, ere 20 they knewe the trueth, nor turnynge theire priuate grudges into the common hurte, yrritinge and prouoking menne vnto anger, and disturbynge the Kynges Coronacion, towarde whiche the Dukes were commynge vppe, that thei mighte paraduenture brynge the matter so farre oute of joynt, that 25 it shold neuer be brought in frame agayne. Whiche stryfe if it shoulde happe, as it were lykelye, to come to a fielde, though both parties were in all other thynges egall, yet shoulde the authoritie bee on that syde where the Kynge is hymselfe. With these parswasions of the Lorde Hastynges, 3 whereof parte hymselfe belieued, of parte he wist the con- trarye, these commocions were sommewhat appeased. But specyally by that that the Dukes of Gloucester and Buck- ingham were so nere, and came so shortelye on with the kynge, in none other maner, with none other voyce or semblaunce, then to his coronacion, causynge the fame to bee blowen about, that these Lordes and knightes whiche 5 were taken hadde contryued the destruccyon of the Dukes of Gloucester and Buckingham, and of other the noble bloode of the realme, to the ende that them selfe woulde alone demeane and gouerne the king at their pleasure. And for the colourable proofe thereof, such of the Dukes 10 seruantes as rode with the cartes of theyr stuffe that were taken (amonge whiche stuffe no meruayle thoughe somme were barneys, whiche at the breakinge vp of that householde muste needes eyther bee broughte awaye or caste awaye) they shewed vnto the people al the waye as they wente, 15 loe here bee the barelles of barneys that this traitours had priuelye conuayed in theyr carryage to destroye the noble lordes with all. This deuise all be it that it made the matter to wise men more vnlykely, well perceyuyng that the intendours of suche a purpose wolde rather haue hadde 20 theyr barneys on theyr backes, then taue bounde them vppe in barrelles, yet muche part of the common people were therewith verye well satisfyed, and said it wer almoise to hange them.

When the kynge approched nere to the citie, Edmonde 25 Sha goldesmithe then mayre, with Willyam White and John

Mathewe sheriffis, and all the other aldermenne in scarlette, with fine hundred horse of the citezens in violette, receiued hym reuerentlye at Harnesey, and rydynge from thence, accoumpanyed him into the citye, whiche hee

The kvnges 30 commyiige to entered the fowrth daye of Maye, the firste and London.

laste yeare of hys raygne. But the Duke of Gloucester bare him in open sighte so reuerentelye to the Prince, with all semblaunce of lowlinesse, that from the great obloquy in which hee was soo late before, hee was sodainelye fallen in soo greate truste, that at the counsayle next assembled, hee was made the onely manne chose and thoughte moste mete, to bee protectoure of the j protec-king and hys realme, so that (were it destenye " ""' '"'" " 5 or were it foly) the lamb was betaken to the w olfe to kepe. At whiche counsayle also the Archebishoppe of Yorke, Chauncelloure of Englande, whiche hadde deliuered vppe the greate seale to the Quene, was thereof greatlye re-proued, and the Seale taken from hym and deliuered to 10 doctour Russell, bysshoppe of Lyncolne, a wyse The bishop manne and a good and of muche experyence, made'Lorde and one of the beste learned menne vndoubt- Chaunceiiour. edlye that Englande hadde in hys time. Diuers Lordes and knightes were appoynted vnto dyuerse rovvmes. The Lorde 15 Chaumberlayne and somme other kepte styll theyr offices that they hadde beefore. Nowe all were it soo that the protectoure so soore thyrsted for the finyshynge of that hee hadde begonne, that thoughte euerye daye a yeare tyll it were atchyeued, yet durste hee no further attempte as longe 20 as he had but halfe hys praye in his hande; well wittinge that yf hee deposed the one brother, all the Realme woulde, falle to the tother, yf hee either remayned in Sainctu-arye, or shoulde happelye bee shortelye conuayde too hys farther libertye. Wherefore incontinente at the nexte metynge 25 of the Lordes at the counsayle, hee preposed vnto them, that it was a haynous deede of the Quene, and procedinge of great malyce tovvarde the Kynges counsayllers, that she should keepe in Saynctuarye the Kynges brother from hym, whose specyall pleasure and coumforte were to haue 30 his brother with hym. And that by her done to none other entente, but to brynge all the Lordes in obloquie and murmure of the people. As thoughe they were not to bee trusted with the Kynges brother, that by the assente of the nobles of the lande wer appoynted, as the Kynges nereste friendes, to the tuicyon of his owne royall parsone. T? ie prosperytye whereof standeth (quod hee) not all in 5 keepynge from enemyes or yll vyande, but partelye also in recreacion and moderate pleasure; which he cannot in this tender youthe take in the coumpanye of auncient parsons, but in the faniylier conuersacyon of those that bee neyther farre vnder nor farre aboue his age, and nath- lo lesse of estate conuenient to accoumpanye his noble ma-gestie. Wherefore with whom rather then with his owne brother? And yf anye manne thinke this consideracion (whiche I thynke no manne thynketh that loueth the Kynge) lette hym consyder that sommetime withoute smal 15 thinges greatter cannot stande. And verelye it redowndeth greatelye to the dishonoure bothe of the kinges highnesse and of al vs that bene about his grace, to haue it runne in euery mans mouth, not in this realme onely, but also in other landes (as euyll woordes walke farre) that the 20 Kynges brother shoulde bee fayne to keepe Saynctuarye. For euerye manne wyll weene, that no manne wyll so dooe for noughte. And suche euyll oppinyon once fastened in mennes heartes, hard it is to wraste oute, and maye growe to more grief than anye manne here canne diuine.

25 Wherefore mee thynketh it were not woorste to sende vnto the Quene, for the redresse of this matter, somme honourable trustye manne, suche as bothe tendereth the Kynges weale, and the honoure of his counsaile, and is also in fauoure and credence wyth her. For al which con- 30 sideracions, none seemeth mee more metelye than oure reuerente father here presente, my Lorde Cardynall, who maye in this matter dooe moste good of anye manne, yf it please hym to take the payne. Whiche I double not of his goodnesse he wyll not refuse, for the Kynges sake and ours, atid wealthe of the younge Duke hymself, the kinges moste honourable brother, and after my soueraygne Lorde hymself, my moste dere nephewe; considered that thereby shall bee ceased the slaunderous rumoure and obloquye 5 nowe goynge and the hurtes auoyded that thereof mighte ensue, and much rest and quyete growe to all the realme. And yf shee bee percase so obstynate, and so preciselye sette vppon her own wyl, that neyther his wise and faithful aduertyseraente canne moue her, nor any mannes reason 10 content her; then shall wee by myne aduyse, by the Kynges authoritye, fetche hym out of that prisone, and brynge hym to his noble presence, in whose contynuall coumpanye he shal bee so well cherished and so honourablye entreated, that all the worlde shall, to our honor and her reproch, 15 perceiue that it was onelye malyce, frowardenesse, or foly, that caused her to keepe him there. This is my minde in this matter for this time, excepte any of your Lorde-shippes anye thinge perceiue to the contrarye. For neuer shal I by Gods grace so wedde my selfe to myne own wyll, 20 but that I shall bee readye to chaunge it vppon youre better aduyses.

When the protectoure hadde said, al the counsayl affyrmed that the mocion was good and reasonable, and to the kynge and the Duke his brother honourable, and a 25 thing that should cease great murmure in the realme, if the mother might be by good meanes enduced to delyucr hym. Whiche thynge the Archebishoppe of Yorke, whome they all agreed also to bee thereto moste conuenyente, tooke vppon hym to moue her, and therein to dooe hys 30 vttermoste deuowre. Howe bee it if shee coulde bee in no wyse entreated with her good wyll to delyuer hym, then thoughte hee and suche other as were of the spiritualtye present, that it were not in anye wyse to be attempted to take him oute agaynste her wil. For it would bee a thynge that shoulde tourne to the greate grudge of all menne, and hyghe dyspleasure of Godde, yf the priueledge of that holye r place should nowe bee broken. Whiche hadde

Saintuarye. i i i i t

SO manye yeares bee kepte, whyche bothe Kynges and Popes soo good hadde graunted, so many hadde confirmed, and whiche holye grounde was more then fyue hundred yeare agoe by Saincte Peter his own parsone in spirite, lo accoumpanyed with greate multitude of aungelles, by nyghte so specyallye halowed and dedicate to Godde, (for the proofe wherof they haue yet in the Abbay Sainct Peters cope to shewe) that from that tyme hytherwarde, was there neuer so vndeuowte a Kinge, that durst that sacred place violate, 15 or so holye a Bishoppe that durste it presume to consecrate. And therefore (quod the Archebishoppe of Yorke) Godde forbydde that anye manne shoulde, for anye thynge earthlye, enterpryse to breake the immunitee and libertye of that sacred Sainctuary, that hath bene the safegarde of so many 20 a good mannes life. And I truste (quod he) with Gods grace, we shal not nede it. But for ani maner nede, I would not we shoulde dooe it. I truste that shee shall bee with reason contented, and all thynge in good maner obtayned. And yf it happen that I brynge it not so to 25 passe, yet shall I towarde it so farrefoorth dooe my beste, that ye shall all well perceiue that no lacke of my deuoure, but the mothers drede and womannishe feare shall bee the let.

Womannishe feare, naye womannishe frowardenesse 30 (quod the Duke of Buck-yngham.) For I dare take it vppon my soule, she well knoweth she needeth no such thyng to feare, either for her sonne or for her selfe. For as for her, here is no manne that will be at warre with women. Woulde God some of the men of her kynne were women too, and then shoulde al bee soone in reste. Howe bee it there is none of her kinne the lesse loued, for that they bee her kinne, but for their owne euill deseruinge. And nathelesse if we loued neither her nor her kinne, yet 5 were there no cause to thinke that we shoulde hate the kynges noble brother, to whose Grace wee oureselfe bee of kynne. Whose honoure if shee as muche desyred as oure dishonoure, and as muche regarde tooke to his wealthe, as to her owne will, she woulde bee as lothe to suffer him 10 from the kinge, as anye of vs bee. For if shee haue anye witte, (as woulde Godde she hadde as good will as she hathe shrewde witte) she reckoneth her selfe no wiser then shee thinketh some that bee here, of whose faithefull mynde she nothing doubteth, but verelye beleueth and knoweth, 15 that they woulde bee as sorye of his harme as her selfe, and yet would haue hym from her yf she byde there. And wee all (I thinke) contente, that bothe bee with her, yf she come thence and bide in suche place where they maie with their honoure bee. 20

No we then yf she refuse, in the deliueraunce of hym, to folowe the counsaile of them whose wisdom she knoweth, whose trouth she well trusteth, it is ethe to perceiue, that frowardnesse letteth her, and not feare. But goeto, suppose that she feare (as who maye lette her to feare her owne 25 shadowe) the more she feareth to delyuer hym, the more oughte wee feare to leaue him in her handes. For if she caste suche fonde doubtes, that shee feare his hurte; then wyll she feare that hee shall bee fette thence. For she will soone thinke, that if menne Avere sette (whiche Godde 30 forbydde) vppon so greate a mischiefe, the saintuarye woulde litle let them. Which good menne mighte, as mee thynk-eth, without sinne sommewhat lesse regarde then they do.

Nowe then if she doubte leste hee mighte bee fetched from her, is it not Hkelye ynoughe that she shall sende him somme where out of the realme? Verely I looke for none other. And I doubte not but shee nowe as sore myndeth 5 it, as wee the lette thereof. And yf she myghte happen to brynge that to passe, (as it were no greate maistrye, wee lettinge her alone) all the worlde woulde saye that wee wer a wyse sort of counsaylers aboute a kynge, that lette his brother bee caste awaye vnder oure noses. And there- lo fore I ensure you faythfully for my mynde, I wyll rather, maugrye her mynde, fetche hym awaye, then leaue hym ther, till her frowardnes or fond feare conuay hym awaye. And yet will I breake no Saintuarye therefore. For verelye sithe the priuileges of that place and other lyke, haue bene 15 of long continued, I am not he that woulde bee aboute to breake them. And in good faith if they were nowe to begynne, I woulde not bee he that shoulde bee aboute to make them. Yet wyll I not saye naye, but that

   Of saintuaries.

It IS a deede of pitie, that suche menne, as the 20 sea or theyr euill dettours haue broughte in pouertye, shoulde haue somme place of libertye, to keepe their bodies oute of the daunger of their cruell creditours. And also yf the crowne happen (as it hathe done) to comme in questyon, whyle eyther parte taketh other as traytours, I wyll well there bee somme 25 places of refuge for bothe. But as for theeues, of whiche these places bee full, and which neuer fall fro the craftc, after thei once falle thereto, it is pitie the saintuarye shoulde serue them. And muche more mannequellers, whome

   Godde badde to take from the aulter and kyll them yf 30 theyr murther were wylfull. And where it is otherwyse there neede wee not the sayntuaryes that God appointed in the olde lawe. For yf eyther necessitie, hys owne defence, or misfortune drawe hym to that dede, a pardon serueth, which eyther the law graunteth of course, or the Kynge of pitie maye.

   Then looke me nowe how few saintuarye menne there bee, whome any fauourable necessitie compelled to gooe thyther. And then see on the tother syde what a sorte 5 there be commonlye therein, of them whome wylfull vn-thriftynesse hathe broughte to nought.

   What a rabble of theues, murtherers, and malicious heyghnous traitours, and that in twoo places specyallye. The tone at the elbowe of the citie, the tother in the verye 10 bowelles. I dare well auowe it, waye the good that they dooe with the hurte that commeth of them, and ye shall fynde it muche better to lacke bothe, then haue bothe. And this I saye, although they were not abused as they nowe bee, and so longe haue bee, that I feare mee euer 15 they wyll bee whyle menne bee afearde to sette theyr handes to the mendement; as thoughe Godde and Saincte Peter were the patrons of vngracious lyuinge.

   Nowe vnthriftes ryote and runne in dette, vppon the boldenesse of these places; yea and ryche menne-p g i jj. f 20 runne thither with poore mennes goodes, there saunuanes. they builde, there thei spende and bidde their creditours gooe whistle them. Mens wyues runne thither with theyr housebandes plate, and saye thci dare not abyde with theyr housbandes for beatinge. Theues bryng thyther theyr stollen 25 goodes, and there lyue thereon. There deuise thei newe roberies, nightlye they steale out, they robbe and reue and kyll, and come in again as though those places gaue them not onely a safe garde for the harme they haue done, but a licence also to dooe more. Howe bee it muche of this 30 mischiefe, if wyse menne woulde sette their handes to it, s myghte bee amended, with greate thank of God and no breache of the priueledge.

The residew sith so long agoe I wote neere what Pope and what Prince, more pyteous then politique, hathe graunted it, and other menne since of a certayne relygious feare haue not broken it, lette vs take a payne therewith, and lette it a Goddes name stande 5 in force, as farrefoorth as reason W7II. Whiche is not fullye so farrefoorth as may serue to lette vs of the fetchynge foorthe of this noble manne to hys honoure and wealthe, oute of that place in whiche he neither is, nor canne bee a Saynctuary manne.

TO A Sainctuarye serueth alway to defende the bodie of that manne that standeth in daunger abrode, not of greate hurte onelye, but also of lawful hurte. For agaynste vnlaw-full harmes neuer Pope nor Kynge entended to priueledge anye one place. For that priueledge hath euery place.

15 Knoweth anye manne anye place wherein it is lawefull one manne to dooe another wrong? That no manne vnlawfuuy take hurt, that libertie, the Kynge, the lawe, and verye nature forbiddeth in euery place, and maketh to that regarde for euerye manne euerye place a Saintuarye. But where 20 a man is by lawful meanes in perill, there needeth he the tuicion of some special priuilege, which is the only ground and cause of al saintuaryes. From whiche necessitie this noble prince is far. Whose loue to his king nature and kinred proueth, whose innocence to al the world his tender 25 youth proueth. And so saintuary as for him, neither none he nedeth, nor also none can haue. Men come not to saintuary as they come to baptisme, to require it by their godfathers. He must ask it himself that muste haue it. And reason, sithe no man hath cause to haue it, but whose 30 conscience of his own faut maketh hym faine neede to require it, what wil then hath yonder babe? which and if he had discrecion to require it, yf nede were, I dare saye would nowe bee right angry with them that kepe him ther,

And I woulde thynke withoute anye scruple of conscience, without any breache of priueledge, to bee sommewhat more homely with them that be there saintuary men in dede. For if one go to saintuary with another mannes goodes, why should not the kyng leauinge his bodye at libertie, 5 satisfy the part y of his goodes euen within the saintuary? For neither king nor pope can geue any place such a priueledge, that it shall discharge a man of his dettes being able to paye.

And with that diuers of the clergy that wer present, 10 whither thei said it for his pleasure, or as thei thought, agreed plainly, that by the law of God and of the church the goodes of a saintuarye man shoulde be deliuered in paiment of his dets, and stollen goodes to the owner, and onelye libertie reserued him to geat his lyuing with 15 the labour of his handes. Verely (quod the duke) I thinke you say very trueth. And what if a mannes wyfe will take saintuary, because she lyste to runne from her husbande; I woulde wene if she can allege none other cause, he may lawfullye, without any displeasure to sainct Peter, take her 20 out of S. Peters churche by the arme. And yf no body maye bee taken out of saintuarye that sayth he wyll bide there; then yf a childe will take saintuarie, because hee feareth to goe to schole, hys mayster must lette hym alone. And as simple as that saumple is, yet is there lesse reason 25 in our case, then in that. For therein though it be a childishe feare, yet is ther at the leastwise some feare. And herein is there none at all. And verelye I haue often heard of saintuarye menne. But I neuer heard erste of saintuarye chyldren. And therefore as for the conclusion 30 of my minde, whoso male haue deserued to neede it, yf thei thinke it for theyr suretye, lette them kepe it. But he canne bee no saintuarye manne, that neither hath wisedom to desire it, nor malice to deserue it, whose lyfe or libertye can by no lawful! processe stande in jeopardie. And he that taketh one oute of saintuary to dooe hym good, I saye plainely that he breaketh no saintuary. 5 When the Duke hadde done, the temporall menne whole, and good part of the spirituall also, thinking none hurt erthly ment towarde the younge babe, condescended in effecte, that if he were not deliuered, he should be fetched. How-beit they thoughte it all beste, in the auoydyng of all maner I o of rumour, that the Lorde Cardinal! shoulde fyrst assaye to geat him with her good will. And thervppon all the counsaile came vnto the sterrechaumber at Westminster. And the Lorde Cardinal!, leauinge the protectour with the counsel! in the sterrechaumber, departed into the saintuary to the Queue, 15 with diuers otlier lordes with him, were it for the respecte of hys honoure, or that slie shoulde by presence of so many perceyue that this erande w as not one mannes minde, or were it for that the protectour entended not in this matter to trust any one manne alone, or els that if she finally wer 20 determined to kepe him, somme of that company had happely secret instruccion incontinent, magry her minde, to take him and to leaue her no respite to conuaye hym, whiche she w as likely to mind after this matter broken to her, yf her time would in any wyse serue her.

' 5 When the Queue and these Lordes were comme together in presence, the Lorde Cardinal! shewed vnto her that it was thought vnto the protectour and vnto the whole coun-sayle, that her kepyng of the kinges brother in that place was the thing whiche highlye souned, not onelye to the 30 great rumoure of the people and theyr obloquye, but also to the importable griefe and displeasure of the kinges royal! majestic. To whose grace it were as singuler coumforte to haue his natural! brother in company, as it was their bothe dishonour, and all theirs and hers also, to suffer hym in saintuarye. As though the tone brother stode in danger and perill of the tother. And he shewed her that the counsel therfore had sent him vnto her, to require her the deliuerye of him, that hee might bee brought vnto the 5 kinges presence at his libertie, oute of that place whiche they reckoned as a prisone. And ther should he be demeaned accordyng to his estate. And she in this doing should bothe dooe great good to the realme, pleasure to the counsell and profyt to her selfe, succour to her frendes 10 that were in distres, and ouer that (which he wiste well she speciallye tenderid) not onely great comfort and honour to the king, but also to the yong duke himself, whose both great welthe it were to bee together, as well for many greater causes, as also for their both disporte and recrea- 15 cion; which thing the lord es estemed no slight, thoughe it seme lyghte, well pondering that their youthe without re-creacion and play cannot endure, nor any estraunger, for the conuenience of their both ages and estates, so metely in that pointe for any of them as either of them for 20 other.

My lord (quod the queue) I saye not nay, but that it were very conuenient that this gentilman whom The Queues ye require were in the company of the kinge hys ""-brother. And in good faith me thinketh it were as great 25 commoditie to them both, as for yet a while, to ben in the custody of their mother, the tender age consydred of the elder of them both, but speciall the yonger, which besides his infancie that also nedeth good loking to, hath a while ben so sore diseased, vexed with sicknes, and is so newly 30 rather a lyttle amended then well recouered, that I dare put no parson erthly in trust with his keping but my selfe onely, considering that there is, as phisicians saye, and as we also

RICH.

finde, double the perill in the recidiuacion that was in the first sicknes, with which disease nature, being forelaborid foreweried and weaked, waxeth the lesse able to beare out a new surfet. And albeit there might be founden other, 5 that would happely doe theyr best vnto him; yet is there none that either knoweth better how to order him, then I that so long haue kept him; or is more tenderly like to cherishe him, then hys own mother that bare him.

No man denieth, good madam, (quod the Cardinal) but lo that your grace were of all folke most necessary aboute your children; and so woulde al the counsell not onely be content, but also glad that ye were, if it might stand with your pleasure to be in such place as might stande with their honour. But yf you appoint your selfe to tary here, then 15 thinke they yet more conuenient that the duke of Yorke wer with the king honorably at his liberte to the comfort of them both, then here as a saintuary man to their both dishonour and obloquy; sith there is not alwaye so great necessitie to haue the childe bee with the mother, but that 20 occasion may sometime be such, that it should be more expedient to kepe him els where. Which in this well appereth that at suche time as your derest sonne, then prince and now king, should for his honour and good order of the countrey kepe householde in Wales farre out of your 25 company, your grace was well contente therewyth your selfe.

Not very well content, quod the Queue. And yet the case is not like j for the tone was then in helthe, and the tother is now sike. In which case I merueile greatly 30 that my lord protectour is so disirous to haue him in his keping, where if the child in his sicknes miscaried by nature, yet might he runne into slaunder and suspicion or fraude. And where they call it a thinge so sore against my childes honour and theirs also that he bydeth in this place; it is all their honours there to suffer him byde, where no manne doubteth hee shall be beste kepte. And that is here, while I am here, whiche as yet intende not to come forthe and jubarde my selfe after other of my frendes; 5 which woulde God wer rather here in suertie with me, then I were there in jubardy with them.

Whye Madame (quod another Lorde) know you any thing why thei should be in jubardye? Nay verely sur, quod shee, nor why they should be in prison neither, as they now be. 10 But it is I trow no great maruaile though I fere, lest those that haue not letted to put them in duresse without colour wil let as lytle to procure their distruccion without cause.

The Cardinall made a countinance to the tother Lord, that he should harp no more vpon that string. And then 15 said he to the Queue, that he nothing doubted, but that those lordes of her honorable kinne, which as yet remained vnder arrest, should vpon the matter examined do wel ynough. And as toward her noble person, neither was nor coulde be any maner jubardy. Whereby should I truste that 20 (quod the Quene), In that I am giltles? As though they were gilty. In that I am with their enemies better beloued, then thei? When they hate them for my sake. In that I am so nere of kinne to the king? And how farre be they of, if that would helpe, as God send grace it hurt not. 25 And therfore as for me, I purpose not as yet to departe hence. And as for this gentilman my sonne, I mynde that he shal be where I am till I see further. For I assure you, for that I se some men so gredye withowte any sub-staunciall cause to haue him, this maketh me much the 30 more farder to deliuer him. Truely madame, quod he, and the farder that you be to delyuer him, the farder bene other men to suffer you to kepe hym, lest your causeles fere might cause you ferther to conuay him. And many be there that thinke that he can haue no priuelege in this place, which neither can haue wil to aske it, nor malyce to deserue it. And therefore they recken no pryuilege broken, "' 5 though thei fetche him out. Which, if ye fynally refuse to deuuer him, I verely thynke they will. So much drede hath my Lorde his vncle, for the tender loue he bereth him, lest your grace shold hap to send him awaye.

A syr, quod the Queue, hath the protectour so tender 10 zele to him, that he fereth nothing but lest he should escape hym? Thinketh he that I.-would sende hym hence, which neyther is in the plight to sende out, and in what place coulde I recken him sure, if he be not sure in this, the sentuarye whereof was there neuer iijtiraunt yet so deuelish, that durste presume to breake?

And I trust God is as strong now to withstande his ad- uersaries, as euer he was. But my sonne can deserue no sentuary, and therefore he cannot haue it. For soth he 7 hath founden a goodly glose, by whiche that place that 2o may defend a thefe, may not saue an innocent. But he is in no jupardy n r hath no nede therof. Wold God he had not. Troweth the protector (I pray God he may proue a protectour) troweth he that I parceiue not where-unto his painted processe draweth? It is not honorable 25 that the duke bide here: it were comfortable for them both that he wer with his brother, because the king lack-eth a playfelowye, be ye sure. I pray God send them - both better playfelowes than hym, that maketh so high a matter vpon such a trifling pretext: as though they coulde 30 none be founden to playe with the kyng, but if his brother, that hath no lust to play for sicknes, come oute of sanctuary, out of hys sauegarde, to play with him. As though princes, as yonge as thei be, could not play but with their peres, or children could not play but with their kyndred, wit h whom for the more part they agree much worse then wyth straungers. But the childe cannot require the priuelege. Who tolde hym so? He shal here him aske it and he will. 5

Howbeit this is a gay matter: Suppose he could not aske it, suppose he woulde not aske it, suppose hee woulde aske to goe owte, if I saye hee shall not, if I aske the priuilege but for my selfe, I say he that agaynst my wyll taketh out him, breaketh the sanctuary. Serueth this liberty for 10 my person onlye, or for my goodes to? ye maye not hence take my horsse fro me; and maye you take my childe fro me? he is also my warde, for, as my lerned counsell sheweth mee, syth he hath nothing by discent holden by knightes seruice, the law maketh his mother his gardaine. Then 15 may no man, I suppose, take my warde fro me oute of sanctuarye, wythout the breche of the sanctuary. And if my pryuelege could not serue hym, nor he aske it for hymselfe, yet sythe the lawe committeth to me the custody of him, I may require it for hym, excepte the lawe giue a 20 childe a gardayne onely for his goodes and hys landes, discharging hym of the cure and saufe kepyng of hys body, for whych only both landes and goodes serue. " And if examples be sufficient to obtayne priue- herebejwine ledge for my chylde, I nede not farre to seeke. andthtlmarke 5 For in thys place in which we now be (and whych ten by Sl More is now in questyon whyther my chylde may take wriuen by hhn benefyte of it) myne other sonne now kyng was blifhlss-born, and kept in hys cradle, and preserued to hisliktsv a more prosperous fortune, which I pray God J "L te n " """ long to continu. And as all you know, this is not the first tyme that I haue taken sanctuarye, for when my lord my husbande was banished and thrust out of his kingdom, I fled hither being great with child, and here I bare the prynce. And when my lorde my husbande re-tourned safe again and had the victorye, than went I hence to welcome him home, and from hence I brought my babe 5 the prynce vnto hys father, when he fyrste toke hym in hys armes. And I praye God that my sonnes palace may be as great sauegard to him now rayning, as thys place was sometime to the kindes enemye. In whych place I entend to kepe his brother sith, c."" lo Wherfore here intend I to kepe him, sins mans law serueth the gardain to kepe the infant. The law of nature Avyll the mother kepe her childe. Gods law pryuelegeth the sanctuary, and the sanctuary my sonne, sith I fere to put hym in the protectours handes that hath hys brother 15 already, and were, if bothe fayled, inheritour to the crowne. The cause of my fere hath no man to doe to examine. And yet fere I no ferther then the law fereth wl: iich, as lerned men tell me, forbiddeth euery man the custody of them, by whose death he may inherite lesse lande then a 20 kingdome. I can no more, but whosoeuer he be that breketh this holy sanctuary; I pray God shorttly sende him nede of sanctuary, when he may not come to it. For taken out of sanctuary would I not my mortall enemy were.

25 The lord Cardinall perceiuing that the quene waxed euer the lenger the farder of, and also that she began to kindle and chafe, and speke sore biting wordes against the protectour, and such as he neither beleued, and was also loth to here, he said vnto her for a finall conclusion, that 30 he woulde no lenger dispute the matter. But if she were content to deuuer the duke to him and to the other lordes there present, he durst lay his owne body and soule both in pledge, not onely for his suerty but also for hys estate.

And if she woulde giue them a resolute aunswere to the contrary, he would forthwith depart there with all, and shyfte whoso would with thys busynes afterwarde: for he neuer entended more to moue her in that matter, in which she thought that he, and all other also saue herselfe, lacked 5 either wit or trouth. AVit, if they were so dul, that they coulde nothing perceiue what the protectour entended: trouthe, if they should procure her sonne to be delyuered into his handes, in whom thei shold perceyue toward the childe any euil intended. id

The quene with these wordes stode a good while in a great study. And for asmuch her semed the Cardinall more redy to depart, then some of the remnant, and the protectour himself redy at hand, so that she verely thought she coulde not kepe him there, but that hee shoulde in- 15 continent be taken thence: and to conuay him elswhere, neyther had shee time to serue her, nor place determined, nor parsons appointed, all thinge vnredy thys message came on her so sodaynely, nothing lesse loking for then to haue him fet out of sentuary, which she thought to be 20 now beset in such places about, that he coulde not be con-uaied out vntaken, and partly as she thought it might fortune her fere to bee false, so well she waste it was either nedeles or boteles: wherfore if she shold nedes go from him, she dempte it beste to deliuer him. And ouer that, of 2 5 the Cardinals faith she nothing doubted, nor of some other lordes neither, whom she there saw. Which as she fered lest they might bee deceiuid; so was she well assured they would not be corupted. Then thought she it should yet make them the more warely to loke to him, and the more 30 sircumspectly to se to his surety, if she with her ovvne ' handes betoke him to them of trust. And at the last she toke the yong duke by the hande, and said vnto the lordes;

My lord (quod she) and all my lordes, I neither am so vnwise to mistrust your wittes, nor so suspicious to mis-truste your trouthes. Of which thing I purpose to make you such a proofe, as if either of both lacked in you, might 5 tourne both me to great sorowe, the realme to much harme, and you to gret reproche. For loe, here is (quod she) this gentilman, whom I doubt not but I could here kepe safe if I woulde, whatsoeuer any man say. And I doubt not also but ther be some abrode so deadly enemies vnto 10 my blood, that if thei wist where any of it lay in their owne body, they would let it out. We haue also had experience The desire of dcsirc of a kingdomc knoweth no kin-a kingdome. j. 'pj- g brother hath bene the brothers bane. And may the nepheus be sure of their vncle? Eche of these 15 children is others defence while they be asunder, and eche of their Hues lieth in the others body. Kepe one safe and both be sure, and nothing for them both more perilouse, then to be both in one place. For what wise merchaunt aduen-tureth all his good in one ship? All this notwithstanding, 20 here I deliuer him, and hys brother in him, to kepe, into your handes, of whome I shall aske them both afore God and the world. Faithfull ye be, that wot I wel, and I know wel you be wise. Power and strenght, to kepe him if ye list, neither lacke ye of yourself, nor can lack helpe in this 25 cause. And if ye cannot els where, then may you leue him here. But only one thing I beseche you, for the trust that his father put in you euer, and for the trust that I put in you now, that as farre as ye thinke that I fere to muche, be you wel ware that you fere not as farre to little.

30 And therewithal! she said vnto the child: Farewel, my own swete Sonne, God send you good keping, let me kis you ones yet ere you goe, for God knoweth when we shal kis togither agayne. And therewith she kissed him, and blessed him, turned her back and wept and went her way, leaning the childe weping as fast. When the lord Cardinal and these other lordes with him, had receiued this yong duke, thei brought him into the sterrechamber odissimu where the protectour toke him in his armes and '"

kissed him with these wordes: Now welcome, my lord, euen with al my very hart. And he sayd in that of likelihod as he thought. Thereupon forthwith they brought him to the kynge his brother into the bishoppes palice at Powles, and from thence through the citie honorably into the Tower, out 10 of which after that day they neuer came abrode.

("When the protector had both the children in his handes, he opened himself more boldly, both to certaine other men, and also chiefely to the h? re betwene duke of Buckingham. Although I know that and'thi 'mark 5 many thought that this duke was priuy to al tenbym More the protectours counsel, euen from the begin- l ritten by hun ning, and some of the protectours frendes said Engiishe, -" i but IS Irans- that the duke was the first mouer of the pro- latedoutof this history tectoure to this matter, sendine: a priuie mes- which he wrote 20 in Laten.

senger vnto him, streight after king Edwards death. But other again, which knewe better the suttle wit of the protectour, deny that he euer opened his enterprise to the duke, vntill he had brought to passe the thinges before rehersed. But when he had imprisoned the quenes kinse- 25 folkes, and gotten bothe her sonnes into his owne handes, than hee opened the rest of his purpose with lesse fere to them whom he thought mete for the matter, and specially to the duke; who being wonne to his purpose, he thought his strength more then halfe encreased. The matter was 30 broken vnto the duke by suttell folkes, and such as were their crafte maisters in the handling of such wicked deuises; who declared vnto him, that the yong king was offended with him for his kinsfolkes sakes, and that if he were euer able, he would reuenge them. Who wold prick him forward therunto, if they escaped (for they would remember their imprisomiient) or els if thei wer put to death, without 5 doubte the yonge king wold be careful for their deathes, whose imprisonment was greuous vnto him. And that with repenting the duke should nothing auaile; for there was no way left to redeme his offence by benefites; but he should soner distroy himself than saue the king, who 10 with his brother and his kinsefolkes he saw in such places imprisoned, as the protectour might with a beck distroy them al; and that it were no doubte but he woulde do it in dede, if there wer any new enterprise attempted. And that it was likely that as the protectour had prouided priuy 15 garde for himself, so had he spialles for the duke, and traines to catche hym, if he should be againste him, and that paraduenture from them whom he least suspected. For the state of thinges and the disposicions of men wer than such, that a man could not wel tell whom he might 20 truste, or whom he might feare. These thinges and such like, being beaten into the dukes minde, brought him to that pointe, that where he had repented the way that he had entred, yet wold he go forth in the same; and since he had ones begon, he would stoutly go through. And 25 therefore to thys wicked enterprise, which he beleued coulde not bee voided, hee bent himselfe and went through; and determined, that since the comon mischief could not be amended, he wold tourne it as much as he might to hys owne commodite.

Than it was agreed that the protectour should haue the dukes aide to make him king, and that the protectours onely lawful sonne should mary the dukes daughter, and that the protectour shold graunt him the quiet possession oi the Erledome of Hertford, which he claimed as his enheri-tance and could neuer obtain it in J ing Edwardes time. Besides these requestes of the duke, the protectour of hys owne minde promised him a great quantite of the kinges tresure and of his howsehold stuffe. And when they wer 5 thus at a point betwene themselfes, they went about to prepare for the coronacyon of the yong king, as they would haue it seme. And that they might turne both the eies and mindes of men from perceiuing of their driftes other where, the lordes, being sent for from al parties of the realme, came 10 thick to that solemnite. But the protectour and the duke, after that that they had set the lord Cardinall, the Arche-bishoppe of Yorke than lorde Chauncellour, the Bishoppe of Ely, the lord Stanley and the lord Hastinges than lord chamberleine, with many other noble men, to commune 15 and deuise about the coronacion in one place; as fast were they in an other place contryuyng the contrary, and to make the protectour kyng. To which counsel, albeit there were adhibit very few, and they very secret; yet began there, here and there about, some maner of muttering amonge the people, 20 as though al should not long be wel, though they neither wist what thei feared nor wherfore; were it that before such great thinges mens hartes of a secret instinct of nature mis-giueth them, as the sea without wind swelleth of himself somtime before a tempest; or were it that some one man, 25 happely somwhat perceiuing, filled mani men with suspicion, though he shewed few men what he knew. Hobeit somwhat the dealing self made men to muse on the mater, though the counsell were close. For litle and little all folke withdrew from the Tower, and drew to Crosbies place in ko Bishops gates strete wher the protectour kept his household. The protectour had the resort, the king in maner dessolate. 1 While some for their busines made sute to them that had the doing, some were by their frendes secretly warned, that it might happelye tourne them to no good, to be to much attendaunt about the king without the protectours appointment j which remoued also diuers of the princes olde 5 seruantes from him, and set newe aboute him. Thus many thinges comming togither partly by chaunce, partly of purpose, caused at length, not comen people only that wane with the winde, but wise men also and some lordes yeke, to marke the mater and muse theron: so ferforth that the lo lord Stanly, that was after Erie of Darbie, wisely mistrusted it, and saied vnto the lord Hasting, that he much misliked these two seuerall counsels. For while we (quod he) talke of one matter in the tone place, litle wote we wherof they talk in the tother place. My lord, (quod the lord Hastinges) 15 on my life neuer doute you. For while one man is there which is neuer thence, neuer can there be thinge ones minded that should sownde amisse toward me, but it should be in mine eares ere it were well oute of their mouthes.

This ment he by Catesby, which was of his nere 2D secret counsail, and whome he veri familiarly vsed, and in his most weighty matters put no man in so special trust, rekening hymself to no man so liefe, sith he well wist there was no man to him so much beholden as was thys Catesby, which was a man wel lerned in the lawes of 25 this lande, and by the special fauour of the lorde chamberlen in good aucthoritie and much rule bare in al the county of Leceter where the Lorde Chamberlens power chiefly laye. But surely great pity was it, that he had not had either more trouthe or lesse wytte. For his dissimulacion onelye 30 kepte all that mischyefe vppe. In whome if the lord Hastinges had not put so speciall trust, the lord Stanley and he had departed with diuerse other lordes, and broken all the daunce, for many il signes that hee sawe, which he nowe const r ues all to the beste. So suerly thoughte he that there could be none harme toward him in that counsaile entended where Catesby was. And of trouth the protectour and the Duke of Buckingham made very good semblaunce vnto the Lord Hastinges, and kept him much in company. And 5 vndoubtedly the protectour loued him wel, and loth was to haue loste him, sauing for fere lest his life shoulde haue quailed their purpose. For which cause he moued Catesby to proue wyth some words cast out afarre of, whither he i could thinke it possible to winne the lord Hasting into their 10 parte. But Catesby, whither he assayed him or assaied him not, reported vnto them, that he founde him so fast, and hard him speke so terrible woordes, that he durst no further breke. And of trouth the lord Chamberlen of very trust shewed vnto Catesbye the mistrust that other began to haue 15 in the mater. And therfore he, fering lest their mocions might with the lord Hastinges minishe his credence, wher-unto onely al the matter lenid, procured the protectour hastely to ridde him. And much the rather, for that he trusted by his deth to obtaine much of the rule that the lorde Hast-

20 inges bare in his countrey; the only desire whereof, was the allectiue that induced him to be partener and one specyall contriuer of al this horrible treson.

Wherupon sone after, that is to wit, on the Friday the day of many Lordes assembled in the The counseii 25 Tower, and there satin counsaile, deuising the ' ' ower. honorable solempnite of the kinges coronacion, of which the time appointed then so nere approched, that the pageauntes and suttelties were in making day and night at Westminster, and much vitaile killed therfore, that after- 30 ward was cast away. These lordes so sytting togyther comoning of thys matter, the protectour came in among them, fyrst aboute ix. of the clock, saluting them curtesly, and excusyng hymself that he had ben from them so long, saieng merely that he had bene a slepe that day. And after a little talking with them, he sayd vnto the Bishop of Elye: JNly lord you haue very good strawberies at your gardayne 5 in Holberne, I require you let vs haue a messe of them.

Gladly my lord, quod he, woulde God I had some better thing as redy to your pleasure as that. And therwith in al the hast he sent hys seruant for a messe of strauberies. The protectour sette the lordes fast in comoning, and therupon 13 prayeng them to spare hym for a little while departed thence. And sone, after one hower, betwene. x. and. xi. he returned into the chamber among them, al changed, with a wonderful soure angrye countenaunce, knitting the browes, frowning and froting and knawing on hys lippes, and so sat 15 him downe in hys place; al the lordes much dismaied and sore meruеiling of this maner of sodain chaunge, and what thing should him aile. Then when he had sitten still a while, thus he began: What were they worthy to haue, that compasse and ymagine the distruccion of me, being so nere 2o of blood vnto the king and protectour of his riall person and his reatme? At this question, al the lordes sat sore astonied, musyng much by whome thys question should be ment, of which euery man wyst himselfe clere. Then the lord chamberlen, as he that for the loue betwene them 25 thoughte he might be boldest witli him, aunswered and sayd, that thei wer worthye to bee punished as heighnous traitors, whatsoeuer they were. And al the other affirmed the same. That is (quod he) yonder sorceres my brothers wife and other with her, meaning the quene. At these 30 wordes many of the other Lordes were gretly abashed that fauoured her. But the lord Hastinges was in his minde better content, that it was moued by her, then by any other whom he loued better. Albeit hys harte somewhat grudged, that he was not afore made of counsell in this mater, as he was of the taking of her kynred, and of their putting to death, which were by his assent before deuised to bee byhedded at Pountfreit, this selfe same day, in which he was not ware that it was by other deuised, that himself should the same day be behedded at London. Then said the protectour; ye shal al se in what wise that sorceres and, that other witch of her counsel, Shoris wife, with their afifynite, haue by their sorcery and witchcraft wasted my' body. And therwith he plucked vp hys doublet sleue to his elbow vpon his left arme, where he shewed a werish withered arme and-small, as it was neuer other. And thereupon euery mannes mind sore misgaue them, well perceiuing that this matter was but a quarel. For wel thei wist, that the queue was to wise to go aboute any such 15 folye. And also if she would, yet wold she of al folke leste make Shoris wife of counsaile, whom of al women she most hated, as that concubine whom the king her husband had most loued. And also no man was there present, but wel knew that his harme was euer such since his birth. 20 Natheles the lorde Chamberlen aunswered and sayd: certainly my lorde if they haue so heinously done, thei be worthy heinouse punishement. What, quod the protectour, thou seruest me, I wene, with ififes and with andes, I tel the thei haue so done, and that I will make good on thy body, traitour. 25 And therwith as in a great anger, he clapped his fist vpon the borde a great rappe. At which token giuen, one cried treason without the c h ambre. Therewith a dore clapped, and in come there rushing men in barneys as many as the chambre might hold. And anon the protectour sayd to the 30 lorde Hastinges: I arest the, traitour. What, me, my Lorde? quod he. Yea the, traitour, quod the protectour. And another let flee at the Lorde Standley which shronke at the stroke and fel vnder the table, or els his lied had ben clefte to the tethe: for as shortely as he shranke, yet

The lord i i i i i i-i mi

Standiey rannc the blood aboute hys eares. Then were they al quickly bestowed in diuerse chambres, 5 except the lorde Chamberlen, whom the protectour bade spede and shryue hym apace, for by saynt Poule (quod he) I wil not to dinner til I se thy hed of. It boted him not to aske why, but heuely he toke a priest at aduenture, and made a short shrift, for a longer would not be suffered, the lo protectour made so much hast to dyner; which he might not go to til this wer done for sauing of his othe. So was he brought forth into the grene beside the chappel within the Tower, and his head laid down vpon a long log of

N timbre, and there striken of, and afterward his body with 15 the hed entred at Windsore beside the body of kinge Edward, whose both soules our Lord pardon.

A merueilouse case is it to here, either the warninges of that he shoulde haue voided, or the tokens of that he could not voide. For the self night next before his death, 20 the lord Standiey sent a trustie secret messenger vnto him at midnight in al the hast, requiring hym to rise and ryde away with hym, for he was disposed vtterly no lenger to bide; he had so fereful a dreme, in which him

Stanley's thoughtc that a bore with his tuskes so raced dl CRITIC 25 ' them both bi the heddes, that the blood ranne aboute both their shoulders. And forasmuch as the protector gaue the bore for his cognisaunce, this dreme made so fereful an impression in his hart, that he was throughly determined no lenger to tary, but had his horse redy, if the 30 lord Hastinges wold go with him to ride so far yet the same night, that thei shold be out of danger ere dai. Ey, good lord, quod the lord Hastinges to this messenger, leneth mi lord thi master so much to such trifles, and hath such faith in dremes, which either his own fere fantasieth or do rise in the nightes rest by reson of his daye thoughtes? Tel him it is plaine witchraft to beleue in suche dremes; which if they wer tokens of thinges to come, why thinketh he not that we might be as likely to make them true by our going if we 5 were caught and brought back (as frendes fayle fleers), for then had the bore a cause likely to race vs with his tuskes, as folke that fled for some falshed, wherfore either is there no peryl nor none there is in dede; or if any be, it is rather in going then biding. And if we should, nedes cost, 10 fall in perill one way or other; yet had I leuer that men should se it wer by other mens falshed, then thinke it were either our owne faulte or faint hart. And therfore go to thy master, man, and commende me to him, and pray him be mery and haue no fere: for I ensure hym

I am as sure of 15 the man that he woteth of, as I am of my own hand. God sende grace, sir, quod the messenger, and went his way.

Certain is it also, that in the riding toward the Tower, the same morning in which he was behedded, his hors twise or thrice stumbled with him almost to the falling; which 20 thing albeit eche man wote wel daily happeneth to them to whom no such mischaunce is toward, yet hath it ben, of an olde rite and custome, obserued as a token often times notably foregoing some great misfortune. Now this that foloweth was no warning, but an enemiouse scorne. The 25 same morning ere he were vp, came a knight vnto him, as it were of curtesy to accompany hym to the counsaile, but of trouth sent by the protector to hast him thitherward, wyth whom he was of secret confederacy in that purpose, a meane man at that time, and now of gret auctorite. This knight 30 when it happed the lord Chamberlen by the way to stay his horse, and comen a while with a priest whome he met in the Tower strete, brake his tale and said merely to him:

RICH.

What, my lord, I pray you come on, whereto talke you so long with that priest, you haue no nede of a pri e st yet; and ther-with he laughed vpon him, as though he would say, ye shal haue sone. But so litle wist that tother what he ment, and 5 so little mistrusted, that he was neuer merier nor neuer so full of good hope in his life; which self thing is often sene a signe of chaunge. But 1 shall rather let anye thinge passe me, then the vain sureti of mans mind so nere his deth. Vpon the very Tower wharfe, so nere the place where his lo hed was of so sone after, there met he with one Hastinges, a purseuant of his own name. And of their meting in that place, he was put in remembraunce of an other time, in which it had happened them before to mete in like maner togither in the same place. At which other tyme the lord 15 Chamberlein had been accused vnto king Edward, by the lord Riuers the queues brother, in such wise that he was for the while (but it lasted not long) farre fallen into the kinges indignacion, and stode in gret fere of himselfe. And for asmuch as he nowe met this purseuant in the same place, 20 that jubardy so wel passed, it gaue him great pleasure to talke with him thereof with whom he had before talked thereof in the same place while he was therin. And therfore he said: Ah Hastinges, art thou remembred when I met thee here ones with an heuy hart? Yea, my lord, 25 (quod he) that remembre I wel: and thanked be God they gate no good, nor ye none harme thereby. Thou wouldest say so, quod he, if thou knewest as much as I know, which few know els as yet and moe shall shortly. That ment he by the lordes of the queues kindred that were 30 taken before, and should that day be behedded at Pounfreit: which he wel wyst, but nothing ware that the axe hang ouer his own hed. In faith, man, quod he, I was neuer so sory, nor neuer stode in so great dread in my life, as I did when thou and I met here. And lo, how the world is turned, now stand mine enemies in the daunger (as thou maist hap to here more hereafter) and I neuer in my hfe so mery nor neuer in so great suerty. O good God, the bundnes of our mortall nature, when he most feared, he was in good suerty: 5 when he rekened him self surest, he lost his life, and that within two howres after. Thus ended this hon- he descrip-orable man, a good knight and a gentle, of gret Lord" ' aucthorite with his prince, of lining somewhat astinges. dessolate, plaine and open to his enemy, and secret to his 10 frend: eth to begile, as he that of good hart and corage forestudied no perilles. A louing man and passing wel be-loued. Very faithful, and trusty ynough, trusting to much. Now flew the fame of this lordes death swiftly through the citie, and so forth farder about like a winde in euery mans 15 ere. But the protector immediatelye after diner, entending to set some colour vpon the matter, sent in al the hast for many sembstauncial men out of the city into the Tower. And at their comming, himself with the Duke of Bukingham, stode harnesed in old il-faring briginders, such as no man 20 shold wene that thei wold vouchsafe to haue put vpon their backes, except that some sodaine necessitie had constrained them. And then the protectour shewed them, that the lor (1 chamberlain, and other of his conspiracy, had contriued to haue sodeinly destroide him and the duke, ther that same 25 day in the counsel. And what thei intended further was as yet not well knowen. Of which their treson he neuer had knowlage before x. of the clock the same forenone. Whiche sodain fere draue them to put on for ther defence such har-neis as came next to hande. And so had God holpen them, 30 that the mischief turned vpon them that wold haue done it. And this he required them to report. Eueri man answered him fair, as though no man mistrusted the mater which of trouth no man beleued. Yet for the further appesing of the peoples mind, he sent humediatli after diner in al the hast, The protectors ne herodc of armes, with a proclamacion to be proclamation. Ynsi Q through the city in the kinges name, con-5 teyning that the lord Hastinges, with diners other of his traytorous purpose, had before conspired that same day to haue slaine the lord protector and the duke of Buckingham sitting in the counsel, and after to haue taken vpon them to rule the king and the realm at their plea-10 sure, and therbi to pil and spoil whom thei list vncon-troled. And much mater was ther in that proclamacion deuised, to the slaunder of the lord chamberlain, as that he was an euil counseller to the kinges father, intising him to many thinges highlye redounding to the minishing of his 15 honor, and to the vniuersal hurt of his realm, by his euyl company, sinister procuring, and vngracious ensample, as wel in many other thinges as in the vicious lining both with ' many other, and also specialli mth Shores wife; which was one also of his most secret counsel of this heynous treson, 20 so that it was the lesse meruel, if vngracious liuyng brought him to an vnhappy ending: which he was now put vnto, by the most drede commaundement of the kinges highnes and of his honorable and faithful counsel, bothe for his demerites, being so openli taken in his falsli conceiued 25 treson, and also lest the delaying of his execucion might haue encoraged other mischiuous parsons, partners of his conspiracy, to gether and assemble themself together in makyng some gret commocion for his deliueraunce, whose hope now being by his wel deserued deth politikely re- 30 pressed, al the realm shold bi Gods grace rest in good quiete and peace. Now was this proclamacion made within ii. houres after that he was beheded, and it was so curiously indited, and so fair writen in parchment in so wel a set hande, and therwith of it self so long a processe, that eueri child might wel perceiue that it was prepared before. ' For al the time betwene his death and the proclaming could scant haue suffised vnto the bare wryting alone, all had it bene but in paper and scribled forth in hast at aduenture. 5 So that vpon the proclaming therof, one that was scole master of Poules of chaunce standing by, and comparing the shortnes of the time with the length of the matter, said vnto them that stode about him, here is a gay goodly cast foule cast awai for hast. And a merchant answered hym, lo that it was writen by profecy. Now then by and bi, as it wer for anger, not for couetise, the protector sent into the house of Shores wife (for her husband dwelled .,. Shores wife.

not With her) and spoiled her of al that euer she had, aboue the value of ii. or iii. M. marks, and sent 15 her body to prison. And when he had a while laide vnto her, for the maner sake, that she went about to bewitch him, and that she was of counsel with the lord chamber-lein to destroy him: in conclusion, when that no colour could fasten vpon these matters, then he layd heinously 20 to her charge, the thing that herself could not deny, that al the world wist was true, and that natheles euery man laughed at to here it then so sodainly so highly taken, that she was nought of her body. And for thys cause (as a goodly continent prince, clene and faultles of himself, sent 25 oute of heauen into this vicious world for the amende-ment of mens maners) he caused the bishop of London to put her to open penance, going before the crosse in procession upon a Sonday with a taper in her hand. In which she went in countenance and pace demure so womanly, and 30 albeit she were out of al array saue her kyrtle only: yet went she so fair and louely, namelye while the wondering of the people caste a comly rud in her chekes (of whiche she , before had most misse) that her great shame wan her much praise. And many good folke also, that hated her Huing, and glad wer to se sin corrected, yet pitied thei more her penance, then rejoyced therein, when thei considred that 5 the protector procured it, more of a corrupt intent then ani vertuous affecion. This woman was born in

The descrip- cion of Shores Loudou, worshipfully frcudcd, honestly brought vp, and very wel maryed, sauing somewhat to sone, her husbande an honest citezen, yonge and goodly 10 and of good substance. Proper she was and faire; nothing in her body that you wold haue changed, but if you would haue wished her somewhat higher. Thus say thei that knew her in her youthe. Albeit some that now se her (for yet she liueth) deme her neuer to haue ben wel visaged. Whose- 15 jugement semeth me somwhat like as though men should gesse the bewty of one longe before departed, by her scalpe taken out of the charnel house; for now is she old, lene, withered, and dried vp, nothing left but ryuilde skin and hard bone. And yet being euen such, whoso wel aduise 20 her visage, might gesse and deuise which partes how filled wold make it a faire face. Yet delited not men so much in her bewty, as in her plesant behauiour. For a proper wit had she, and could both rede wel and write, mery in company, redy and quick of aunswer, neither mute 25 nor ful of bable, sometime taunting without displesure and not without disport In whom the king therfore toke special 1 pleasure. Whose fauour, to sai the trouth, (for sinne it wer to belie the deuil) she neuer abused to any mans hurt, but to many a mans comfort and relief: 30 where the king toke displeasure she would mitigate and appease his mind: where men were out of fauour, she wold bring them in his grace. For many that had highly offended, shee obtained pardon. Of great forfetures she gate men remission. And finally in many weighty sutes, she stode many men in gret stede, eidier for none, or very smal re-wardes, and those rather gay then rich; either for that she was content with the dede selfe well done, or for that she delited to be suid vnto, and to show what she was able to 5 do wyth the king, or for that wanton women and welthy be not alway couetouse. I doubt not some shal think this woman to sleight a thing to be written of and set amonge the remembraunces of great matters; which thei shal specially think, that happely shal esteme her only by that thei 10 now see her. But me semeth the chaunce so much the more worthy to be remembred, in how much she is now in the more beggerly condicion, vnfrended and worne out of acquaintance, after good substance, after as gret fauour with the prince, after as gret sute and seking to with al those that 15 those days had busynes to spede, as many other men were in their times, which be now famouse, only by the infamy of their il dedes. Her doinges were not much lesse, albeit thei be much lesse reme m bred, because thei were not so euil. For men vse if they haue an euil turne, to write it in marble: 20 and whoso doth vs a good tourne, we write it in duste, which is not worst proued by her: for at this daye shee beggeth of many at this daye lining, that at this day had begged if she had not bene.

Now was it so deuised by the protectour and his 25 counsel, that the self day in which the lord Chamberlen was behedded in the tower of London, and about the selfsame hower, was there, not with- Riuers and out his assent, behedded at Poontfraite, the ' "" " fore-remembred lordes and knightes that were taken from 30 the king at Northampton and Stony Stratford. Which thinge was done in the presence and by the order of syr Richard Ratclii knight, whose seruice the protector speci-

Sur Richard Y ' ed in the counsel and in thexecucion of Ratchf. such lawles enterprises, as a man that had ben long secret with him, hauing experience of the world and a shrewde wit, short and rude in speche, rough and bous-5 tiouse of behauiour, bold in mischief, as far from pitie as from al fere of God. This knight bringing them out of the prison to the scafold, and shewing to the people about that thei were traitors, not suffring them to speke and declare their innocence, lest their wordes might haue in- lo clined men to pity them, and to hate the protectour and his part, caused them hastly without jugement, processe, or maner of order to be behedded, and without other earthly gilt, but only that thei were good men, to true to the king and to nigh to the quene. Now when the lord 15 Chamberlen, and these other lordes and knightes were thus behedded and ridde out of the way: then thought the protectour, that while men mused what the mater ment, while the lordes of the realme wer about him out oi their owne strenghtis, while no man wist what to thinke nor 20 whome to trust, ere euer they should haue space to dispute and disgest the mater and make parties, it wer best hastly to pursue his purpose, and put himself in possession of the crowne, ere men could haue time to deuise ani wais to resist. But now was al the study, by what meane thys 25 matter being of it self so heinouse, might be first broken to the people, in such wise that it might be wel taken. To this counsel they toke diuerse, such as they thought metely to be trusted, likely to be indused to the parte, and able to stand them in stede, either by power or policy. Among 30 whom, they made of counsail Edmond Shaa shaa, Maier knight, thcu Maicr of London, which, vpon trust of his owne aduauncement, whereof he was of a proud hart highly desirouse, shold frame the cite to their appetite. Of spiritual men thei toke such as had wit, and were in aucthoritie among the peple for oppinion of ther lerning, a, nd had no scrupilouse consience. Among these had thei John Shaa clerke, brother to the Maier, . Doctour Shaa.

and freer Penker, proumcial of the Augustme 5 freers, both doctors of diuinite, both gret prechars, both of more learning then vertue, of more fame then lerning. For thei were before gretly estemed among the peple, but after that neuer. Of these two the tone had a sermon in praise of the protectour before the 10 coronacion, the tother after, both so fid of tediouse flatery, that no mans eares could abide them. Penker in his sermon so lost his voice that he was faine to leaue of and come downe in the middes. Doctour Shaa by his sermon lost his honestie, and sone after his life, for very shame of the 15 worlde, into which he durst neuer after come abrode. But the frere forced for no shame, and so it harmed him the lesse. Howbeit some dout and many thinken that Penker was not of counsel of the mater before the coronacion, but after the comen maner fell to flattery after, namely 20 sith his sermon was not incontinent vpon it, but at S. Mary hospytall at the Ester after. But certaine is it, that Doctour Shaa was of counsel in the beginning, so farre forth that they determined that he should first breke the mater in a sermon at Poules Crosse, in whiche he shold, by the 25 t aucthorite of his preaching, encline the peple to the pro-tectours ghos t ly purpose. But now was al the labour and study in the deuise of some conuenient pretext, for which the peple should be content to depose the prince and accept the protector for kinge. In which, diuerse thinges 30 they deuised. But the chief thing and the weighty of al that inuencion rested in this that they should allege bastardy, either In king Edward himself, or in his children, or both. So that he should seme dishabled to inherite the crowne by the duke of Yorke, and the prince by him. To lay bastardy in kynge Edward sowned openly to the rebuke of the protectours owne mother, which was mother 5 to them both; for in that point could be none other colour, but to pretend that his own mother was one aduouteresse which notwithstanding, to farther this purpose, he letted not j but natheles he would that point should be lesse, and more fauorably, handled, not euen fully plain and directly, 10 but that the matter should be touched aslope craftely, as though men spared in that point to speke al the trouth for fere of his displeasure. But the other point concerning the bastardy that they deuised to surmise in king Edwards children, that wold he should be openly declared and 15 inforsed to the vttermost. The coloure and pretext wherof cannot be wel perceiued, but if we first repete you some thinges longe before done about king Edwardes mariage.

After that king Edward the fourthe had deposed kmge Henry the sixt, and was in peasyble possession of the 20 realme, determining himself to mary, as it was requisite bothe for himself and for the realme, he sent ouer in embassiate the Erie of Warwike with other noblemen in his company vnto Spaine, to intreate and conclude a mariage betwene king Edward and the kinges doughter of 25 Spain. In which thing the Erie of Warsvik founde the parties so toward and willing, that he spedely, according to his instruccions, without any difficulty, brought the matter to verye good conclusion. Now happed it that in the meane season, there came to make a sute, by peticion to 30 YX z2,- the king, dame Elizabeth Gray which was after beth Gray. j jg quenc, at that tyme a widow borne of noble blood, specyally by her mother, which was Duches of Bedford ere she maried the lord Wodefeld her father. Howbcit this dame Elizabeth her self, being in seruice with quene Margaret, wife vnto king Henry the VI., was marled vnto one Gray a squier whom king Henry made knight vpon the field that he had on at against king Edward. And litle while enjoyed he that knighthod, for he was at that same field 5 slaine. After which done, and the Erie of Warwik being in his embassiate about thafore remembred mariage, this pore Lady made humble sute vnto the king, that she might be restored vnto such smal landes as her late husband had giuen her in jointure. Whom when the king beheld, 10 and hard her speke, as she was both faire, of a good fauor, moderate of stature, wel made and very wise: he not only pitied her, but also waxed ennamored on her. And thus " taking counsaile of his desyre determined in al possible hast to mary her. And after he was thus appointed, and 15 hadde betwene them twain ensured her; then asked he counsel of his other frendes, and that in suche maner, as thei might ethe perceiue it boted not greatly to say nay. Notwithstanding the Duches of York his mother r,, - J ne kinges was SO sore moued therewith, that she diswaded " 'her. 20 the mariage as much as she possible might, alleging that it was his honor, profite, and surety also, to mary in a noble progeny out of his realm, whereupon depended gret strength to his estate by the afiinytie and great possibilitie of encrease of his possessions. And that he could not well otherwise do,-5 standing that the Earle of Warwik had so far moued already. Whiche wer not likely to ta. e it well, if al his viage were in suche wise frustrate, and his appointmentes deluded. And she said also that it was not princely to mary hys owne subject, no gret occasion leading thervnto, no possessions 30 or other commodityes depending thervpon, but onely as it were a rich man that would mary his mayde, onely for a "" litle wanton dotage vppon her parson. In which mariage manye moe commend the maidens fortune then the mais-ters wisdom. And yet therin she said was more honesty, then honor in this mariage. Forasmuch as there is betwene no merchant and his own maid so gret difference, as 5 betwene the king and this widovve. In whose parson albeit ther was nothing to be mishked, yet was there, she saide, nothing so excellent, but that it might be founden in diuers other, that wer more metely (quod she) for your estate, and maydens also, wher as the only widowhed of Elizabeth lo Gray, though she wer in al other thinges conuenient for you, shold yet suffice, as me semeth, to refrain you from her mariage, sith it is an vnfitting thing, and a veri blemish, and highe disparagement, to the sacre magesty of a prince, that ought as nigh to approche priesthode in clenes as he 15 doth in dignitie, to be defouled with bigamy in his first mariage.

The king when his mother had said, made her answer part in ernest, part in play merely, as he that wiste himself out of her rule. And albeit he would gladly that she The kynges.,,,.,.

2D answer to his shold take it wcl, yct was at a pomte m nis owne mynde, toke she it wel or otherwise. Howbeit somwhat to satisfy her he saide, that albeit mariage being a spiritual thing, ought rather to be made for the respecte of

God where his grace enclineth the parties to loue together, as 25 he trusted it was in his, then for the regard of any temporal aduauntage; yet natheles him semed that this mariage euen worldly considred was not vnprofitable. For he reckened the amitye of no earthly nacion so necessari for him, as the frendship of his own. Which he thought likely to beare 30 him so muche the more herty fauor in that he disdayned not to marye with one of his own land. And yet yf oute-ward aliance wer thought so requisite, he wold find the meanes to enter therinto, much better bi other of his kin, wher al the parties could be contented, than to mary himself, whom hee shoulde happelye neuer loue, and for the possibility of more possessions lese the fruit and pleasure of this that he had alredy. For smal pleasure taketh a man of al that euer he hath beside, yf he bee wiued 5 against his appetite. And I dout not, quod he, but there be, as ye saye, other that be in euery point comparable with her. And therfore I let not them that like them to wedde them. No more is it reason that it mislike any man, that I mary where it liketh me. And I am sure that lo my cosein of Warwik neither loueth me so litle, to grudge at that I loue, nor is so vnresonable to loke that I shold, in choise of a wife, rather be ruled by hys eye, then by mine own; as though I wer a ward that wer bound to mary by thapointment of a gardain. I wold not be a kyng with 15 that condicion, to forbere mine own lyberty in choise of my own mariage. As for possibilitie of more inheritaunce by new affinity in estraunge landes, it is ofte the occasion of more trouble then profite. And we haue alredy title, by that meanes, to so much as suffiseth to get and kepe wel 20 in one mans dales. And as for the bigamy, let the bishop hardely lay it in my wai, when I come to take orders. For I vnderstand it is forbidden a prieste, but I neuer wiste it yet that it was forbidden a prince.

The Duchesse with these wordes nothyng appeased, and 25 seing the king so set thereon that she coulde not pull him backe, so hyghelye she dysdained it, that vnder pretext of her duetye to Godwarde, shee deuised to disturbe this mariage, and rather to help that he shold mary one dame , ' Elizabeth Lucy.

Elizabeth Lucy, whom the kmg had also not long 30 before gotten with child. Wherefore the kinges mother objected openly against his mariage, as it were in discharge of her conscience, that the kinge was sure to danle Elisabeth

Lucy and her husband before God. By reson of which wordes, such obstacle was made in the mater, that either the Bishoppes durst not, or the king would not, procede to the solempnisacion of this weding, til these same wer clerely 5 purged, and the trouth wel and openly testified. Wherupon dame Elysabeth Lucy was sent for. And albeit that she was by the kinges mother and many other put in good comfort, to affirme that she was ensured vnto the king: yet when she was solempnely sworne to say the trouth, she lo confessed that they were neuer ensured. Howbeit she sayed his grace spake so louing wordes vnto her, that she verely hopid he wold haue maried her. This examinacion solempnly taken, when it was clerely perceiued that there was none impediment: the king, with gret feast and honor- i5Thekin-es solcmpnitc, marled dame Elisabeth Grai mariage. j gj. crowncd qucnc that was hys enemies wife, and many time had praied full hartly for his losse. In which God loued her better, then to graunt her her bone.

But when the Erie of Warwick vnderstode of this 20 mariage, he tooke it so highly that his embasiate was deluded, that for very angre and disdaine, he at his retourne assembled a gret puisaunce against the king, and came so fast vppon him or he could be able to resist, that he The Vm'y as faiuc to voidc the realme and fie into Hol- 22 fledde. lauud for succour. Wher he remayned for the space of ii. yeres, leuing hys new wife in Westminster in The prince sauctuary, whcr she was deliuered of Edward borne. priucc, of whom we before haue spoken.

In which mene time the Erie of Warwik toke out of prison 50 j jj g jjg y and set vp againe king Henry the vi. which the vi. set up. yg g before by king Edward deposed and that much what by the power of the Erie of Warwike; which was a wise man and a couragiouse wariour, and of such strength, what for his landes, his auiaunce and of the Erie of fauer with al the people, that he made kinges 'a'' '-and put down kinges ahiiost at his pleasure, and not impossible to haue attained it himselfe, if he had not rekened. it a greater thing to make a king then to be a king. But 5 nothing lasteth alway, for in conclusion king Edwarde returned, and with much lesse number then he had, at Barnet on thestre daye felde, slewe the Erie of Warwik Therie of with many other great estates of that partie, and Warwiksiam. so stably attained the crowne againe, that he peassybly 10 enjoyed it vntil his dieng day: and in such plight left it, that it could not be lost, but by the discorde of his verye frendes, or falshed of his fained frendes.

I haue rehersed this busines about this manage som-w hat the more at lenght, because it might therby the better 15 appere vpon how slipper a grounde the protector builded his colour, by which he pretended king Edwardes children to be bastardes. But that inuencion simple as it was, it liked them to whom it suffised to haue somwhat to say, while they wer sure to be compelled to no larger proofe 20 then themselfe list to make. Now then as I began to shew you, it was by the protectour and his counsaile concluded, that this doctour Sha should, in a sermon at . Doctoure

Pomes Crosse, sygnine to the people, that nei- shawesser-ther king Edward himself, nor the Duke of ' 25

Clarence, were lawfully begotten, nor were not the very children of the duke of Yorke; but gotten vnlawfully by other parsons by thaduoutry of the duches their mother. And that also dame Elisabeth Lucy was verely the wife of king Edward, and so the prince and all his children bas- 30 tardes that were gotten vpon the queue. According to this deuise, doctour Shaa the Sonday after at Poules Crosse in a gret audience (as alway assembled gret numbre to his preching) he toke for his tyme spuria viiulavmia non agent radices alias. That is to say, bastard slippes shal neuer take depe roote. Therupon when he had shewed the great grace that God giueth and secretly infowndeth in right generacion 5 after the lawes of matrimony, then declared he that comenl)'-those children lacked that grace, and for the punishment of their parentes were for the more parte vnhappie, which were gotten in baste and speciallye in aduowtrie. Of which, though some, by the ignoraunce of the world and the trouth hid ic fro knowlege, enherited for the season other mennes landes, yet God alway so prouideth, that it continueth not in their blood long, but the trouth comming to light, the rightful inheritors be restored, and the bastard slip pulled vp, ere it can be roted depe. And when he had laid for the proofe 15 and confirmacion of this sentence, certain ensamples taken out of the olde testament and other auncient histories, then began he to descend into the praise of the lord Richarde late duke of York, calling him father to the lord protectour, and declared the title of hys heires vnto the 2o crowne, to whom it was after the death of King Henry the sixte entailed by authoritye of parliamente. Then shewed he that his very right heire of his body lawfully begotten, was onely the lord protector. For he declared then that king Edward was neuer lawfully maried vnto the quene, 25 but was before God husband vnto dame Elizabeth Lucye, and so his children bastardes. And besides that, neither king Edward himself, nor the duke of Clarence among those that wer secret in the housholf, wer reckened very surely for the children of the noble Duke, as those that by 30 their fauours more resembled other knowen men then him. From whose vertuous condicions he said also that kynge Edward was far of. But the lord protectour he said, that very noble prince, the special paterne of knightly prowes, as well in all princely behaueor as in the liniamentes and fauor of his visage, represented the verye face of the noble duke his father. This is, quod he, the fathers owne figure, this is his own countenance, the very prent of his visage, the sure vndoubted image, the playne expresse likenes of 5 that noble Duke.

Nowe was it before deuised, that in the speaking of these wordes, the protector should haue comen in among the people to the sermonwarde, to thend that those words meting with his presence, might haue been taken among the 10 hearers, as thoughe the Holye Ghost had put them in the preachers mouth, and should haue moued the people euen ther to crie, king Richard, king Richard, that it might haue bene after said, that he was specially chosen by God and in maner by miracle. But this deuise quailed either by the 15 protectors negligence, or the preachers ouermuche dihgence. For while the protector found by the way tarying lest he should preuent those woordes, and the doctor fearing that he should com ere his sermon could come to those wordes hasted his matter therto; he was com to them and past 20 them, and entred into other matters ere the protector came. Whom when he beheld coming, he sodainly lefte the matter, with which he was in hand, and without ani deduccion ther-unto, out of al order, and oute of al frame, began to repete those wordes again; this is that verye noble prince, the 25 special patrone of knightly prowes, which as well in al princelye behaueor, as in the lineamentes and fauor of his visage, representeth the very face of the noble duke of York his father. This is the fathers own figure, this his own countenance, the very printe of his visage, the sure vn- 30 doubted ymage, the plain expresse lykenes of the noble duke, whose remembrance can neuer dye while he liueth. Whyle these wordes wer in speaking, the protector accom-

RICH.

panied with the duke of Buckingham, went thorow the people into the place where the doctors comonly stand in the vpper story, where he stode to hearken the sermon. But the people wer so farre fro crying king Richard, 5 that thei stode as thei had bene turned into stones, for wonder of this shameful! sermon. After whiche once ended, the preacher gate him home and neuer after durst looke out for shame, but kepe him out of sight lyke an owle. And when he once asked one that had bene his old frend, what the lo people talked of him, al wer it that his own conscience wel shewed him that thei talked no good, yet when the tother answered him that there was in euery mans mouth spoken of him much shame, it so strake him to the heart, that within fewe dales after he withered and consumed away.

15 Then on the Tewesday folowing this sermon, there came vnto the geld hall in London the duke of Buckingham, accompanied with diuers lordes and knightes, mo then hap-pely knewe the message that thei brought. And there in the east ende of the hall where the maire kepeth the hust- 20 inges, the maire and al the aldermen being assembled about him, all the commons of the citie gathered before them, after silence commaunded vpon greate pain in the protectors name, the Duke stode vp, and (as he was neither vn-learned, and of nature marueilouslye well spoken) hee saide 25 vnto the people with a clere and a loude voice in this maner of wyse.

The duke of Frendcs, for the zeale and heartye fauour oracionr that wc bearc you, we be comen to breake vnto you, of a matter ryghte great and weighty, and no lesse 30 weightye, then pleasing to God and profitable to al the realm; nor to no part of the realm more profitable, then to you the citezens of this noble citie. For why, that thyng that we wote well ye haue long time lacked and sore longed for, that ye woulde haue geuen great good for, that ye woulde haue gone farre to fetche, that thynge wee bee comme hyther to bringe you, withoute youre labour, payne, coste, aduenture or jeopardie. What thynge is that? certes the suretye of your owne bodyes, the quiete of youre wiues and youre doughters, the safegarde of youre goodes; of all whiche thynges in tymes passed ye stoode euermore in doubte. For who was there of you all, that woulde recken hym selfe lorde of his own good, among so many grennes and trappes as was set therfore, among so much pilling and 10 polling, among so many taxes and tallages, of whiche there was neuer ende, and often time no nede; or if any wer, it rather grew of riote and vnresonable wast, then any neces-sarye or honorable charge? So that there was dayly pilled fro good men and honest, gret substaunce of goodes to be 15 lashed oute among vnthriftes so farforth that fiftenes suffised not, nor ani vsual names of knowen taxes; but vnder an easy name of beneuolence and good will, the commissioners so much of euery man toke, as noman would with his good wil haue giuen. As though the name of beneuolence, had 20 signified that euery man shold pay, not what himself of his good wil list to graunt, but what the king of his good will list to take. Which neuer asked litle, but euery thing was hawsed aboue the mesure; amercementes turned into fines, fines into raunsomes, smal trespas to misprision, misprision 25 into treson. Wherof I thinke no man loketh that we should remembre you of examples by name, as though

Burdet.

Burdet were forgotten, that was, for a worde spoken in hast, cruelly behedded, by the misconstruing of the lavves of thys realme for the princes plesure: vith no 30 les honour to Markam then chief Justyce, that left his office rather then he would assent to that judgement, then to the dishonesty of those, that either for fere or flatterie gaue that judgement. What, Coke your own worshipful neibour, alderman and mayer of this noble citie, who is of you eyther so negligent that he knoweth not, or so forgetfull that 5 he remembreth not, or so harde hearted that he pitieth not, that worshipful mans losse? What speke we of losse?

his vtter spoile and vndeserued distruccyon, only for that it happed those to fauour him, whome the prince fauored not. We nede not, I suppose, to reherse of these any 10 mo by name, sith ther be, I doubte not, many here present, that either in themself or their nighe frendes, haue knowen as well their goodes as their parsons greatly endaungered, either by fained quarels, or smal matters agreuid with heinouse names. And also there was no crime so great, 15 of whiche there could lack a pretext. For sithe the king preuenting the time of his enheritaunce attained the crowne by batayl; it suffised in a riche man for a pretext of treson, to haue ben of kinred or alliaunce, nere famiuarite or leger aquaintaunce, with any of those that were at any 2 3 time the kinges enemies, which was at one time and other, more then halfe the realme. Thus wer nether your goods in surety and yet they brought your bodies in jubardi, besyde the comen aduenture of open warre, which albeit penwarr. OCCasion of much 25 mischief, yet is it neuer so mischeuouse, as where any peple fal at distaunce among themself, nor in none erthly nacion so dedely and so pestilent, as when it happeneth among vs, and among vs neuer so long continued dissension, nor so many battailes in the season, nor so cruel and 30 so deadly foughten, as was in that kinges dales that dead is, God forgiue it his soule. In whose time and by whose occasion, what about the getting of the garland, keping it, lesing and winning againe, it hath cost more Englishe blood then hath twise the winning of Fraunce. In which inward warre among our self, hath ben so great effucion . Civil warre.

of the auncient noble blood of this realme, that scarcely the half remaineth, to the gret infebling of this noble land, beside many a good town ransakid and 5 spoiled, by them that haue ben going to the field or cumming from thence. And peace long after not much surer then war. So that no time was ther in which rich men for their mony, and gret men for their landes, or some other for some fere or some displesure were out of peryl. For 10 whome trusted he that mistrusted his own brother? Whom spared he that killed his own brother? or who could par-fitely loue him, if hys owne brother could not? what maner of folke he most fauoured, we shall for hys honour spare to speke of, howbeit thys wote you wel al, that whoso was 15 beste, bare alway lest rule, and more sute was in his dayes vnto Shores wife, then to al the lordes in England, except vnto those that made her their proctoure; which simple woman was wel named and honest, tyll the kyng byreft her from her husband, a right honest substauncial yong 20 man among you. And all were it that with this and other importable dealing, the realme was in euery part annoyd: yet specially ye here the citezens of this noble citie, as well for that among you is most plenty of all such thinges as minister matter to such injuries, as for that you were 25 nereste at hande, sith that nere here about was comonly his most abyding. And yet bee ye the people whom he had as singuler cause wel and kyndly to entreate,

London the as any part of his realme, not onely for that the kinges special 1,.,,.,., 1 chaumber.

prince by this noble citye, as his special cham 30 ber and the speciall wel renoumed citye of his realme, much honorable fame receiueth among all other nacions: but also for that ye, not without your great coste and sundry perils and jeopardies in all his warres, bare euer your specyallfauoure to his parte. Whiche youre kynde myndes borne to the house of York, sith he hath nothing worthely acquited, ther is of that house that now by Gods grace better shal, which thing 5 to shewe you is the whole some and effect of this our pre-sente errande. It shall not, I wote well, nede that I rehearse you agayn that ye haue alreadye harde, of him that can better tell it, and of whom I am sure ye wil better beleue it. And reason is that it so be. I am not so proude to lolooke therfore, that ye shoulde recken my wordes of as great authoritie as the preachers of the worde of God, namelye a manne so cunninge and so wise that no manne better woteth what he should say, and thereto so good and vertuous that he would not say the thyng whiche he wist he 15 shoulde not say, in the pulpet namely, into which none honest man commeth to lie,which honorable preacher ye wel remember substancially declared vnto you at Poules crosse on Sunday last passed, the righte and tide that the most excellent prince Richard, duke of Gloucester, now pro- 20 tectour of this realme, hath vnto the crown and kingdom of the same. For as the worshipful man groundly made open vnto you, the children of king Edward the fourth wer neuer lawfully begotten, forasmuch as the king (liuing his very wife dame Elizabeth Lucy) was neuer lawfully married vnto the 25 Queue their mother, whose bloode, sauing that he set his volupteous pleasure before his honor, was full vnmetely to bee matched with his, and the mengling of whose bloodes together, hath bene the effusion of great parte of the noble bloode of this realme. Wherby it maye wel seme that 30 mariage not well made, of which ther is so much mischief growen. For lack of which lawfull accoupling, and also of other thinges, which the said worshipful doctor rather signified then fully explaned, and which thynges shal not be spoken for me, as the thing wherin euery man forbereth to say that he knoweth, in auoidinge dyspleasure of my noble lord protector, bearinge as nature requireth a filial reuerence to the duches his mother; for these causes, I say, before remembred, that is to wit, for lack of other issue lawfully 5 comming of the late noble prince Richard duke of York, to whose roial bloode the crown of England and of Fraunce is by the high authoritie of parliament entailed, the right and title of the same is, by the just course of enheritance accordinge to the comon law of this lande, deuolute and 10 comen vnto the most excellent prince the lord protector as to the very lawfully begotten sonne of the fore remembred noble duke of Yorke. Which thing well considred, and the greate knightly prowes pondred, with manyfolde vertues w hich in his noble parson singularly abound, the nobles and 15 commons also of this realm, and specially of the north partes, not willing any bastard blood to haue the rule of the land, nor the abusions before in the same vsed any longer to continue, haue condiscended and fullye determined to make humble peticion vnto the most puisant prince, the 20 lord protector, that it maye like his grace, at our humble request, to take vpon him the guiding and gouernance of this realm, to the velth and encrease of the same, according to his very right and just title. Which thing I wote it wel he wil be loth to take vpon him, as he whose wisdom well 25 perceiueth the labor and study both of minde and of bodye that shal come therewith, to whom so euer so wel occupy the roume, as I dare say he wil if he take it. Which roume I warne you well is no childes office. And that the greate wise manne well perceiued, when hee sayde: Veh regno 30 cuius rex puer est. Woe is that Realme, that hathe a chylde to theyre Kynge. Wherefore soo muche the more cause haue we to thank God, that this noble parsonage which is so ryghteousely intitled thereunto, is of so sadde age, and therto of so great wisedome joined with so great experience; whiche albeit he wil be lothe, as I haue said, to take it vpon him; yet shall he to oure peticion in that behalf the 5 more graciously encline if ye, the worsshipfuu citezens of this the chiefe citie of this realme, joyne wyth vs the nobles in our said request. Which for your owne weale we doubte not but ye will, and natheles I hartelye praye you so to doe, wherby you shall doe gret profite to all this realme beside lo in chosing them so good a king, and vnto your selfe speciall commodite, to whome hys majesty shall euer after beare so muche the more tender fauour, in howe much he shall per-ceiue you the more prone and beueuolently minded toward his eleccion. Wherin, dere frendes, what mind you haue, 15 wee require you plainely to shew vs.

When the duke had saied, and looked that the people whome he hoped that the mayer had framed before, shoulde, after this proposicion made, haue cried, king Richarde, king Richard; all was husht and mute, and not one 20 word aunswered therunto. Wherewith the duke was meruailously abashed, and taking the maier nerer to him, with other that were about him priuey to that matter, saied vnto them softlye. What meaneth this, that this peple be so stil? Sir, quod the mayer, parcase they perceyue you 25 not well. That shal we mende (quod he) if that wyll helpe. And by and by somewhat louder, he rehersed them the same matter againe in other order and other wordes, so wel and ornately, and natheles so euidently and plaine, with voice gesture and countenance so cumly 30 and so conuenient, that euery man much meruailed that herd him, and thought that they neuer had in their Hues – heard so euill a tale so well tolde. But were it for wonder or feare, or that eche looke d that other shoulde speake fyrste; not one woorde was there aiinswered of all the people that stode before, but al was as styl as the midnight, not so much as rowning among them, by whych they myght seme to comen what was best to doe. When the mayer saw thys he wyth other pertiners of that counsayle, drew aboute the 5 duke and sayed that the people had not ben accustomed there to be spoken vnto but by the recorder, whiche is the mouth of the citie, and happely to him they Fitzwiiham will aunswere. With that the recorder, called ' ''' '"-Fitz Wyllyam, a sadde man and an honest, whiche was jo so new come into that office that he neuer had spoken to the peple before, and loth was with that matter to beginne, notwithstanding thereunto commaunded by the mayer, made rehersall to the comens of that the duke had twise rehersed them himselfe. But the recorder so tern- 15 pered his tale, that he shewed euery thing as the dukes wordes and no part his owne. But all thys nothing no chaunge made in the people which, alway after one, stode as they had ben men amased, wherupon the duke rowned vnto the mayer and sayd: Thys is a maruelouse obstinate 20 silence. And therewith he turned vnto the peple againe with these wordes: Dere frendes, we cume to moue you to that thing which peraduenture we not so greately neded, but that the lordes of thys realme and the comens of other parties might haue suffised, sauing that we such 25 loue bere you, and so much sette by you, that we woulde not gladly doe withoute you that thing in which to bee parteners is your weale and honour which, as it semeth, eyther you se not or way not. Wherfore we require you giue vs aunswer one or other, whither you be mynded as all 30 the nobles of the realme be, to haue this noble prynce now protectour to be your kyng or not. At these wordes the people began to whisper among themselfe secretely, that the voyce was neyther loude nor distincke, but as it were the sounde of a swarme of bees, tyl at the last in the nether ende of the hal, a bushement of the dukes seruantes, and

"Nashefeldes and other longing to the protectour, with some 5 prentises and laddes that thrust into the hal amonge the prese, began sodainelye at mennes backes to crye owte as lovvde as their throtes would gyue, king Richarde, kinge Rycharde, and threwe vp their cappes in token of joye. And they that stode before, cast back theyr heddes mer- lo uailing thereof, but nothing they sayd. And when the duke and the maier saw thys maner, they wysely turned it to theyr purpose. And said it was a goodly cry and a joy-full to here, euery man with one voice, no manne sayeng nay. Wherfore frendes, quod the duke, sins that we par- 15 ceiue it is al your hole mindes to haue this noble man for your king, whereof we shall make his grace so efifectuall reporte, that we doubte not but it shall redounde vnto your great weal and commoditye; we require ye that ye to morow go with vs and wee with you vnto his noble grace, 20 to make our humble request vnto him in maner before remembred. And therewith the lordes came downe, and the company dissolued and departed, the more part al sad, som with glad semblaunce that wer not very mery, and some of those that came thyther with the duke, not able to 25 dissemble theyr sorow, were faine at his backe to turne their face to the wall, while the doloure of their heart braste oute at theyr eyen. Then on

the morowe after, the mayre with all the aldermen and chiefe comeners of the citie in
The mayer their bcstc maucr apparailed, assembling them-
30 ikv!? irdls together resorted vnto Baynardes castell casiei. where the protector
lay. To which place repaired also according to theyr appointmente the duke of
Buckingham, with dyuers noble menne with him, beside manye knightes and other
gentlemen. And thereupon the duke sent worde vnto the lord protectour, of the being
there of a great and honourable coumpanye, to moue a great matter vnto his grace.
Whereupon the protectour made difficultie to come oute vnto them, but 5 if he first
knewe some part of theyr errande, as though he doubted and partelye dystrusted
the commyng of suche noumber vnto him so sodainlye, withoute any warnyng or
knowledge, whyther they came for good or harme. Then the Duke when he had
shewed this vnto the maire and other, 10 that they mighte thereby see howe lytle the
protectour loked for this matter, thei sent vnto him by the messenger suche louyng
message againe, and therewith so humblye besought hym to vouchesafe that thei might
resort to hys presence, to purpose their intent, of which they would vnto 15 none other
parson any part disclose, that at the laste hee came foorth of his chamber, and get
not down vnto them, but stode aboue in a galarye ouer them, where they mighte see
hym and speake to him, as though he woulde not yet come to nere them tyll he wist
Avhat they mente. And 20 thereuppon the Duke of Buckingham fyrste made humble
peticion vnto him, on the behalfe of them all, that his grace woulde pardon them and
lycence them to purpose vnto hys grace the intent of their commyng withoute his
displeasure, withoute whiche pardon obtayned, they durst 25 not be bold to moue him
of that matter. In whiche albeit thei ment as muche honor to hys grace as wealthe to
al the realm beside, yet were they not sure howe hys grace woulde take it, whom they
would in no wyse offende. Then the protector as hee was very gentle of hymselfe,
and also 30 longed sore to wit what they mente, gaue hym leaue to purpose what hym
lyked, verely trustyng for the good minde that he bare them al, none of them ani thing
would intende vnto hym warde, where with he ought to be greued. Wlien the duke
had this leaue and pardon to speake, then waxed he bolde to shewe hym theyr intent
and purpose, with all the causes mouing them thereunto as ye before haue harde, 5
and finally to beseche hys grace, that it wold lyke him of his accustomed goodnes and
zeale vnto the realm, now with his eye of pitie, to beholde the long continued distres
and decay of the same and to sette his gracious handes to the redresse and amendement
therof, by taking vppon him the lo crowne and gouernaunce of this realme, according
to his right and tytle lawfully descended vnto hym, and to the laude of God, profyte
of the land, and vnto his grace so muche the more honour and lesse paine, in that
that neuer prince raigned vpon any people, that were so glad to line 15 vnder hys
obeysaunce as the people of this realme vnder his.

When the protector had hard the proposicion, he loked very strangely therat, and
answered: That all were it that he partli knew the thinges by them alledged to be true;
20 yet such entier loue he bare vnto king Edward and his children, that so muche more
regarded hys honour in other realmes about, then the crowne of any one, of which he
was neuer desyrous, that he could not fynde in his hearte in this poynte to enclyne
to theyr desyre. For in all other nacyons 25 where the trueth wer not wel knowen,
it shold paraduenture be thought, that it were his owne ambicious minde and deuise,

to depose the prince and take himself the crown. With which infami he wold not
haue his honoure stayned for anye crowne. In which he had euer parceyued muche
30 more labour and payn, then pleasure to hym that so woulde so vse it, as he that
woulde not were not worthy to haue it. Notwithstanding he not only pardoned them
the mocion that they made him, but also thanked them for the loue and hearty fauoure
they bare him, praylnge them for his sake to gene and beare the same to the prynce,
vnder whom he was and would be content to lyue, and with his labour and counsel as
farre as should like the kyng to vse him, he woold doe his vttermost deuor to set the
realm in good state. 5 'hiche was alreadye in this litle while of his protectorship (the
prayse geuen to God) wel begon, in that the malice of such as wer before occasion
of the contrary, and of new intended to bee, were nowe partelye by good pohcye,
partly more by Goddes special prouidence then mans prouision 10 repressed. Vpon
this answer geuen, the Duke by the pro-tectours lycence, a lytle rouned, as well with
other noble men about him as with the mayre and recorder of London. And after
that vpon lyke pardone desyred and obtayned, he shewed aloude vnto the protectour
that for a fynal conclu- 15 sion, that the realm was appointed king Edwardes lyne
shoulde not any longer reigne vpon them, both for that thei had so farre gone, that it
was now no surety to retreate, as for that they thought it for the weale vniuersal to
take that wai although they had not yet begonne it. Wherfore yf it 20 would lyke hys
grace tq take the crowne vpon him, they woulde humblye beseche hym thereunto. If
he woulde geue them a resolute aunswere to the contrarye, whyche they woulde bee
lothe to heare, than muste they needes seke and shold not faile to fynd some other
noble manne 25 that woulde. These wordes muche moued the protectoure, whiche
els, as euery manne may witte, would neuer of likelyhoode haue inclyned therunto.
But when he saw ther was none other way, but that eyther he must take it or els he and
his bothe goe fro it, he saide vnto the lordes and 30 commons: Sith we parceiue wel
that al the realm is so set, whereof we be very sorye that they wil not suffer in any wise
king Edwardes line to gouerne them, whom no manne earthly can gouerne again their
willes, and we wel also per-ceue, that no manne is there, to whom the crowne can by
so just tytle appertayn as to our self, as verye ryghte heyre lawfullye begotten of the
bodye of oure moste deere father 5 Rycharde late Duke of Yorke, to whiche tytle is
nowe joyned your elleccion, the nobles and comons of this realm, whiche wee of all
titles possible take for most effectual: we be content and agre fauourably to incline to
your peticion The protector id Tcqucst, and accordyug to the same, here him tobe " "
' take vppon vs the royall estate, preeminence kynge. j kyugdomc of the twoo noble
realmes,

England and Fraunce, the tone fro this day forward by vs and our heires to rule,
gouerne and defend, the tother by Goddes grace and youre good helpe to geat again and
sub- 15 dewe, and establish for euer in due obedyence vnto this realme of Englande,
thaduancement wherof we neuer aske of God longer to lyue then we entende to
procure. With this there was a great shout, crying, kyng Richard, king s Rychard. And
then the lordes went vp to the kyng (for 20 so was he from that time called) and the
people departed, talkyng diuersly of the matter euery man as his fantasye gaue hym.
But muche they talked and marueiled of the maner of this dealing, that the matter was

on bothe partes made so straunge, as though neither had euer communed 25 with other thereof before, when that themself wel wist

V there was no man so dul that heard them, but he per-ceiued well inough, that all the matter was made betwene them. Howbeit somme excused that agayne, and sayde all must be done in good order though. And menne must 30 sommetime for the manner sake not bee a-knowen what they knowe. For at the consecracion of a bishop, euery man woteth well by the paying for his bulles, that he pur-poseth to be one, and thoughe he paye for nothing elles.

And yet must he bee twise asked whyther he wil be bishop or no, and he muste twyse say naye, and at the third tyme take it as compelled ther vnto by his owne wyll. And in a stage play all the people know right wel, that he that playeth the sowdayne is percase a sowter. Yet if one 5 should can so lyttle good, to shewe out of seasonne what acquaintance he hath with him, and calle him by his owne name whyle he standeth in his magestie, one of his tormentors might hap to breake his head, and worthy for marring of the play. And so they said that these matters 10 bee Kynges games, as it were stage playes, and for the more part plaied vpon scafoldes. In which pore men be but the lokers on. And thei that wise be, wil medle no farther. For they that sometyme step vp and playe with them, when they cannot play their partes, they disorder the play and do 15 themself no good.,.,., The nexte daye the protectoure with a 1 Ins that IS here ' ' bet yene this great trainc wente to Westmynster halle and marke and this"

marke wasnot there whcn hc had placed himself in the court written by master More of the kingcs bcnch, declared to the audience, 20 in this history written by him that lic woulde take vpon him the crowne in in English, but i i i is translated that placc thcrc, whcr the kmg hmiself sitteth tory which ho and ministreth the law; because he considred that it was the chiefest duety of a kyng to minister the lawes. Than with as pleasant an oracion 25 as he could, he went about to win vnto him the nobles, the marchantes, the artificers, and in conclusion al kinde of men, but specially the lawyers of this realme. And fynally to thentent that no man shoulde hate hym for feare, and that his deceitful clemency mighte geat him 30 the good wyll of the people, when he had declared the dyscomoditie of discorde, and the commodyties of Concorde and vnitie, he made an open proclamacion, that

So THE HISTORIE OF ha did put oute of his minde all enymities, and that he there did openly pardon all offences committed against him. And to the entente that he might shew a proofe thereof, he commaunded that one Fogge, whom he had 5 long deadly hated, shold be brought than before him. Who being brought oute of the saintuary by (for thither had he fled, for fere of hym) in the sight of the people, he tooke him by the hand. Whiche thyng the common people rejoysed at and praised, but wise men tooke it for a vanitye. lo In his returne homewarde, whom so euer he met he saluted. For a minde that knoweth it self giltye, is in a maner dejected to a seruile flattery.

When he hadde begonne his reygne the daye of June, after this mockishe eleccion, than was he crowned the 15 day of the same moneth. And that solemnitie was furnished for the most part with the selfe same prouision that was appointed for the coronacion of his nephew".

Now fell ther mischieues thick. And as the thinge euill gotten is neuer well kept, through all the time of his 20 reygne, neuer ceased there cruel death and slaughter, till his owne destruccion ended it But as he finished his time with the beste death, and the most righteous, that is to wyt his own; so began he with the most piteous and wicked, I meane the lamentable murther of his innoocent 25 nephewes, the young king and his tender brother. Whose death and final infortune hathe natheles so far comen in question, that some remain yet in doubt, whither they wer in his dayes destroyde or no. Not for that onely that Perken Pcrken Wcrbeckc, by many folkes malice, and 30 Werbecke. niore folkes foly, so long space abusyng the worldc;, was, as wel with princes as the porer people, reputed and taken for the yonger of those two, but for that also that all thynges wer in late dales so couertly demeaned, one thing pretended and an other ment, that there was nothyng so plaine and openly proued, but that q j yet for the comen custome of close and couert " suspect, dealing, men had it euer inwardely suspect, as many well counterfaited jewels make the true mistrusted. Howbeit 5 concerning the opinion, with the occasions mouing either partie, we shal haue place more at large to entreate, yf we hereafter happen to write the time of the late noble prince of famous memory king Henry the seuenth, or parcase that history of Perkin in any compendious processe lo by it selfe. But in the meane time for this present matter, I shall rehearse you the dolorous end of those babes, not after euery way that I haue heard, but after that way that I haue so hard by suche men and by such meanes, as me thinketh it wer hard but it should be true. King Richarde 15 after his coronacion, takyng his way to Gloucester to visit, in his newe honor, the towne of which he bare the name of his old, deuised as he roode to fulfil that thing which he before had intended. And forasmuch as his minde gaue him that, his nephewes liuing, men woulde not recken 20 that hee could haue right to the realm, he thought therfore without delay to rid them, as though the killing of his kinsmen could amend his cause and make him a kindly king. Whereuppon he sent one John Grene, ! ' ' John Grene.

whom he specially trusted, vnto sir Robert Robert Brak- 25 Brakenbery constable of the Tower, with a st"aw7orth"e letter and credence also, that the same sir ' "-Robert shoulde in any wise put the two children to death. This John Grene did his errande vnto Brakenbery kneling before our Lady in the Tower, who plainely 30 answered that he would neuer putte them to death to dye therfore, with which answer Jhon Grene returning recounted the same to Kynge Richarde at Warwick yet in his way. RICH.

Wherwith he toke such displeasure and thought, that the same night, he said vnto a secrete page of his: Ah whome shall a man trust? those that I haue broughte vp my selfe, those that I had went would most surely serue me, euen 5 those fayle me, and at my commaundemente wyll do nothyng for me. Sir, quod his page, there lyeth one on your paylet without, that I dare well say, to do your grace pleasure, the thyng were right harde that he wold refuse, Syr James meaning this by sir James Tyrell, which was a

JO Tyrell. v 2iw of right goodlyc parsonage, and for natures gyftes, worthy to haue serued a muche better prince, if he had well serued God, and by grace obtayned as muche trouthe and good wil as he had strength and witte. The man had an high heart, and sore longed vpwarde, not rising 15 yet so fast as he had hoped, being hindered and kept vnder by the meanes of sir Richarde Ratclife and sir William

Catesby, which longing for no moo parteners

Authority.,, loueth no of the prmccs fauour, and namely not for hym, whose pride thei wist would beare no pere, 20 kept him by secrete driftes oute of all secrete trust. Whiche thyng this page wel had marked and knowen. Wherefore thys occasion offered, of very speciall frendship he toke his time to put him forward, and by such wise doe him good, that al the enemies he had except the deuil, could 25 neuer haue done him so muche hurte. For vpon this pages wordes king Richard arose. (For this communicacion had he sitting at the draught, a conuenient carpet for such a counsaile) and came out in to the pallet chamber, on which he found in bed sir James and sir Thomas Tyrels, of parson 30 like and brethren of blood, but nothing of kin in condi-cions. Then said the king merely to them: What, sirs, be ye in bed so soone? And calling vp syr James, brake to him secretely his mind in this mischieuous matter. In whiche he founde him nothing strange. Wherfore on the morow he sente him to Brakenbiiry with a letter, by which he was commaunded to dehuer sir James all the kayes of the Tower for one nyght, to the ende he might there accomplish the kinges pleasure, in such thing as he had 5 geuen him commaundement. After which letter deliuered and the kayes receiued, sir James appointed the night nexte ensuing to destroy them, deuysing before and preparing the meanes. The prince, as soone as the protector left that name and toke himself as king, had it shewed vnto 10 him, that he should not reigne, but his vncle should haue the crowne. At which worde the prince sore abashed, began to sigh and said: Alas I woulde my vncle woulde lette me haue my lyfe yet, though I lese my kingdome. Then he that tolde him the tale, vsed him with good wordes, 15 and put him in the best comfort he could. But forthwith was the prince and his brother bothe shet vp, and all other remoued from them, onely one called black Wil or William Slaughter except, set to serue them and see them sure. After whiche time the prince neuer tyed his pointes, nor 20 ought rought of hymselfe, but with that young babe hys brother, lingered in thought and heauines til this tratorous death deliuered them of that wretchednes. For sir James Tirel deuised that thei shold be murthered in their beddes. To the execucion wherof, he appointed Miles jyjjies purest Forest, one of the foure that kept them, a felowe fleshed in murther before time. To him ., Jhon DIghton.

he joyned one John Dighton, his own horse,,: keper, a big brode square strong knaue. Then al the other beeing remoued from them, thys Miles Forest and 3 John Dighton, about midnight (the sely children lying in their beddes) came into the chamber, and sodainly lapped them vp among the clothes, so bewrapped them and entangled them, keping down by force the fetherbed and pillowes hard vnto their mouthes, that within a while smored and stifled, theyr breath failing, thei gaue vp to God their innocent soules into the joyes of heauen, leaning 5 to the tormentors their bodyes dead in the and hys brother bed. Whichc after that the wretches parceiued, first by the struling with the paines of death, and after long lying styll, to be throughly dead; they laide their bodies naked out vppon the bed, and fetched sir James lo to see them. Which vpon the sight of them, caused those murtherers to burye them at the stayre foote, metely depe in the grounde vnder a great heape of stones. Than rode sir James in great hast to king Richarde, and shewed him al the maner of the murther, who gaue hym gret thanks and, 15 as som say, there made him knight. But he allowed not, as I haue heard, the burying in so vile a corner, saying that he woulde haue them buried in a better place, because thei wer a kinges sonnes. Loe the honourable corage of a kynge! Wherupon thei say that a prieste of syr Robert 2c Brakenbury toke vp the bodyes again, and secretelye entered them in such place, as by the occasion of his deathe, whiche onely knew it, could neuer synce come to light. Very trouthe is it and well knowen, that at such time as syr James Tirell was in the Tower, for Treason committed agaynste the moste 25 famous prince king Henry the seuenth, bothe Dighton and he were examined, and confessed the murther in maner aboue writen, but whither the bodies were remoued thei could nothing tel. And thus as I haue learned of them that much knew and litle cause had to lye, wer these two 30 noble princes, these innocent tender children, borne of moste royall bloode, brought vp in great wealth, likely long to Hue to reigne and rule in the realme, by traytorous tiranny taken, depryued of their estate, shortly shitte vp in prison, and priully slaine and murthered, theyr bodies cast God wote where by the cruel ambicion of their vnnaturall vncle and his dispiteous tormentors. Which thinges on euery part wel pondered, God neuer gaue this world a more notable example, neither in what vnsuretie standeth 5 this worldly wel, or what mischief worketh the prowde enterprise of an hyghe heart, or finally what wretched end ensueth such dispiteous crueltie. For first to beginne with the ministers, Miles Forest at sainct Martens pecemele rotted away. Dighton in dede yet walketh on aliue in lo good possibilitie to bee hanged ere he dye. But sir James Tirel dyed at Tower hill, beheaded for treason. King Richarde himselfe, as ye shal herafter here, slain in the fielde, hacked and hewed of his enemies handes, haryed on horsebacke dead, his here in despite torn and togged lyke 15 a cur dogge. And the mischief that he tooke, within lesse then thre yeares of the mischiefe that he dyd. And yet all the meane time spente in much pain and trouble outward, much feare anguish and sorow within. For I haue heard by credible report of such as wer secrete with his 20 chamberers, that after this abhominable deede done, he neuer hadde quiet in his minde, hee neuer thought himself sure. Where he went abrode, his eyen whirled about, his body priuily fenced, his hand euer inward ,,,,.,,., troubles of on his dager, his countenance and maner like tyraumes. 25 one alway ready to strike againe, he toke ill rest a nightes, lay long wakyng and musing, sore weried with care and watch, rather slumbred then slept, troubled wyth feareful dreames, sodainly sommetyme sterte vp, leape out of his bed and runne about the chamber, so 30 was his restles herte continually tossed and tumbled with the tedious impression and stormy remembrance of his abominable dede. Nowe hadde he outward no long time in rest. For hereupon sone after began the conspiracy, or rather good confederacion, betwene the Duke of Buckingham and many other gentlemen against him. Thocca-sion wheruppon the king and the Duke fell out is of 5 diuers folke diuerse wyse pretended. This duke, as I haue for certain bene enformed, as soone as the duke of Gloucester vpon the death of kyng Edward came to York, and there had solemne funeral seruise for king Edward, sente thither in the most secret wise he could, one Persal lo his trusty seruant, who came to John Warde, a chamberer of like secret trust with the Duke of Gloucester, desiring that in the most close and couert maner, he might be admitted to the presence and speche of his maister. And the duke of Gloucester, aduertised of hys desyre, caused 15 him in the dead of the night after al other folk auoyded, to be brought vnto him in his secret chamber, wher Persall after his masters recommendacion shewed him, that he had secretly sente hym to shew him, that in this new worlde he would take such part as he wold, and wait vpon 20 him with a. M. good felowes if neede wer. The messenger sent back with thanks, and some secret instruccion of the protectors mind, yet met him again with farther message from the duke his master, within few dayes after at Not-ingham j whither the protector from York, with many gen-25 tlemen of the north countrey to the number of sixe. C. horses, was comen on his way to London ward. And 'after secrete meting and communicacion had, eftsoone departed. Wherupon at Northampton the duke met with the protector himself, wyth CCC. horses, and from thence still contynued 30 the partner of all his deuises, till that after his coronacion thei departed as it semed very great frendes at Gloucester. From whence as sone as the duke came home, he so lightli turned from him and so highly conspired against him, that a man would marueil wherof the chaunge grew. And surely the occasion of theyr variaunce is of diuers men diuersly reported. Some haue I heard say, that the duke a litle before the coronacion among other thinges, required of the protector the duke of Herfordes landes, to which 5 he pretended himself just inheritor. And forasmuch as the title which he claimed by inheritance, was somewhat enterlaced with the title to the crowne by the line of king Henry before depriued; the protector conceiued such in-dignacion, that he rejected the dukes request with many 10 spitefuu and minatory wordes. Which so wounded his hert with hatred and mistrust, that he neuer after could endure to loke aright on king Richard, but euer feared his own life, so farfoorth that when the protectoure rode through London toward his coronacion, he fained himself 15 sick, because he wold not ride with hym. And the tother taking it in euil part, sent hym worde to ryse, and come ride or he wold make him be caried. Wherupon he rode on with euil wil, and that notwithstanding on the morow rose from the feast faining himself sicke, and kyng Richard 20 said it was done in hatred and dispile of him. And they say that euer after continually ech of them lined in suche hatred and distrust of other, that the duke verilye looked to haue bene murthered at Gloucester. From which nathles he in fair maner departed. But surely some right 25 secrete at the dales deny this; and many right wise men think it vnlikely (the depe dissimuling nature of those bothe men considered, and what nede in that grene world the protector had of the duke, and in what peril the duke stode if he fell once in suspicion of the tiraunt) that either 30 the protector wold geue the duke occasion of displeasure, or the duke the protector occasion of mistrust. And vtterly men think, that yf kyng Richard had any such oppinion conceiued: he would neuer haue suffred him to escape his handes. Very trouth it is, the duke was an high minded man, and euyll could beare the glory of an other, so that I haue heard of som that said thei saw it, that the duke at 5 such time as the crown was first set vpon the protectors hed, his eye could not abide the sight thereof, but wried hys hed an other way. But men say that he was of trouth not wel at ease, and that both to king Richard wel knowen, and not yl taken, nor ani demaund of the dukes vncourteisly lo rejected, but he both with gret giftes and high behestes, in most louing and trusty maner departed at Gloucester. But sone after his coming home to Breknock, hauing ther in his custody, by the commaundement of king Richard, doctor Morton bishop of Ely, who as ye before herd was 15 taken in the counsel at the Tower, waxed with him familier. Whose wisedom abused his pride to his own deliueraunce and the dukes destruccion. The bishop was a man of gret natural wit, very wel lerned, and honorable in behaueor, lacking no wise waies to win fauor. He had bene fast 20 vpon the part of king Henry while that part was in wealth, and natheles left it not nor forsoke it in wo, but fled the realme with the quene and the prince, while king Edward had the king in prison, neuer came home but to the field. After which lost, and the parte vtterly subdued, the tother 25 for his faste faith and wisedom, not only was contente to receiue him, but also woed him to come and had him from thence forth bothe in secret trust and very speciall fauor. Whiche he nothing deceiued. For he being as ye haue heard after king Edwardes death, first taken by the tirant 30 for his trouth to the king, found the meane to set this duke in his top, joined gentlemen together in aid of king Henry, deuising first the maryage betwene him and king Edwardes doughter, by whiche his faith declared and good seruice to bothe his masters at once, with infinite benefite to the realm, by the conjunccion of those twoo bloodes in one, whose seueral titles had long enquieted the land, he fled the realm, went to Rome, neuer minding more to medle with the world til the noble prince king Henry the. vii. 5 gate him home again, made him archbishop of Canturburye and chaunceller of England, wherunto the Pope joined thonor of Cardinal. Thus lining many dayes in as much honor as one man mighte well wish, ended them so godly, that his death with Gods mercy wel changed his life. Thys 10 man therfore as I was about to tell you, by the long and often alternate proofe, as wel of prosperitie as aduers fortune, hadde gotten by great experience, the verye mother and maistres of wisdom, a depe insighte in politike worldli driftes. Wherby perceiuing now this duke glad to comen 15 with him, fed him with faire wordes and many pleasaunt praises. And parceiuing by the processe of their com-municacions the dukes pride now and then balke oute a lytle breide of enuy toward the glory of the king, and therby feling him ethe to fal out yf the matter were well handled: 20 he craftelye sought the waies to pricke him forwarde taking alwaies thoccasion of his comming and so keping himself close within his bondes, that he rather semed him to folow hym then to lead him. For when the duke first began to praise and bost the king, and shewe how much profit the 25 realm shold take by his reign; my lord Morton aunswered; Surely, my lord, foly wer it for me to lye, for yf I wold swere the contrary, your lordship would not I weene beleue, but that if the vvorlde woold haue gone as I would haue wished, king Henryes sonne had had the crown and not king 30 Edward. But after that God had ordered hym to lese it, and kinge Edwarde to reigne, I was neuer soo mad, that I would with a dead man striue against the quicke. So was I to king Edward faithfull diapleyn, and glad wold haue bene that his childe had succeded him. Howebeit if the secrete judgement of God haue otherwyse prouided; I purpose not to spurne againste a prick, nor labor to set vp 5 that God puueth down. And as for the late protector and now kyng. And euen there he left, saying that he had alredy medled to muche with the world, and would fro that day medle with his boke and his beedes and no farther.

Then longed the duke sore to here what he would lo haue sayd, because he ended with the king and there so sodeinly stopped, and exhorted him so familiarly betwene them twain, to be bold to say what soeuer he thought, wherof he faithfully promised there should neuer come hurte, and paraduenture more good then he would wene, 15 and that himselfe intended to vse his faithful secret aduise and counsayle, whiche he saide was the onely cause for whiche he procured of the kyng to haue him in his custody, where he myght recken himself at home, and els had he bene put in the handes of them, with whome he should not 2D haue founden the lyke fauor. The bishop right humbly thanked him and said; In good faith, my lord, I loue not much to talk muche of princes, as thing not all out of peril, thoughe the word be without fault, forasmuch as it shal not be taken as the party ment it, but as it pleaseth the 25 prince to conster it. And euer I think on Esops tale, that when the lion had proclamed that on pain of deth there should none horned beast abide m that wood, one that had in his forehed a bonch of flesh, fled awaye a great pace. The fox that saw him run so faste, asked him whither he -70 made al that hast. And he answered, in faith I neither wote nor reck, so I wer once hence because of this pro-clamacion made of horned beastes. What, fole, quod the fox, thou maist abide wel inough, the lyon ment not by thee.

for it is none home that is in thine head. No mary, quod he, that wote I wel ynough. But what and he cal it an horn, wher am I then? The duke laughed merely at the tale, and said; My lord I warant you, neither the lyon nor the bore shal pyke anye matter at any thyng here spoken, 5 for it shall neuer come nere their eare. In good fayth, sir, said the bishop, if it did, the thing that I was about to say, taken as wel as afore God I ment it, could deserue but thank. And yet taken as I wene it wold, might happen to turne me to litle good and you to lesse. Then longed the 10 duke yet moch more to wit what it was. Wherupon the byshop said; In good faith, my lord, as for the late protector, sith he is now king in possession, I purpose not to dispute his title. But for the weale of this realm, wherof his grace hath now the gouernance, and wherof I am my i 5 self one poore member, I was about to wish, that to those good habilities wherof he hath already right many, litle nedyng my prayse, it might yet haue pleased Godde for the better store, to haue geuen him some of suche other. excellente vertues mete for the rule of a realm, as our Lorde 20 hath planted in the parsone of youre grace. Thus ends Sir Thomas Mo re's work.

That the history of the reign of Richard III may he complete the remainder is given as in the continuation of Hardyn s Chronicle. 25

By whiche wordes the duke perceiuyng that the byshop bare unto him his good heart and favoure, mistrusted not to entre more plaine communicacion with him so farre, that at the last the bishoppe declared him selfe to be one of them that would gladly helpe that Rychard, who then 30 vsurped the croune, might be deposed, if he had knowen ho we It might conueniently be brought to passe that suche a person as had true title of inheritaunce vnto the same, might be restored therunto. Vpon this the sayd duke, knowyng the byshoppe to be a man of prudence and 5 fidehtee, opened to him all his whole heart and entent, saiyng, my lord, I haue deuised the way how the blod both of king Edward and of king Henry the sixt, that is left, beyng coupled by mariage and affinitee may be restored vnto the croune, beyng by just and true title due vnto them 10 bothe, (for kyng Rycharde he called not the brother of kyng Edward the fourth, but his enemy and mortal fooe). The way that the duke had deuised was this, that they should with al spede and celerite find meanes to sende for Henry earle of Richemonde (whom the rumour went immediatly 15 vpon knowledge of king Edwardes death to haue bene deliuered out of prison with Fraunces duke of Britayn) and the same Henry to helpe with all their power and strength, so that the sayd Henry would fyrst, by his faithfull othe, promise that immediatly vpon the obteygnyng the croune, 20 he would mary and take to wyfe Elyzabeth, the elder doughter of Edwarde the fourth. The bishop of Ely right wel alowed bothe the deuice and purpose of the duke, and also the maner and way howe the matter should be brought to effecte, and found meanes that Reynold Breye, seruaunt 25 with Margarete mother of the sayd Henry then maried to Thomas Stanley, came to the duke into Wales, and the dukes minde throughly perceyued and knowen, with great spede returned to the sayd Margarete, aduertisyng the same of all thinges whiche was betwene the duke and him con- 30 cernyng as wel the common weale of the realme, as also the aduauncement of her and her blood had bene debated.

Nowe it came so to passe that the duke of Buckyngham and the lady Margarete mother to the sayd Henry, had bene in communicacion of the same matter before, and that the sayd lady Margarete had deuised the same meane and way for the deposycion of kyng Richard and bringyng in of Henry her sonne, the whiche the duke nowe brake vnto the by shop of Ely, wherupon there rested no more, forasmuche 5 as she perceiued the duke nowe willyng to prosecute and further the sayd deuice, but that she should fynde the meanes that this matter might be broken vnto quene Elizabeth, the wife of kyng Edward the fourth then beyng in sanctuary. And hereupon she caused one Lewes that was 10 her physician, in his owne name and as though it came of him seife, to breake this matter vnto the quene, saiyng that if she would consent and agree thervnto, a meane might be found how to restore againe the blood of kyng Edwarde and kyng Henry the sixt vnto the croune, and to be aduenged 15 of kyng Richard for the murther of kyng Edwardes children, and then declared that there was beyond the sea Henry earle of Richemond, whiche was of the blood of kyng Henry the sixt, whom yf she would be content that he mary might Elisabeth her eldest doughter, there should of his syde 20 be made right many frendes, and she for her part might helpe in like maner, wherby no doubte it should come to passe that he should possesse the croune by most rightful inheritaunce. Whiche matter, when she hearde it, it liked her exceadyngly well, insomuche as she counceled the sayd 25 phisycian to breake the same vnto his mastresse the ladye Margarete and knowe her mynde therein, promisyng vpon her woorde that she would make all the frendes of kyng JSdwarde to take part with the sayd Henry if he would be sworne that when he came to the possessyon of the croune, 30 he would immediatly take in mariage Elisabeth her eldest doughter, or els if she lyued not that tyme, that then he would take Cicile her yongest doughter.

Whereupon the sayd Lewes retourned vnto the lady Margarete his mastresse declaryng vnto her the whole mynde and entent of the quene. So that then it was shortly agreed betwene these two women, that with all spede this matter 5 should be set forwarde, insomuche that the lady Margarete brake this matter vnto Reynold Bray, willyng him to moue and set forwarde the same with all suche as he should perceiue either able to do good or willyng therunto. Then had the quene deuised that one Christopher (whom the I o foresayd Lewes the physician had promoted into her seruice) shuld be sent into Britayne to Henry to geue him knowledge of their myndes here, and that he should prepare and appoinct him selfe redy and to come into Wales, where he should fynd ayd and helpe ynough ready to receyue him.

15 But then shortly after it came vnto her knowledge that the duke of Buckyngham had of him selfe afore entended the same matter, wherupon she thought it should

be mete to sende some messenger of more reputation and credyte then was this Christopher, and so kepte him at home, and 2o then sent Hughe Conewaye with a great somme of moneye, willyng him to declare vnto Henry all thynges, and that he should hast him to come and to lande in Wales as is aforesayd. And after him one Rycharde Guilforde out of Kente sent one Thomas Ramney with the same message, 25 the whichetwo messengers came in maner both at one tyme into Britayn to the erle Henry, and declared vnto him al their commissyons. The whiche message, when Henry had perceiued and throughly hard, it rejoysed his heart, and he gaue thankes vnto God, ful purposyng with all conuenient 30 spede to take his journey towardes England, desiryng the ayde and helpe of the duke of Britayne, with promyse of thankeful recompence when God should send him to come to his right. The duke of Britayne notwithstandyng that he had not long after bene required by Thomas Hutton purposely sent to him from kyng Rychard in message with mony eftsones to imprison the sayd Henry erle of Riche-mond and there continually to kepe and holde the same from commyng into England, yet with al gladnesse and 5 fauour inclyned to the desyre of Henry and ayded him as he might with men, monye, shyppes and other necessaries. But Henry whyle he might accordingly appoinct and farnishe him selfe, remayned in Britayne sendyng afore the foresayd Hugh Coneway and Thomas Ramney, whiche. ii. 10 were to him very true and faithful, to beare tidynges into England vnto his frendes of his commyng, to the ende that they might prouidently ordre al thinges, as wel for the commodious receiuyng of him at his commyng, as also foreseyng suche daungers as might befall, and auoydyng suche trappes 15 and snares as by Rychard the thirde and his complyces might be set for him and for al his other company that he should bryng with him.

In the meane tyme, the frendes of Henrye with al care, study, and dilygence wrought all thyngs vnto their purpose 20 belongyng. And though al this wer as secretly wrought and conueighed as emong so greate a numbre was possible to bee, yet priuie knowledge thereof came to the eares of kyng Richard, who although he were at the firste hearyng muche abashed, yet thought beste to dissemble the matter 25 as thoughe he had no knowledge thereof, while he might secretely gather vnto hym power and strength, and by secrete spiall emong the people get more perfect knowledge of the whole matters and chief autoures and contriuers of the same. And because he knewe the chief and principall 30 of theim, as vnto whom his owne conscience knewe that he had geuen moste just causes of enemite, he thought it necessary first of all to dispatche the same duke out of the waie. Wherfore, vnto the duke he addressed letters enfarced and replenished with al humanitee, frendship, familiaritee and swetnesse of wordes, willyng and desiryng the same to come vnto hym with all conueniente spede.

r And ferther gaue in commaundement to the messenger that caried the letters that he should in his behalfe make many high and gaie promises vnto the duke and by all gentle j meanes persuade the same to come vnto hym. But the I duke, mistrustyng the faire woordes and promises so sodainly 10 offred of hym, of whose wily craftes and meanes he knewe sondery examples afore practised, desired the kyng his perdon, excusyng hym self that he was deseased and sicke, and that he might bee asserteined, that if it possible wer for hym to come, he would not absent hym self from his grace.

15 This excuse the kyng would not admitte, but eftsones directed vnto the duke other letters of a more rough sorte, not without menacyng and threatenyng onlesse he would accordyng to his dutie repaire vnto him at his callyng, whervnto the Duke playnly made aunswere that he would 20 not come vnto hym whom he knewe to bee his enemie.

And immediately the duke prepared hym self to make warre against hym, and perswaded all his complices and partakers of his intent with all possible expedicion, some in one place and some in another, to sturre against kyng Richarde. And 25 by this meanes and maner, at one tyme and houre, Thomas Marques of Dorcester reised an armie within the countye of Yorke, beeyng hym self late come furthe of sanctuary, and by the meanes and helpe of Thomas Rowell, preserued and saued from perell of deathe. And in Deuonshire, Edwarde 30 Courtenay with his brother Peter, bishoppe of Excester, reised in like maner an armie, and in Kente, Richard Guylforde accompaignied with certain other gentlemen raysed vp the people, as is aforsaied, and all this was dooen in maner in one momente. But the kyng, who had in the meane tyme gathered together greate power and strength, thynkyng it not to be best by pursuyng euery one of his enemies to disparkle his compaignie in small flockes, determined to lette passe all the others, and with all his whole 5 puysaunce to set upon the chief hed, that is to sale the duke of Buckyngham: so takyng his journey from London he wente towardes Salisbury to the entente that he might set vpon the saied duke, in case he mighte haue perfecte knowledge that the same laie in any felde embatailed. And now 10 was the kyng within twoo dales journey of Salisbury when the duke attempted to mete him, whiche duke beyng accompaignied with great strength of Welshemen, whom he had enforced thereunto and coherced, more by lordly com-maundement then by liberall wages and hire, whiche thyng 15 in deede was the cause that thei fell from hym and forsoke- hym. Wherfore he beeyng sodenly forsaken of his menne, was of necessite constrained to flee, in whiche doyng, as a man caste in sodain and therfore great feare, of this his sodain chaunge of fortune, and by reason of the same fear 20 not knowyng where to bee come, nor wher to hide his hed, nor what in suche case best to doo, he secretely conueighed hym self into the house of Homffray Banaster, in whom he had conceiued a sure hope and confidence to finde faithfull and trustie vnto hym, because the same had been and then 25 was his seruaunt, entendyng there to remain in secrete vntill he might either raise a newe armie, or els by some meanes conueigh hym self into Britain to Henry erle of Richemonde. But as sone as the others, whiche had attempted the same enterprise against the kyng, had knowledge that the duke 30 was forsaken of his compaigny and fled and could not bee founde, thei beeyng striken with sodain feare, made euery man for himself suche shift as he might, and beyng in vtter

RICH.

despaire of their helth and life, either gotte theim to sanctuaries or desert places, or els assaied to escape ouer sea, and many of them in deede arriued sauely in Britain, emong whom wer these whose names ensue. Peter Curtney bishop 5 of Excestre with his brother Edward erle of Deuonshire, Thomas Marques of Dorcestre with his sonne Thomas beyng a very young childe, John Bourshere, John Welshe, Edwarde Wooduile a stoute manne of armes and brother to Elizabeth the queue, Robert Willoughby,

Giles Daubeney, 10 Thomas Harondell, Jhon Cheiny with his twoo brethren, William Berkeley, William Brandon with Thomas his brother, Richard Edgecome, and all these for the moste parte knightes. Also Jhon Halwell, Edward Pointz an excellent good capitain and Christopher Urswicke, but Jhon 15 Morton bishop of Ely at the self same tyme together with sondrye of the nobles and gentlemen sailed into Flaunders.

But Richarde the kyng, who was now come to Salisbury and had gotten perfect knowledge that all these parties sought to flie the realme, with all diligence and haste that 20 mighte bee, sent to all the porte townes there aboute, to make sure steye that none of theim might passe vntaken, and made proclamacion that whosoeuer would bryng him knowledge, where the duke of Buckyngham wer to bee had, should haue for his reward, if he wer a bondman, his 25 fredome, and if he were free, his pardon and besides that, a thousande pounde of money.

Furthermore because he vnderstod by Thomas Hutton newly returned out of Britain, of whome afore is mencioned, that Fraunces duke of Britain would not onely not hold 30 Henry erle of Richemond in prisone for his sake, but also was ready to help the same Henry with menne, money and shippes in all that he might against hym, he set diuerse and sondery shippes in places conueniente by all the sea coastes to Britain ward, that if Henry should come that waie, he might either bee taken before his arriuall, or els might bee kepte from landyng in any coaste of Englande. And furthermore in euery coaste and corner of the realme, laied wounderfull waite and watche to take partely any other of 5 his enemies, and specially the saied duke of Buckyngham. Where vpon the saied Homffrey Banaster (were it for mede or for losyng his life and goodes,) disclosed hym vnto the. kynges inquisitours, who immediately toke hym, and furth-with all brought him to Salisbury where kyng Richard was. 10 The duke beyng diligently examined vttered without any maner refusall or stickyng, all suche thynges as he knewe, trustyng that for his plain confession he should have libertie to speake with the kyng, whiche he made moste instaunt and humble peticion that he might doo. But as sone 15 as he had confessed his offence towardes kyng Richarde, he was out of hande behedded. And this death the duke receiued at the handes of kyng Richarde whom he had before holpen in his affaires and purposes beyonde all Godes forbode. 20

While these thynges wer in hande in Englande, Henry erle of Richemond made redy his hoste and strength to the number of fiue thousand Britons and fiftene shippes, the daie appoincted of his departure beeyng now come, whiche was the twelfe daie of the monethe of Octobre, in the year of 25 our lorde God a thousande foure hundred foureskore and foure, and the seconde yere of the reigne of kyng Richard and hauyng a faire wynde, hoysed vp the sailes and set forwarde, but toward the night came suche a tempest that thei wer dispersed one from another, some into Briten and 33 some into Normandy. But the ship in whiche Henry was, with one other ship, tossed all the night with the wanes of the sea and tempest, when the mornyng came, it waxed somewhat calme and faire weder, and thei wer come toward the Southe parte of Englande, by a hauen or porte called Poole, where the saied Henry saw all the shores and bankes sette full of harnessed men, whiche were souldiours apoincted 5 there to waite by kyng Richard, as wee haue saied before, for the comyng and landyng of the erle. While Henry ther abode he gaue commaundement, that no manne should lande before the comyng of the other shippes. And in the meane tyme that he waited for them, he sent a httle bote lo with a few in it aland to knowe what thei wer that stoode on the shore, his frendes or enemies. Too whom those souldiours, beeyng before taught what thei should sale, answered that thei were the frendes of Henry, and wer appoincted by the duke of Buckyngham there too abide his 15 commyng and to conducte hym to those castelles and holdes, where his tentes pauihons and artillary for the warre laie, and where remaigned for hym a greate power that entended nowe with all spede to set vpon kyng Rychard while he was nowe fled for feare and cleane without 20 prouision, and therefore besought hym to come alande.

Henry suspectyng this to bee but fraude, after that he sawe none of his shippes apered, hoised vp the sailes, hauyng a meruelous good wynde, euen appoincted hym of God to deliuer hym from that greate jeoperdy, and sailed 2 5 backe again into Normandye. And after his landyng there, he and his compaignie after their laboures, arested them for the space of three dales, determinyng too go from thence afoote into Britain, and in the meane while sente messengers vnto Charles the Frenche kyng, the sonne of Lewes that 30 a little before departed, besechyng hym of libertee and licence too passe thorough Normandy into Britain. The young kyng Charles, beeyng sory for his fortune, was not only ready and well pleased to graunte his passage, but also

KYNG RYCHARDE THE THIRDE. loi sente hym money to helpe hym furthe in his journey. But Henry before that he knewe the kyng his mynde (not doubtyng of his greate humanitee and gentlenesse), had sente awaie his shippes towardes Britain, and had sette hym self forewardes in his journey, but made no greate haste till 5 the messengers returned, which greate gentlenesse when he receiued from the kyng, rejoysed his hert and with a lusty stomacke and good hope sette forwarde into Britain, there to take farther counsaill of his affaires.

And when he was in Britain, he receiued from his 10 frendes out of Englande knowledge that the duke of Buckingham was behedded, and that the Marques of Dor-cester with a great numbre of the noble men of Englande had been ther a little before to seke hym, and that thei wer now in Veneti a cite in Britain. The whiche thynges beeyng 15 knowen to therle, he on the one parte did greatly lamente the death and euill chaunce of his chief and principall frende, but yet on the other part he greately rejoysed in that he had so many and noble menne to take his parte in the battaill. And therefore conceiuyng a good hope and 20 opinion that his purpose should well frame and come to passe, determined with hym self with all expedicion to set furthward, and there vpon wente to a place in Britain called Rhedon, and from thence sent the Marques with all the other noble men that thei should come vnto hym. 25 Then when thei heard that Henry was safe returned into Britain rejoysed not a little, for thei had thoughte he had landed in Englande, and so fallen into the handes of kyng Richarde, and thei made not a little hast till thei were come vnto hym. The whiche when thei mette after great joye- o and gladnesse as well of their parte as of his, thei began to talke of their prepensed matters, and now was Christmasse come, on the which daie thei altogether assembled in the churche and tlier sware faith and truthe one to another. And Henry sware firste, promisyng that as sone as he should possesse the crowne of Englande, that he would marye Elizabeth the daughter of kyng Edwarde the fourth 5 and afterwarde thei sware feaultee and homage vnto hym, euen as thoughe he had already been kyng, and so from that tyme furthe did take hym, promisyng hym that thei would spende bothe their lifes and gooddes with hym, and that Richard should no lenger reigne ouer theim. When this lo was dooen, Henry declared all these thynges to the duke of Britain, praiyng and desiryng hym now of helpe, and that he would aide hym with a greater numbre of men, and also to lende hym a frendely and honeste some of money, that he might now recouer his righte and enheritaunce of the croune 15 of Englande, vnto the whiche he was called and desired by all the lordes and nobilitee of the realme, and whiche (God willyng) he was moste assured to possesse, and after his possession he would moste faithfully restore the same again. The duke promised hym aide, vpon the trust whereof he 20 began to make redy his shippes that thei might with all expedicion be redy to saile, that no tyme should bee lost. In the whiche tyme kyng Richard was again retourned to London, and had taken diuerse of theim that wer of this conspiracy that is to sale George Browne, Roger Clififorde, 25 Thomas Selenger, knightes. Also Thomas Ram, Robert Clififorde and diuerse other whom he caused to bee put to death.

After this he called a parliament, wherein was decreed that all those that wer fled out of the land should bee 30 reputed and taken as enemies too the realme, and all their landes and goodes to be forfaite and confiscate. And not content with that preay, whiche was no small thyng, he caused also a great taxe and some of money to bee leuied of the people. For the large giftes and liberalitee that he first vsed, to bye the fauoures and frendshippis of many, had now brought hym in nede. But nothing was more like then that Thomas Stanley should haue been reputed and taken for one of those enemies, because of the workyng of Margaret 5 his wife, whiche was mother vnto Henry erle of Richemonde, the whiche was noted for the chief hed and woorker of this conspiracy. But forasmuche as it was thought that it was to small purpose that women could dooe, Thomas beeyng nothyng fauty was deliuered and commaunded that he 10 should not suffre Margaret his wife to haue any seruauntes about her, neither that she should not go abrod, but bee shutte vp and that from thence furth she should sende no message neither to her sonne nor to any of her other frendes, whereby any hurte might bee wrought against the 15 kyng, the whiche commaundement was accomplished. And by the autoritie of the same parliamente a peace was concluded with the Scottes, whiche a litle before had skirmished with the borderers. Whiche thyng brought to passe, the kyng supposed all conspiracy to bee clene auoyded, foras-20 muche as the duke with other of his compaignie wer put to death, and also certaigne other bannished. Yet for all this, kyng Richard was dailye vexed and troubled, partely mis-trustyng his owne strength, and partely fearyng the commyng of Henry with his compaigny, so that he liued but in a 25 miserable case. And because that he would not so con-tinewe any longer, he determined with hym self to putte awaie the cause of this his feare and businesse, either by policie or els by strengthe. And after that he had thus purposed with hym self, he thought nothyng better then too 30 tempte the duke of Britain yet once again either with money, prayer or some other speciall rewarde, because that he had in kepyng therle Henry, and moste chiefly, because he knewe that it was onely he that might deuuer hym from all his trouble by deliueryng or imprisonyng the saied Henry. Wherefore incontinently he sente vnto the duke certain ambassadoures the whiche should promise vnto hym, S beside other greate

rewardes that thei broughte with theim, to geue hym yerely all the reuenewes of all
the landes of Henry and of all the other lordes there beyng with hym, if he would after
the receite of the ambassadoures put theim in prisone. The ambassadoures, beeyng
departed and come ID where the duke laie, could not haue communicacion with hym,
for as muche as by extreme sicknesse his wittes were feble and weake. Wherfore one
Peter Landose his treasurer a manne bothe of pregnaunt wit and of greate autoritee,
tooke this matter in hande. For whiche cause he was 15 afterwarde hated of all the
lordes of Britain. With this Peter the Englishe ambassadoures had communicacion,
and declaryng to hym the kyng his message desiered hym instantly, forasmuche as
thei knewe that he might bryng their purpose to passe, that he would graunt vnto kyng
20 Richard his request, and he should haue the yerly reuenues of all the landes of the
saied lordes. Peter, consideryng that he was greately hated of the lordes of his owne
nacion, thought that if he mighte bryng to passe through kyng Richard to haue all
these greate possessions and yerly 25 reuenewes, he should then bee hable too matche
with theim well inough and not to care a rushe for theim, where vpon he answered
the ambassadours that he would dooe that kyng Richard did desire, if he brake not
promise with hym. And this did he not for any hatred that he bare vnto Henry, for
30 he hated hym not, for not long before he saued his life where the erle Henry was
in greate jeoperdy. But suche was the good fortune of Englande, that this craftie
compacte took no place, for while the letters and messengers ranne betwene

Peter and kyng Richard, Jhon bishoppe of Ely beeyng then in Flaundres was certified
by a prieste, whiche came out of Englande whose name was Christopher Urswicke,
of all the whole circumstaunce of this deuise and purpose. Where vpon with all spede
the saied bishop caused the saied priest 5 the same dale to cary knowledge thereof into
Britain to Henry erle of Richemond, willyng hym with all the other noble menne to
dispatche theim selfes with all possible haste into Fraunce. Henry was then in Venetie,
when he heard of this fraude without tariaunce sent Christopher vnto 10 Charles the
Frenche kyng desiryng licence that Henry with the other noble menne might safely
come into Fraunce, the whiche thyng beeyng sone obteigned, the messenger returned
with spede to his lorde and prince.

Then therle Henry settyng all his businesse in as good 15 stale and ordre as he
mighte, talked litle and made fewe a counsaill herof, and for the more expedicion,
he caused the Erie of Penbroucke secretely to cause all the noble menne to take their
horses, dissemblyng to ride vnto the duke of Brytain: but when thei came to the
vttermoste partes there 20 of, thei should forsake the waie that led them towarde the
duke, and to make into Fraunce with al that euer thei might. Then thei, doyng in euery
thyng as thei wer bidden, lost no tyme but so sped theim that shortely thei obteigned
and gatte into the countie of Angeow. Henry then within 25 twoo dales folowyng,
beyng then still at Venety tooke foure or fiue of his seruauntes with hym and feigned as
though he would haue ridden thereby to visite a frende of his; and forasmuche as there
wer many English menne lefte there in the towne, no manne suspected any thyng, but
after that he 30 had kepte the right waie for the space of fiue miles, he forsoke that
and turned streight into a wood that was thereby, and toke vpon hym his seruauntes
apparell, and put his apparell vpon his seruaunt and so tooke but one of theim with
hym, on whom he waited as thoughe he had been the seruaunte and the other the

maister. And with all con-uenient and spedy haste so set furthe on their journey that c no tyme was lost, and made no more tariaunce by the waie, then onely the baityng of their horses, so that shortely he recouered the coastes of Angeow, where all his other com-paignie was.

But within foure dales after that the erle was thus escaped ID Peter receiued from kyng Richarde the confirmacion of the graunte and promises made for the betraiyng of Henry and the other nobles. Wherefore the saied Peter sent out after hym horses and menne with suche expedicion and spede to haue taken hym, that scacely the erle was entered Fraunce 15 one houre but thei wer at his heles. The English menne then beyng aboue the numbre of three hundred at Veneti, hearyng that the erle and all the nobles wer fled so sodainly and without any of their knowledge, were astonied and in maner despaired of their liues.

20 But it happened contrary to their expectacion for the duke of Britain, takyng the matter so vnkyndely that Henry should bee so vsed with hym that for feare he should bee compelled to flee his land, was not a litle vexed with Peter, too whom (although that he was ignoraunte of the fraude 25 and crafte that had been wrought by hym) yet he laied the whole faute in hym, and therefore called vnto hym Edward Poynynges and Edward Wooduille, deliueryng vnto theim the foresaied money that Henry before had desired the duke to lende hym towarde the charge of his journey, and com- 30 maunded theim to conueigh and conducte all the Englishe-men his seruauntes vnto hym paiyng their expenses, and to deliuer the saied some of money vnto the erle. When the erle sawe his menne come and heard the comfortable newes, he not a litle rejoysed, desiryng the messengers that returned to shewe vnto the duke, that he trusted ere long tyme to shewe hymself not to bee vnthankfull for this great kindnesse that he now shewed vnto him. And within fewe daies after, the erle wente vnto Charles the Frenche kyng, too whom after he had rendred thankes for the great benefites and kindnesse that he had receiued of hym, the cause of his commyng firste declared, then he besought hym of his helpe and aide, whiche should bee an immortall ben elite to hym and his lordes, of whom generally he was called vnto the 10 kyngdome, forasmuche as thei so abhorred the tiranny of kyng Richard. Charles promised hym helpe and bade hym to bee of good chere and to take no care, for he would gladly declare vnto him his beneuolence. And the same tyme Charles remoued and took with hym Henry and all jr the other noble menne.

While Henry remained there, Jhon erle of Oxenforde (of whom is before spoken) whiche was put in prisone by kyng Edward the fourthe in the castle of Hammes with also James Blount capitain of that castle, and Jhon Forskewe 20 knighte, porter of the towne of Caleis, came vnto hym. But James the capitain, because he lefte his wife in the castle, did furnishe the same with a good garison of menne before his departure.

Henry, when he sawe therle, was out of measure glad 25 that so noble a manne and of greate experience in battaill, and so valiaunt and hardy a knighte, whom he thought to bee moste faithfuu and sure, for somuche as he had, in the tyme of kyng Edward the fourthe, continuall battaill with him in defendyng of king Henry the sixt, thought that now-.3 he was so well appoincted that he could not desire to bee better, and therefore communicated vnto hym all his whole affaires, to bee ordred and ruled only by hym. Not long after Charles the Frenche kyng remoued again to Paris, whom

Henry folowed, and there again moued and besoughte the kyng as he had moste fauourably and kyndly entreteigned hym all this tyme, not onely in wordes but also in dedes, 5 that it would likewise please him yet so muche further to extend his fauoure and beneuolence vnto hym, that now he would aide and helpe hym forwarde in his journey, that not onely he, but also all the lordes and nobilitee of England mighte justely haue cause to knowledge and confesse that ID by the meane of his fauoure and goodnesse thei were restored again to the possession of their enheritaunces, whiche without him thei could not well bryng to passe.

In the meane while, his fortune was suche, that many Englishe menne came ouer dayely out of Englande vnto 15 hym, and many whiche then were in Paris, emong whom were diuerse studientes that fell vnto his parte bothe more and lesse, and specially there was one, whose name was Richard Foxe a prieste, beeyng a manne of a synguler good witte and learnyng, whom Henry streight waie retaigned 20 and committed all his secretes unto hym and whom also afterwarde he promoted too many high promocions, and at the laste he made hym bishop of Winchester.

Kyng Richard then, hearyng of all this conspiracie and of the greate aide that daily wente ouer vnto Henry, thought 25 yet for all this, that if he might bryng to passe that Henry should not couple in mariage with the bloud of king Edward, that then he should dooe well inough with hym and kepe hym from the possession of the croune. Then deuised he with hym self al the waies and meanes that might be how 30 to bring this to passe. And first he thought it to bee best with faire and large promises to attempte the queue, whose fauoure obteigned, he doubted not but shortely to finde the meanes to haue bothe her daughters out of her handes into his owne, and then rested nothyng but if he hym selfe might finde the meanes afterward to mary one of the same daughters, whereby he thought he should make all sure and safe to the vtter disapoyntyng of Henry. Where vpon he sent vnto the quene, then beeyng in the sainctuary, diuerse and sondry 5 messengers that should excuse and pourge hym of his facte afore dooen towardes her, settyng furthe the matter with pleasaunte woordes and high promises bothe to her and also her Sonne Thomas lorde Marques of Dorset, of all thynges that could bee desired. These messengers, beeyng menne 10 of grauitee, handled the quene so craftely that anone she began to bee alured and to herken vnto theim fauourably, so that in conclusion she promised to bee obedient to the kyng in his requestes (forgettyng the injuries he had done to her before, and on the other parte not remembryng the 15 the promise that she made to Margarete, Henries mother). And first she deliuered both her daughters into the handes of kyng Richard, then after she sent priuely for the lord Marques her sonne beyng then at Paris with Henry (as ye haue heard) willyng him to forsake Henry with whom he 20 was, and spedely to retourne into England, for al things was pardoned and forgeuen, and she againe in fauoure and frendshyp of the kyng, and it should be highly for his ad-uauncement and honoure.

Kyng Richard (when quene Elizabeth was thus brought 25 into a fooles paradice) after he had receyued al his brothers daughters from the sanctuary into his palayce, thought there nowe remayned nothyng to be done, but onely the castyng awaye and destroying of his owne wyfe, whiche thyng he had wholy purposed and decreed within hym selfe. And there 30 was nothyng that feared him so muche from this most cruell and detestable murtlier as the losyng of the good opinion that he thought the people had conceyued of him, for as ye haue heard before, he feigned him selfe to be a good man and thought the people had estemed him euen so. Not-withstandyng shortly after, his foresayd vngracious purpose ouercame all this honest feare. And first of all, he found him 5 selfe greued with the barrennes of his wife, that she was vnfruit-ful and brought him furth no chyldren, complainyng therof very greuously vnto the nobles of his realme, and chiefly aboue other vnto Thomas Rotheram, then archebishop of Yorke (whom he had deliuered a lytle afore out of prison), the lo whiche bishop dyd gather of this, that the quene should be ryd out of the way, ere it were long after (suche experience had he of kyng Richardes compleccion, who had practised many lyke thynges not long before) and the same tyme also he made diuerse of his secrete frendes preuy of the same his 15 conjecture.

After this he caused a rumour to runne among the commen people (but he would not haue the aucthor knowen) that the quene was dead, to thentent that she heryng this meruei lous rumoure, should take so greuous a 20 conceyte that anone after she should fall into some great disease, so that he would assay that way, in case it should chaunce her afterward to be sicke, dead or otherwyse murdred, that then the people might impute her deathe vnto the thought she toke, or els to sickenesse. But when 25 the quene heard of so horrible a rumour of her death sprong abroade among the common people, she suspected the matter and supposed the world to be at an ende with her, and incontinently, she went to the kyng with a lamentable countenaunce, and with wepyng teares asked him, whether 30 she had done any thyng whereby he might judge her worthy to suffer death. The kyng made answere with a smilyng and dissimulyng countenaunce and with flatteryng wordes, byddyng her to be of good comforte and to plucke vp her heart for there was no suche thyng-toward her that he knewe. But howe soeuer it fortuned, either by sorowe or els by poysonyng, within fewe dayes after the quene was dead and afterwarde was buryed in the abbey of Westmynster. This is the same Anne, one of Rycharde the earle of Warwickes 5 daughters, which once was contracted to prince Edwarde, kyng Henry the sixt his sonne.

This kyng beyng thus deliuered of his wyfe fantasied apace Lady Elizabeth his nece, desiryng in any wyse to mary with her, but because that al men, yea and the mayden her 10 selfe, abhorred this vnlawfull desire, as a thyng moost detestable, he determined with him selfe to make no great haste in the matter, chiefly for that he was in a pecke of troubles, fearyng least that of the noble men some would forsake him and runne vnto Henry his part, the other at the 15 least would fauoure the secrete conspiracy made againe him, so that of his ende there was almost no doubte. Also the more part of the commen people were in so great dispayre, that many of them had rather to be accompted of the nombre of his enemies, then to put them selfes in 20 jeopardy both of losse of body and goodes in takyng of his part.

And amongest those hoble men whom he feared, fyrst was Thomas Standley and Willyam his brother, Gilberte Talbote, and other a great nombre, of whose purpose though 25 kyng Rychard was ignoraunte, neuerthelesse he trusted not one of them, and least of all Thomas Standley, because he had maryed Henryes mother, as it may well appeare by this that foloweth. For when the sayd Thomas would haue departed from the courte vnto his owne mansyon for his 33 recreacion (as he sayd) but the trueth was, because he would be in a readynesse to receyue Henry and ayde him at his commyng into the realme. But the kyng dyd let him, and would not suffre him to departe, vntyll suche tyme he had lefte in the courte behynde him George Strange, his sonne and heyre, for a pledge. And whyle kyng Rycharde was thus wrapped in feare, and care of the tumulte that was to come, 5 lo, euen then tidynges came that Henry was entered into the land, and that the castell of Hammes was prepared to receyue Henry by the meanes of the erle of Oxenforde whiche then was fled, with James Blunte keper of the castel, vnto Henry.

10 Then kyng Rycharde, thynkyng at the begynnyng to stey all this matter, sent furth with al hast the greater part that were then at Calyce to recouer the sayd castell agayne. Those that were in the castel, when they sawe their aduer-saries make towardes them, spedely they armed them selfes 15 to defence, and in all hast sent messengers to Henry, desiryng him of ayde. Henry furthwith sent the erle of Oxenforde with a chosen sorte of menne to assyst them, and at their fyrst commyng they layde siege not farre from the castel. And whyle kyng Rychardes menne turned backe 20 hauing an eye towardes them, Thomas Brandon, with thirty valeaunt menne of the other syde, gatte ouer a water into the castel, to strength them that were within. Then they that were within layde harde to their charge that were without; on the other syde, the erle of Oxenford so valiantly 25 assayled them of the backe side that they were glad to make proclamacion to them that were within, that yf they would be content to geue over the castel, they should haue fre lybertie to depart with al that euer they had. The erle of Oxenford hearyng this, whiche came onely to saue his 30 frendes from hurte, and namely James Bluntes wyfe, was contented with this condicion and departed in saufegard with all his frendes, returnyng backe to Henry, whiche was at Paris. After this, kyng Rychard was enfourmed that the

Frenche kyng was wery of Henry and his company, and would do nothyng for him, wherby Henry was now not able in maner to healpe him selfe, so that it was not possible that he should preuaile or go forwarde in thenterprise that he thought to haue taken in hand against kyng Rychard. 5 Kyng Rychard beyng brought thus into a fooles paradice, thought himself to be out of all feare, and that there was no cause why he should, beyng so sure, once to wake out of his slepe or trouble him selfe any furder, and therfore called backe his nauy of shyppes that then was redy upon the sea, 10 whiche was fully furnyshed to haue scoured the seas. But yet for the more suretie, least he should be sodenly oppressed, he gaue commaundement to the great men dwellyng by the sea syde (and specially the Welshmen) to watche night and day, least his aduersaries should haue any oportunitee to 15 entre into the lande. As the fashyon is in tyme of warre that those that dvvel by the seas syde should make becons in the highest places there aboute, whiche might be sene afarre of, so that when it should chaunce their enemies to ariue toward the lande, by and by they should fyre their 20 bekyns and rayse the countrey, to the entent that quickely from place to place they might be ascerteyned of al the whole matter, and also to arme them selfes spedely against their enemies.

And so to come to our purpose againe, kyng Richard 25 through the aforesayd tidynges, beganne to be more care-lesse and rechelesse, as who say, he had no power to withstand the desteny that hong ouer his head. Such is the prouident justyce of God, that a man doeth leste knowe, prouide and beware when the vengeaunce of God is euen at 30 hand for his offences. And to go furth, at that tyme when Henry the erle of Rychemond remained in Fraunce en-treatyng and suyng for ayde and helpe of the Frenche men,

RICH.

many of the chief noble men, whiche had the realme in gouernaunce (because of the yong age of Charles the kyng), fell somewhat at dissencion, of the whiche variaunce, Lewes the prynce of Orlyaunce was the chiefe and heade, whiche 5 because he had maried John the kynges syster loked to haue bene chiefe gouernoure of all the realme. By the whiche meanes it came to passe, that one manne had the principal gouernaunce of the realme. And therfore Henry therle was constrayned to sue vnto al the nobles seuerally lo one after another desiryng and praiyng them of ayde and helpe in his purpose, and thus the matter was prolonged. In the meane tyme Thomas the Marques of Dorcet (of whom we spake afore) was priuely sent for to come home by his mother, partely mystrustyng that Henry should not 15 preuayle, and partly for the great and large promises that kyng Rychard had made to her for hym before. Whiche letters when the sayd Marques had receyued, he beleuyng all thynges that his mother wrote vnto him, and also thynkyng that Henry should neuer prevaile, and that the 20 Frenche men dyd but mocke and dalay with him, he sodenly in the night tyme conueighed him selfe out of Paris and with great spede made towardes Flaunders. The whiche thyng when therle and other of the Englishe lordes heard of, they were sore astonned and amased, and with all 25 spede purchased of Charles the kyng a licence and com-maundement that the Marques might be steyed, whersoeuer he were found within the dominion of Fraunce, chiefly for that he was secrete of their counsel and knewe al their purpose. The commaundement was quickly obteyned and 30 postes made forth euery way, among whom one Humfrey Cheyney playing the part of a good blodhound so truly smelled out and folowed the trace, that by and by he found out and toke the Marques, and so handled and persuaded him with gentle and good wordes, that shortly after he was content to retourne.

Then Henry, beyng delyuered of this chaunce, thought it best to prolonge the matter no further least he should loose bothe the present oportunitee and also wery his 5 frendes that looked for him in England. Wherfore he made haste and set forewarde with a smal army obteyned of the Frenche kyng, of whom he also borowed some money, and some of other his frendes, for the whiche he lefte the Marques and John Burchere behynde for a pledge. And 10 so settyng forward came to Roan, and whyle he taried ther and prepared shippyng at the hauen of Seyn, tidynges came to him that kyng Richardes wyfe was dead, and purposed to mary with the lady Elizabeth, kyng Edwardes eldest doughter beyng his nece, and that he had maried Cicile her 15 syster to a mans sonne of the land farre vnderneth her degre. At the whiche thing, Henry was sore amased and troubled, thinkyng that by this meanes al his purpose was dashed, for that there was no other waye for him to come to the kyngdome but onely by the mariage of one of kyng 20 Edwardes doughters. And by this meanes also he feared least his frendes in England would shrynke from him for lacke of an honest title. But after they had consulted vpon the matter, they thought it best to tary a lytle to proue yf they might get more helpe and make mo frendes. And 25 among all other, they thought it best to adjoyne the lorde Harbart vnto them, whiche was a man of great power in Wales, and that should be brought to passe by this meanes, for that the lorde Harbart had a syster maryable, whom Henry would be content to mary if he would take their part. 30 And to bryng al this matter to passe messengers were sent to Henry the erle of Northumberland, whiche had maried the other syster, so that he should bryng this matter aboute, but the wayes were so besette that the messengers could not come to him.

And in the meane season came veray good tydynges from John ap Morgan, a temporal lawyer, whiche signified 5 vnto them that sir Ryce ap Thomas, a noble and valiaunt man, and John Sauage fauoured his part earnestly, and also sir Reynolde Bray had prepared a great sum me of mony to wage battaile on his part and to helpe him, and therfore he would they should make hast with all that euer they could, lo and make towarde Wales.

Then Henry spedely prepared him selfe because he would lynger his frendes no longer. And after that he had made his praier vnto almightye God that he might haue good successe in his journey, onely with. ii. M. men and a 15 fewe shyppes in the calendes of August he sayled from the hauen of Seyne, and the vii. day after whiche was the xxii. day of August, he ariued in Wales aboute sonneset and landed at Milford hauen, and in the part whiche is called the Dale, where he heard that there was diuers layd in wayt 20 for him, to kepe him backe. From thence in the mornyng betimes he remoued toward a toune called Harford, within X. myle of the Dale, where he was very joyfully receiued. Here he had contrary tidynges brought to that he heard in Normandy afore, that Sir Ryce ap Thomas and John Sauage, 25 with al that euer they coulde make, were of kyng Rychardes part.

Notwithstandyng, they had suche tidynges sent them from the men of Pembruche by a valiaunt gentleman, whose name was Arnold Butteler, that it rejoysed al their heartes, 30 w iiche was, that if al former offences might be remytted, they would be in a redynesse to sticke vnto their owne Gespare the erle. Then Henries company by this meanes beyng encreased, departed from Herford. v. myle toward

Cardigane, and then while he refreshed his men, sodeynly came a rumoure vnto him that the lord Harbart, whiche dwelled at Carmerdine, was nigh at hand with a great armye of menne. At the whiche rumoure there was a great sturre amongest them, euery man toke him selfe to his weapon 5 and made them selfes redy if nede were to fight, and a lytle while they were al afrayd, tyll suche tyme as Henry had sent out horsmen to try the trueth, whiche when they came againe, declared that al thinges was quiet and that there was no suche thyng. But most of all maister Gryffythes, a 10 very noble man, dyd comfort them and gladden their heartes whiche although before he had joyned himselfe to the lorde Harbert, at that very tyme he cleued to Henry with suche company as he had, although they were but fewe, and the same tyme came John ap Morgan vnto him. Henry went 15 styl forwarde and taried almost in no place, because he would make sure worke and the better spede, he inuaded suche places afore that they were armed against him, the whiche places he bette doune with very lytle strength. But afterwarde, hauyng knowledge by his spyes that the lord 20 Harbert and Sir Ryce were in a redynes to geue him battaile, he determined to set vpon them, and either to put them to flight or els to make them sweare homage and feaultee vnto him, and to take them with him in his host against kyng Rychard. And because he would ascertayne his frendes 25 in England howe al the matter went forwarde with him, he sent his moost trusty frendes to the lady Margarete his mother, to Standley, to Talbot, and to other of his most especial frendes with certayne commaundementes. The effecte of the commaundementes were, that he intended with 30 the helpe of his frendes to passe ouer Seuerne and by Shrewesbury to make toward London. Therefore he desired them with those that were of their councel, in tyme and place coniienient, to mete him. So the messengers goyng forth with these commissyons, Henry went forward toward Shrewesbury, and in the way met with sir Ryce ap Thomas with a great nomber of men whiche came vnto him and was 5 of his part. For two dayes afore Henry promysed him to be chiefe ruler of all Wales as sone as he came to the croune (if he would come vnto him) whiche afterward he gaue to him in dede. In the meane tyme the messengers execu-tyng the message diligently returned backe agayne with lo large rewardes of them to whom they were sent, and came to Henry the same day he entred into Shrewesburye and shewed howe all his frendes were in a redynesse to do the vttermost that lay in them. This tidynges put Henry in suche great hope, that he went furth with a courage and 15 came to the toune of Newporte and there set up his tentes vpon a lytle hyl, and there lay all night. That night came to him Sir Gylbert Talbot with aboue two hundred men. After that they went furth to Stafforde and whyle they were there, Willyam Standley came to him with a few 20 after him, and when he had talked a lytle with him, returned backe againe to his boost whiche he had prepared. From thence he went to Lichefelde and that night lay without the toune, but in the mornyng betime he entred into the citee and was receyued honourably. A day or ii afore, Thomas 25 Standley was there with fyue. M. men armed, whiche, when he knewe of Henries commyng, furthwith went afore to a village called Aderstone there to tary tyl Henry came. This he dyd to auoyde suspection, beyng afrayd lest king Richard knowyng his intent would haue put his sonne to 30 death, whiche, as I telled you before, was left with him as a pledge for his father. But kyng Rychard in the meane tyme, which then was at Nottyngham, hearyng that Henry with a few more of banished men was entred into Wales, so lightly regarded the matter, that he thought it was not muche to be past vpon, for that he came in with so fewe in nombre, and that the lorde Harbarte and Sir Ryce, whiche were rulers of all Wales, would eyther kyll him, or els take him and bryng him aliue. But afterward, when he remem- 5 bred him selfe that oftentymes a smal matter in batel, if it be not loked vnto betymes, would make at the laste a great sturre, he thought it best to remedy the matter betymes and commaunded Henry the earle of Northumberlande with other of the nobles of the realme (whom he thought had set 10 more by him then by their owne goodes) to rayse vp an army and to come to him with spede. Also he sent dmers messengers with letters to Robert Brakynbury, keper of the Towre of London, commandyng him to come vnto him in all hast, and to bryng with him, as felowes in battaile, 15 Thomas Burschere, Walter Hungreford and diuers other knightes, whom he dyd not a lytle suspecte.

In this tyme it was shewed that Henrye was come to Shrewesbury without any hurt. With the whiche tydynges, the kyng began to rage and make exclamacion against 20 them, that contrary to their faithes they had vtterly deceyued him, and then he beganne to mystrust all menne, and wyste not whom he might truste, so that he thoughte it best to sette fourth him selfe against his aduersaries. And furthwith he sent out spyes to knowe which way Henry dyd take. They 25 when they had done their diligence retourned backe againe and shewed him howe that Henry was come to Lichefelde. The whiche thyng after he knewe, because no we there was a great nombre of souldiers come together, by and by his men set in aray, he commaunded them forwarde, and to go 30 iiii and iiii together, and by that way whiche they kept they heard say, their enemies were commyng. The suspecte persons he put in the middes, he him selfe with those he trusted came behynd, with wynges of horsemen rimnyng on euery side. And thus kepyng their order, aboute sonne-set came vnto Leicestre.

When Henry in the meane season had remoued from 5 Lichefeld vnto the next village called Tamworth, in the mydway he met with Walter Hungerford, Thomas Burschier and many other more, whiche had promised to ayde him afore. And for because they perceyued that they were suspected of kyng Rychard, and least they shoulde be lo brought violently vnto him, beyng their enemy, they forsoke Robert Brakenbury their capitayne and in the night tyme stole priuely away and went to Henry. Unto whom there chaunced by the waye that was worthy to be marked, whiche was that Henry, although he was a man of 15 noble courage and also his company did dayly encrease, yet for al that he stode in great feare because he was vncertayne of Thomas Stanley whiche, as I telled you before, for the feare of puttyng his sonnes to death, inclyned as yet vnto no part, and that the matter was not 2D so slender of kyng Rycharde, as reporte was made to him of his frendes.

Wherfore, as all afrayde without a cause, he toke onely twenty men with him, and steyed in his journey as a man in dispayre and halfe musyng with him self what was best to 25 be done. And to aggrauate the matter, tidynges was brought him that kyng Rychard was commyng nere to mete him with a great and houge boost of men. And whyle he thus lyngered for feare behynd, his boost came afore to the toune of Tamworthe, and because it was then darke night, 30 he lost bothe his company and also his waye, then wandr "ng from place to place, at last came to a lytle village, iii. myle from his hoost, beyng ful of feare, and lest he should fal into the daunger of the scoutwatche he durst not aske a question of any man, and partly for the feare that was present, and partely for that was to come he lay there that night and toke this for a signe or a pronosticacion of some great plage that was to come, and the other part of his hoost was no lesse abashed seyng his absence for that tyme. When in the 5 mornyng Henry came to them in the light of the day he excused the matter that he was not absent because he had lost his way, but rather of purpose, because he would common with his preuy frendes whiche would not be sene in the day. After that he went priuely to Aderstone where Thomas 10 Standley and Willyam his brother dyd dwell. Here Henry, Thomas, and Willyam mette and toke other by the hand with louyng salutacions and were glad one of another. Then after they counceled together of their metyng with kyng Richard whom they perceiued not then to be farre from 15 them. That day when it drewe toward night, in the euenyng John Sauage, Brytanne Sanforde, Symon Digby with many other had forsaken kyng Rychard and came to Henry with a great power of menne, whiche power and strength sette Henry aloft againe. In the mean season kyng Rychard 20 whiche purposed to go thrpughe thicke and thinne in this matter came to Bosvvorth a lytle beyond Lecester where the place of battail should be (as a man would say the high justice of God, whiche could not be

auoyded, hangyng ouer his head, h3, d called him to a place where he should suffer
25 worthy punishement for his detestable offences) and there he set vp his tentes and
rested that night. Afore he went to bed, he made an oration to his company with great
vehe-mencye, perswadyng and exhortyng them manfully to fight. And afterward, as
it was sayd, he had a terrible dreame in 30 his slepe, semyng that he sawe horrible
deuilles appeare vnto him and pullyng and halyng of him that he could take no rest,
whiche vision fylled him full of feare and also of heuy care when he waked. For
by and by after, beyng sore greued in his mynd, he dyd prognosticate of this dreame
the euil lucke and heuye chaunce that after came to him, and he came not with so
chereful a countenaunce vnto his com-5 panye as he was wonte to do. Then, least
they should thynke that he had this heauynesse for the feare of his enemies, he stode
vp and rehersed vnto them al his dreame. But I thynke that this was not a dreame, but
rather his conscience pricked with the sharpe styng of his mischeuous 10 offences,
whiche although they do not pricke alway, yet moost commonly they wyll byte moost
towarde the latter daye, representyng vnto vs not onely them selfe, but also the terrible
punishement that is ordeyned for the same, as the sight of the deuill tearyng and halyng
vs, so that therby (if 15 we haue grace) we may take an occasyon to be penitent, or
els for lacke of the same dye in desperacion. Nowe to come to my purpose againe,
the next day after, kyng Richard hauyng al thinges in a readynesse went furth with the
armye out of his tentes, and began to sette his men in aray; fyrst 20 the forwarde set
furth a merueilous length bothe of horsemen and also of footemen, a veray terrible
companye to them that should see them afarre of; and in the formost part of al he
ordered the bowmen as a strong fortresse for them that came after, and ouer this John
the duke of 25 Northfolke was head captaine. After him folowed the kyng with a
mighty sorte of men.

   And in this while, Henry, beyng departed from the communicacion of his frendes,
without any tariyng pytched his tentes nere his enemies and laye there all night and
30 commaunded his men to be in a redynesse. In the mornyng he sent also to Thomas
Standley, beyng then in the middes betwixt bothe hostes, that he should come nere
with his armye. He sent him worde againe that he should set his men in an ordre tyl
he came; with the whiche answere, otherwise then he had thought or then the matter
did require, he was not a Httle abashed and stode as it were in doubt. Yet for all that
he taryed not, but with all spede set his men in an order, the forwarde was but slender,
because 5 his nombre was but fewe, the archers were set in the formost parte. Ouer
them John the erle of Oxenford was heade capitain. In the right wyng he set Gilbert
Talbot. In the left he put John Sauage; And he hymself with the helpe of Thomas
Stanley folowed with one com. paignie of horsemen 10 and a fewe footemen, for all
his whole compaignie were scant fine thousande besides bothe the Stanleis with their
compaignie, of the whiche William Stanley had thre thousande. The kyng his armie
was double to all this. And so when bothe armies were all in a redynesse and began for
to 15 come within the sight of other, thei bragged furthe them selfes of bothe parties,
lokyng onely for the signe and token of strik i ng together. Betwixt bothe hostes, there
was a marresse whiche Henry left on his right hande purposely as a defence of his
menne, he found the meanes also to haue 20 the brighte sunne on his backe, that it
might dasill the yies of his enemies.

But the kyng, when he sawe Henry passe ouer the marresse, commaunded his men with all violence to set vpon theim. Thei by and by with a sodain clamor let arowes 25 flee at theim. On the other side thei paied them home manfully again with the same. But when thei came nere together thei laied on valeauntely with swerdes. Therle of Oxforde fearyng least in the meane tyme kyng Richardes multitude should haue compassed in his men, whiche were but a few, 3 he commaunded them by hues thei should not moue forward past ten foote, the whiche commaundement knowen, thei knit them selfe together and seased not in fightyng: their aduersaries beeyng afraied suspected some craft or gyle and began to breake of, and many of the same part wer not muche greued therwith, because thei were as glad the kyng should be loste as saued, and therefore thei fought vith lesse 5 corage. Then therle of Oxford, with his men thicke together, stroke on more freshlier. The other of the other part did likewise the same. And while the first wardes of the battail had fought so manfully, Richard perceiued by his spies Henry afar of with a fewe compaigny of armed men. After- lo ward comyng nere, Richard knewe him by signes and tokens, then beeyng inflamed with an anger, furiously stroke the horse with the spurres and ran out of the one side of the hoste, and like a lion ran at hym. On the other side Henry, perceiuing hym commyng, was very desirouse to mete him.

15 Richard at the first settyng furth killed diuerse that stoode before him, again he threwe doune Henryes banner and William Brandon the bearer also, he ran at Cheiny, a man of great might, whiche came for to mete hym, and with great violence ouerthrewe hym to the grounde, and thus he made 20 hymself a waie through them for to come to Henry. But Henry kepte better tacke with hym then his men would have thought, whiche then was almoste in despaire of the victory. And euei at that time lo there came William Stanley to aide them with thre thousand men, and euen at 25 the very same tyme the residue of kyng Richardes men wer put to flight. Then Richard fightyng alone in the middest of al his enemies was ouerthrowne and slain. In the meane tyme therle of Oxford in the forward, after he had fought manfully a little while, put the residue to flight of whom he 30 si ewe a great numbre. But a great numbre more, whiche folowed Richard more for feare then for loue, helde their handes from fightyng and went awaie without hurte, for that thei looked not for his safegard, but rather for his destruccion.

There wer slain at this conflict not many more than one. M. of the whiche these wer noble men: Jhon duke of Norffolke, Walter Feris, Robert Brakyngbury, Richard e Radcliffe and many other more. And within. ii. daies after, William Catisby lawyer with certain other of his felowes was put to 5 deth at Leicester, and emonges those that ran awaie was Fraunces Louell, Humfray Stafford, with Thomas his brother, and many other more that ran into sanctuary at Colchester in Essex. Ther was of the captiues a great numbre, because that when kyng Richard was slain, euery man cast doune 10 his wepon and yeld hym self to Henry, of the whiche the more parte would haue dooen so at the beginnyng, if it had not been for feare of kyng Richardes spies, whiche then wandred in euery place. And emongest these, the nobles wer therle of Northumberlande, the erle of Surrey, of the 15 whiche therle of Surrey was put in prisone, the other as a frend was receiued into fauor. Henry at that feld lost not aboue a. C. men, ernohgest whom the chief was William Brandon whiche bare Henries banner. This battaill was fought in the. xxvii. dale of the monethe of Auguste, in the 20 yere of our lorde. M. cccc. lxxxvi. the conflict indured more then two houres. Richard might (as the fame went) a saued hym self if he would a fled awaie, for those that were about hym, when thei sawe his men from the beginnyng fight but faintly and that some were ronne awaie to the other part, 25 suspected treason and willed hym to flie, and when the matter was manifest that all hope of victory was paste, thei brought hym a swift horse. He puttyng aside all hope and trust that was in fliyng, made (as it was saied) this answere, that this dale he would haue either an end of battail or els 3 of his life, suche was his great audacite and manfulnes whiche because he did se certainly that in this dale he should obtain the kyngdome quietly all daies of his life or els lose bothe foreuer, he entred in emongest tlielm, as it was declared before, intendyng vtterly eidier to lose all or els to win all. And so the wretche died, hauyng the ende that al suche wer wont to haiie, whiche in the stede of lawe, honesty and al 5 godlinesse folowe their owne appetite, villany and all wicked-nesse. And plainly this is an example whiche cannot bee expressed, to feare them whiche will not suffre one houre to bee otherwise spent then in cruelte, mischief and al deuelishe fasions. Henry when he had thus obtained the victory he lo fell doune on his knees and, with many praiers and thankes, referred all to the goodnesse of God. Then after he stoode vp beeyng wonderfully replenished with joye, and wente vp vpon a little hill and there gaue greate commendacions to his souldiours, commaundyng theim that were hurte to bee 15 heled and the ded to bee buried; afterward he gaue im-mortall thankes to his noble capitans promisyng them that he would neuer forget their benefite. The multitude in the meane time with one voyce and one minde proclamed him kyng. When Thomas Stanley sawe that, he toke kyng 20 Richarde his croune whiche was founde emongest the spoile, and by and by put it vpon Henries hed as though he had been then created kyng by the eleccion of the people as it was wont to be in the old tyme, and this was the first token of his fehcite. After this kyng Henry with his compaigny 25 and carriage wente to Leicestre towarde nighte too bed, where, after he had refreshed his compaignie well for the space of twoo daies, that thei might the better go towarde London, Kyng Richardes body was brought naked ouer a horse backe, the hed and the amies hangyng on the one 30 side and the legges on, the other, and caried into the Grey Friers of Lecester, and surely it was but a miserable sight to looke vpon, yet it was good inough consideryng his wretched liuyng, and there without any solempnitee was buried two dales after. He reigned two yeres two monethes and one dale, he was but of a small stature hauyng but a deformed body, the one shulder was higher than the other, he had a shorte face and a cruell loke whiche did betoken malice, gyle and deceit. And while he did muse vpon any thyng 5 standyng, he would bite his vnder lippe continually, wherby a manne might perceiue his cruell nature within his wretched body striued and chaffed alwaie within hymself, also the dagger whiche he bare aboute hym, he would alwaies be choppyng of it in and out. He had a sharpe and pregnaunt 10 witte, subtile and to dessimule and fain very mete. He had also a proude and cruell mynde, whiche neuer wente from hym to the houre of his death, whiche he had rather suffer by the cruell sworde, thoughe all his compaignie did forsake hym, then by shamefull flight he would fauoure his life, 15 whiche after might fortune by sicknesse or other condyng punyshemente shortely too perishe.

p. 1, line 1. kyng Edwardc. the jvcvrth. His reign commenced (see Nicolas' Chronology of History, p. 305) 4th March, 1461. He was crowned 28th or 29th June following and died 9th April, 1483.

7. that is to witte. The phrase is more full than usual, "that is" meaning exactly the same as "to witte." So that the meaning is doubly expressed. It = "that is to say" or "namely."

8. Edwarde the Prynce, afterwards Edward V.

9. Elizabeth, affianced during her father's lifetime to the dauphin, but afterwards married to Henry VH.

11. Cecily, the promised bride of the King of Scots, afterwards married to Viscount Welles. Halle adds after "fayre'": " firste wedded to the Vicounte Welles, after to one Kyne, and lived not in great wealthe." See below, 115. 16.

12. Brigette became a nun in a convent at Dart ford. The convent at Dartford was founded, in honour of St Mary and St Margaret, by King Edward IH. See Dugdale, Monasticon, II. 357. Halle has " at Sion" before "in Dertforde."

13. her whose name she bare. St Bridget was the daughter of Dubtach, a man of Leinster, and niece on her mother's side of St Ultan, who collected the accounts of her virtues and had them put into poetry. She took the veil in order to escape marriage, and became abbess of Kildare.

15. Anne, contracted first to Philip of Burgundy and afterwards married to Thomas Howard who became Duke of Norfolk.

16. Katheryne, affianced first to the infant of Spain, but married William Courtenay, Earl of Devon. Halle says " Katheryne, the youngest daughter was maried to Lorde William Courtney, sonne to therle of Devonshire, whiche, c."

23. greate funerall honoiire. The account of King Edward's funeral is given in Sandford's Genealogical History, pp. 391 392. "The manner of this King's interment was thus; first, the corpse was covered from the Navel to the knees and so laid upon a board all naked, and so continued ten or twelve hours, that all the Lords both Spiritual and Temporal then being in London or about might look on him, and the Lord Mayor and his brethren saw him so lying, and then he was seared (i. e. embalmed). Then, on the morrow after, he was brought into the Chapel of St Stephen (now the House of Commons)

RICH. Q where there were three masses sung, the first of our Lady, the second of the Trmity, the third of Requiem; and in the afternoon there was sung Dirige and Cominendai7i, and at night well watched with his nobles and servants. He rested in this order eight days, and on Wednesday being the 17th day of the month of April above said, the body was conveyed into the Abbey of Westminster, borne by several Knights and Esquires that were for his body, having upon the corpse a rich and large black cloth of gold with a cross of cloth of silver, and above that a rich canopy of cloth imperial, fringed with gold and black silk, borne by four Knights, having at the corners four banners, also borne by four Knights, the first of the Trinity, the second of our Lady, the third of St George, and the fourth of St Edward. My Lord Howard bare the King's banner before the body, the Officers of Arms about him on every side.

In the Herse in Westminster Abbey above the body and Cloth of Gold aforesaid was a personage like to the similitude of a king, in habit Royal, crowned with a crown

Royal on his head, holding in one hand a Sceptre and in the other hand a ball of Silver gilt with a cross patee.

When the mass and all other solemnities were performed the body was placed in a chariot drawn by six horses, and so with that pomp that was required went to Charing Cross, where the Chariot was censed, and from thence to Syon, where it was received that night with the usual ceremonies; from thence on the next morning they departed in good order to Eton where they were received by the procession of Windsor, and at the Castle gate the Archbishop of York and the Bishop of Winchester censed the corpse; and from thence they passed to the new Church where in the quire was ordained a marvellous well-wrought Herse being that night watched with a good company of Nobles and Esquires of the body, and was there buried with all solemnities befitting so great and so victorious a King, and had this rhiming Epitaph composed for him registred in a Book in the College of Arms." (Then follow 26 Latin hexameters in praise of the King.)

P. 1, line 5. beloued with. We now use by after heloned. In Shakespeare the phrase is always beloved?(never by').

12. in effecte. We should now say in fact, cf. 4. 19.

13. in that that. The modern use would omit one "that" but cf. for the repetition 21. 33.

15. growen, old past part, oi to grozv, now contracted into 'i77 w. Cf. Gascoigne's Steel Glas, "Yet now I stand prinking me intheglasse, when the crowes foote is growen under mine eye."

16. straunge, i. e. reserved, distant, shy about exhibiting. Cf. Shaks. Co? H. of Err. II. 2. 112, "Look strange and frown." So Troil. II. 3. 250, "If he were proud, or covetous of praise, or strange, or self-affected."

17. parsonage, i. e. personage, Lat. persona, whence we get our word parson = clergyman, who was the representative person of the parish.

23. consyder. This seems to be a sort of conditional tense = If any one should consider; the relative ivho so being equivalent to if any.

24. voyded. Halle reads here "advoided them." Cf. Shaks. Corio-lanus, IV. 5. 88, "If I had feared death, of all the men i' the world I would have z' ctvthee."

The style of this History is somewhat Euphuistic, i. e. it has numerous instances of sentences, nicely balanced in order and number of words, and with occasional instances (as here in voyded, vainquisshed) of alliteration, after the manner of Lyly's Eiiphues, and other works of the Elizabethan times. Cf. 4. 14, 15; 8. 28, 29, S: c.

28. boo7-clye hux Y. Fxom door=rusic, hence sfoii, strong, large.

P. 3, line 2. j-i7 = lessened. Ci. C? i cer, Frankeleines Tale, 1169, "And on his way than is he forth y-fare In hope to ben lessyd of his care."

wcl. in the sense of quite, entirely. Cf. Shaks. Tivo Gentlemen, I. I. 81, "A silly answer and fitting well a sheep."

lefte, left off, ceased. Cf. Lyly's E7iphues, 73, "As the dry beech kindled at the roote, never Icavcth untill it come to the toppe."

5. towarde, in expectation. Cf. Shaks. As You Like It, v. 4. 35, "There is, sure, another flood tozvard."" such as no manne looked for ey. ez. edi. Cf. Matt, xi, 13.

14. trybute cute of Fraimce. This was the annual pension of 50,000 crowns settled to be paid to Edward IV. by Louis XI. after their treaty at Picquigny. See Lingard, iv. 100.

16. Baruiycke, i. e. Berwick-upon-Tweed, yielded to Edward by the Scotch in 1482.

19. Halle adds after '-estoned " " then those highe humilitees."

21. parte, mien, carriage. ' wwevikidsa., Arte of English Poesie, "ij), " Y of state." Sliaks. 2 Hen. VI. IV. i. 19, " t of gentleman."

delonayre d (y, Fr. de bon air. Cf. Troilus and Cressida, 1. 3- 35,

"Courtiers as free, as debonair, unarmed, As bending angels."

24. Wyndesore. Here Halle reads " Haverynge at the Bower."

in, used with the pres. part, as we often find on or a, to give more fulness to the expression. Cf. i Sam. ii. 13, "While the flesh was in seething."

28. chere meant originally yi?, then it was applied to that which had an effect on the face, which gladdened or enlivened; to mirth and spirit, then to the entertainment which caused them. Cf. Lever's Sermons, p. 79, "They rose up by rebellion and have lost all the chere of that feast."

30. vioe, more. Cf. Puttenham, Arte of En- lish Poesie, 55, " mo and more excellent examples."

P. 4, line 6. tozvardoiesse, docility, capability of being taught. Cf. Grindal, Remains, 450, "This kind of dispensation. seemeth not convenient to be used, but where there is good proof of great tozvardness in learning."

10. kinde, kin, relationship. Cf. Shaks. Pericles, v. I. 68, "Came of a gentle kind, and noble stock."

11. haddeholden place, i. e. had had any effect, had had their proper influence. Cf. for a like phrase Burton's Anatomy, p. 352, "They were both cured by reading when no prescribed physic would take place"" (i. e. have any effect). And p. 359, "When this last engine would take no place (have no influence) they left him to his own ways."

15. binden. This is the Old English form of the plural number.

17. bereue. For the use of this verb not followed as it commonly is by the preposition of, cf. Chaucer, Wife of Bathes Prologue, 475,

"But Age alias that al wole envenyme Hath me biraft my beaiitee and my pith."

10. entreate, treat of. Cf. Lyly's Euphues, p. 53, "For me to intreat of the one, being a novise, I may well make you weary."

24. a noble manne ajid a mightie. This order of adjectives was not imcommon in Old English. Cf. Luke xxiii. 50, "A good man and a just."

28. kinge Henrye his bloode,. Q. r g'H. Qnty"sh ood. A common mistake in Elizabethan English. See 5.2.

29. a goodlye Prince, i. e. Edward the Lancastrian Prince of Wales, murdered by the retainers of Edward IV. after the battle of Tewkesbury.

P. 5, line I. preuente o anticipate. Cf. Bacon's Advancemetii (W. Aldis Wright), p. 261, "Man is not io prevent his time." 3. Wakcfielde. The battle was fought 31 Dec. 1460.

5. j-a j- = princes. Shaks. Kingjojut, II. i. 395,

"How like you this wild counsel, mighty statesv 6. stomacke, temper, courage. Cf. Bp Pilkington's Works, p. 59, "With such words of fear and power must all stubborn stomachs be pulled down."

18. at the lest ivise. We should now say at least.

19. fatitye, guilty, in fault. Cf. Golden Boke, Let. 6, "O how sorowfuu am I, for in all these am I fatityey This pronunciation is common enough in some parts of England still.

23. wist, past tense of an Old English verb, witan =. o know, connected with both zuise and wit. Cf. Bp Pilkington's Works, p. 443, "A wise man should not say, Had I wist this or that, I would have provided for this and that."

26. egall, equal, Fr. egal, Lat. aeqiialis. See Puttenham, Arte of English Poesie, p. 57, "Vertue itselfe is not in every respect of egdll value and estimation,"

27. vndcr ' Xiix ox to. Cf. Sir Thomas More's Utopia (Pitt Press Series), 97. 17, where speaking of gold he says, "And then who doeth not playnelye se howe farre it is under iron?"

28. ill fetured, ill made or formed. Feature is Lat. facticra from facio, to make, fashion. We should only now use it of the face. See

Shaks. Sonnet xxix. 6,

"Feattired like him, like him with friends possessed."

30. hard fauonred, ugly. See Burton's Anat. of Mel. p. 4S2, "an old hard favoured man fast asleep in a bower."

states, see on 1. 5. Halle has " such as in estates is called a warlike visage, and emong commen persones, a crabbed face."

31. warlye, weird-like, used of things having a malignant influence. The MTiter uses this word as a sort of euphemism, rather than employ of a great prince such an epithet as hideous or ugly. Of other men he would have used another word.

P. 6, line I. adoe. This noun is now not much employed, but is known from the title of Shakespeare's play "Much ado about nothing." Cf. Gosson, School of Abuse, p. 28, "As one said at the shearing of hogs, great cry and little wool, much ado and small help." An example of " i7iore adoe " is in Milton, Tractate on Education (Pitt Press Series), p. 8.

2. borne oufwarde, carried forth, as for burial, feet foremost.

5. elks, otherwise, else. The orthography is that of the rd in A. S., which form was preserved for a long time in Middle English.

7. 72one, we should now say w. Cf. Ilawes, Pastime of Pleasure, cap. X.,

"They hadde none order nor no stedfastnes."

8. metely. In Early English this word is often found as an adjective. Cf. Berners' Froissart, vol. I. c. 275, "He was a knight tn-etely to be the leader of men of arms."

Cf. also Chaucer, Romaunt of the Rose (Bell's Ed.), vol. vii. p. 40,

"Fetys he was and wel beseye With metely mouth and yen greye."

II. dyspence, expenditure. See Spenser, Faerie Queene, b. II. c. i,

"Was poured forth with plentiful dispence.

13. get, instead oigat. Cf. 75. 17.

14. pil, rob, pillage. See Thos. Lever, Sermons, p. 29, "And the poore flocke. most miserablyejZ o', and spoyled."

15. dissifnuler, dissimulator, dissembler, concealer of the truth. Fr. dissimtder, Lat. dissi? nulare. For the verb dissifuule see Forjnularies of Faith, p. 159, "All they which. will wink thereat and dissimitle iv 16. lozvlye of counteynaunce, humble in manner. Yox countenance in the sense oi ntan ter, see Shaks. As You Like It, il. 7. 108,

"And therefore put I on the countenance Of stem commandment."

17. cotimpinable = ix tndi y. Apparently the same word as com-paniable, for which see Bacon, Hen. VII. (Pitt Press Series), p. 217. 4, '-companiable and respective and without jealousy." Also Chaucer, Shipman s Tale, line 4, "A wyf he hadde of excellent beautee and com-paignable and revelous was she." Halle has instead " familier."

? = omitting. Cp. Bacon, Hen. VII (Pitt Press Series) p. 159.15. " King Ferdinand would not let to counsel the King in his own aflairs."

19. ofter. The original has after, but this appears to be a misprint. Oftei' is not very common in English, but More uses it. Works, p. 984,

"I dare say that ther are but few, but that they had wel lever abide the paine to be ihrise acquited by proclamacion, and peradventure ofter, then once beare a fagot for heresy."

2 1. inuche zvhat. What is used in older English frequently as if it could take the place of an indefinite noun. Cf. Spenser, F. Q. vi. 9. 7, "And gave him for to feed Such homely what as serves the simple clowne,"

i. e. such plain food of any kind.

So Spenser, Siep. Caend., July, line 29,

"Come downe and learne the little wiat That Thomalin can sayne,"

a sense which survives in the word somewhat. An example nearest like that in our text is Spenser, Shep. Calend., Sept., 104,

"Then plainly to speak of shepherds, most what Bad is the best," i. e. for the most part. And so here the sense is "Friend and foe was for the most part indifferent." Cf. below, 62. 32.

28. borne, i. e. born. For the usage, cf. Shaks. K. yohn, ii. 104,

"Geffrey was thy elder brother born.

29. drifte, intention, meaning, plan. Cf. Shaks. Rotiieo, IV. r. 114, "In the meantime shall Roaieo by my letters know our drift."" 32. then he that wer, i. e. than any one that was than if he were. The connexion of the whole sentence is: His design secretly communicated to some one did not fail to help forward Clarence to his death; which death Edward in outward appearance resisted, c.

33. welth, well-being. Cf. For? nularies of the Faiths p. 167, To use our tongues in truth to h. zvealth of our neighbours." Compare also the Prayer-Book Collect in Coj? im. Office, "That she may study to preserve thy people committed to her charge, in wealth, peace, and godliness." Ilis zaelth of course means Clarence's welfare.

P. 7, line I. forethought, to devise, plan, consider beforehand. Cf. Earle's Micro-Cosmographie, p. 76,. foi'ethinks what will come hereafter."

3. decease, iwe. 'L2X. decedere. Cf."Lyly s Fuf hues, p. 10, "Certes I deeme you would be content if I were deceased."

9. enterprised, undertook, attempted. Cf. Bp Pilkington's Works, p. 137, "It is written of Gedeon, when he enterprised that venturous act to fight against God's enemies."

II. as wel 2 likely, or as easily.

13. j-d? = same. We still use the word compounded with same selfsame. For selfe see Gascoigne's Steel Glas, p. 25,

"And flesh and blood in this self oxx. is tryed."

15. Reddecrosse strete. Red Cross Street ran between Golden I ane and the end of the present Jewin Street, terminating at St Giles' Church, Cripplegate. See Maitland's History of London, ir. 908.

17. lettcn in, i. e. let in.

21. toivard, being toward zv; z = being connected with, or engaged about him. The precise sense of the word as here used is of rare occurrence. Halle has " being his servaunte."

-22. inkelynge, inkling, suspicion. Cf. Lyiy's Euphues, "That my father have no inkling hee'reoff."

23. of noughtcy for no reason, without cause.

26. forcminded, i. e. had previously set his mind on. I have not met with this word elsewhere.

27. at erste = for the first time. Erst, though in form the superlative from 6'; r, is generally used in the sense oiformerly, as in Shaks. Pericles, I. r. 49, "Sick men. gripe not at earthly joys as erst they did," but when preceded by at, erst = first. Cf. Chaucer, Second Nun s Tale, 151,

"And then at erst to hym thus seyde she."

30. spede, success, good speed. Cf. Shaks. Wittier"s Tale, III. 2. 146, "With mere conceit and fear of the queen's speed."" 32. vsnrpacion. As the Latin word itsiirpaiio is often used without the sense of wrongful seizure, so the English word seems to be here. See Shaks. Venus and Adonis, 591, "A sudden Xc. Msiirps her cheek."

33. wiste. See above, p. 5, 1. 23.

? = helped, old past tense oi to help. Cf. Shaks. K. John, "Sir Robert never holp to make this leg.""

P. 8, line 4. fortherlye, favourable, such as to further his intention.

8- abuse = io make a wrong use of, employ wrongfully.

tone. tother, contraction for the one. the other.

If. therefore, for it, i. e. ere they expected it. Cf. Shaks. 2 Hen. VI. I, 4. 3, "We are therefore provided."

16. yrkcd, annoyed, gave pain to. See Shaks. As Vou Like It, 11. r. 22, "it irks me."

19. liable, able, as if from Lat. habilis. Cf. Sir Thomas More, Utopia, 24. 8, "A man not only liable to delite him with your pro-founde learnyng."

20. perceiued. In the original it is received, but probably this is a misprint. Halle has " perceived."

21. dyspayred. We now generally use the verb with a preposition 1 after it.

27. commodity, advantage. Cf. Sir Thos. More's Utopia, 11. i-, "For the commoditie of the common wealth."

26. ?;; t' = themselves; frequent in this History.

29. aduertisemente, instruction, information, notice. Cf. Bp Coverdale's Works, p. 217, "Besides this we ought not to cease with warning and advertisement. h3X they may leave off from their obstinate wickedness."

31. the Lorde Marqnes Dorsette. This was Thomas Grey, previously Lord Grey of Groby, and then in 1472 created Earl of Huntingdon, and in 1475 Marquis of Dorset. He resigned the earldom of Huntingdon in 1479, which title was then conferred on William Herbert, Earl of Pembroke.

P. 9, line 4. bare hym sore, exactly = Lat. cegre ferre, "to be annoyed at." The phrase is not common in English and is probably only a rendering of the Latin.

5. captayne of Calyce. From the reign of Edward III. to that of Queen Mary, Calais was in the possession of the English.

6. Lorde Ryuers. This was Richard Woodville, who was created Earl of Rivers in 1466. This title was extinct in 1496.

8. that they lokedfor, that they expected to have had. See above, 10. presence, the royal presence. Spenser, F. Q. ill. 9.-26, ' She came m presence with right comely grace." vndcrsctte, propped up. See Daniel, Civil IVars, Vlll. 27, "Now when she had of fatal Lancaster Seen all the pillars crushed and ruined That ttnderset it."

13. by whiche, wherefore, from which cause.

look, i. e. expect. Cf. (for this use with the infinitive) Shaks. Temp. V. 292, "As you look to have my pardon."

i lyke, likely. Cf. Lyly's Etiphues, p. 99, "It is lyke to fare with thee as with the eagle."

23. happelye, haply, perchante. Cf. Shaks. Measjtre for Measure, IV. 2. 98, 'Happily You something know."

24. jz) r, unstable, insecure. See Barnes, Works, p. 283, "I know they be slipper that I have to do wyth, and there is no holde of them."

25.-onderpropped, supported, upheld. Cf. Shaks. King John, v. 2. 99,

What penny hath Rome borne. To underprop this action?"

26. but, unless. Cf. Shaks. Merchant of Venice, v. i. 208,.

"I'll die for't but some woman had the ring." gree, agree. Cf. Shaks. Merchant of Venice, II. 2. 108, "How grcc you now?"

27. Mrt=that which. Cf. P. B. 3 Collect in Mo7-ning Prayer, " to do always that is righteous in thy sight."

28. for hatred of ech of others parson. This may be = for the hatred which each one bears to the other's person; but it would be better English to omit the second of, and then the sense would be simple.

30. goeforwarde, make progress, to be successful. Cf. Shaks. Mids. N'ight s Dream, IV. 2. 6, "The play is marred, '. goes not forward. " 31. shall haiie more place, i. e. shall be more used, be more prevalent, and more influential

P. 10, line I. infect, infected, tainted. See Shaks. Troilns and Cressida, l. 3. 187, "Many are infect, Ajax is grown self-willed."

1. drazve down. to mine. Here the verb is neuter, and signifies to come, as in the common phrase, "the time draws near," c. Cf. 12. 7, but if, unless. Cf. Sir T.

Elyot, Governotir, b. I. c. 14, "A man may not be an oratour, bnt if he have gotten the knowledge of all thinges, and artes of greatest importance."

5. d?-iftcs, designs, intentions. See Shaks. Ahuh Ado, II. i. 403, "I will tell you my drift. ' 6. dreue, to drive. The word is used in the sense of come, but probably the sentence was a sort of alliterative proverb of the time.

10. agretteth, makes grievous, or painful and annoying. Cf. South, Sermofts, viii. i, "Pains that afflict the body are afflictive just so long as they actually possess the part which they agg?-ieve. We still use commonly enough the past participle aggrieved.

14. 7iere appears to hq.-= never; an instance is given in Halliwell's Glossary from MS. Arund. Coll. Ar. 27, fol. 130,

"A semilier seemlier) to min sithe sight?) saw I ner non."

15. byandby = Ti m. e. dmie y, presently. The expression is common in this book. Cf. Shaks. Two Gentlemen, I. 3. 87,

"The uncertain glory of an April day. Which now shews all the beauty of the sun, And by and by a cloud takes all away."

19. affinitie, relationship by marriage. See Daniel, Civil Wars, ' With unlucky stars he married. For by the means of this affinity Was lost all that his father conquered."

20. beare that zveyghte, i. e. have that influence.

24. j- = same, see above, sclfe 7iighte, p. 7, 1. 13.

30. states. Here the meaning seems to be a little wider than above 5. 5, though here the sense princes will suffice. But probably it includes all persons of high position. Cf. The estates of the realm.

P. II, line I. woorship, i. e. honour, being treated as a person of worth. Cf. Shaks. Wint, Tale, i. 2. 314, "Whom I from meaner form have benched and reared to worship."

3. growen, see above, p. 2, 1. 15.

7. conrtesye of me ines knees, i. e. the reverence shewn by the l)ending of the knee. Cf. Shaks. Rich. II. i. 4. 33,

"A brace of draymen bid God speed him well, And had the tribute of his stipple knee."" 9. sithen, since, more commonly written sithence or sith. The present form is found in Wycliffe, 2 Pet. iii. 4, "For sithen the fadris dieden all thingis lasten fro the beg 'nnyng of creature."

gaine-called, i. e. called back again. This sense of gain in compounds is rare. Most frequently it is, as in gainsay, equal to against. But we find gaincome = coming again, in Chaucer, Testament of Cresside, 55,

But whan he saw passed the day and hour Of her gaincovie, in sorow gan oppresse His woful heart."

Also the Ayenbite of Inwyt = the remorse agaht + bite) of conscience, while again buying and again buyer are common in Old English for redemption and redeemer.

lo. oughte zuee brcvare. In the oldest English the infinitive having a distinctive termination needed no preposition to precede it. In modern language to is inserted after all but a very few verbs which are called auxiliaries (and with them the verb to daj-e). But this was not so constantly observed in Elizabethan English. Cf. Shaks. ytil. C(sary I. I. 3, "You ought not ivalky ir. eftesoones, presently. Cf. Shaks. Pericles, v. i. 256, Eftsoons I'll tell thee why,"

14. coseyns. It is customary for royal personages to use the word cousin of all princes and dignified persons who are their friends though not blood relations. Cf. 61. 11.

16. the lesse losse wer they, i, e. They (my children) w ould be the less loss, on whom though God should do his pleasure (an euphemistic expression for their being removed by a natural death) yet the realm would find Kings.

22. looke, expect. Cf. 7. 2.

a6. grieues, grievances, vexations. Cf. Shaks. 1 Hen. IV. iv. 1. 69,

Find our gi'iefs heavier than our offences."

29. kinred. Here as distinguished from affinity, the word implies consanguinity, blood relationship.

30. stirety, security, safety. Cf. More's Utopia, 134. 17, "They prefer the same greate rewardes with pardone and suertie of their lives."

31. therezuithal. Al in this word, as in 7vithal, adds nothing to the meaning of the word, which is simply equivalent to therewitji. Cf. Latimer, Sermons, p. 161, "The arte of shutyng. is a gift of God that he hath geven us to excell all other nacions ztyth all."''"

P. 12, line I. rccomforting, consoling, cheering. See Spen. F. Q. IV. 8. 5, ' Him to rccomfoi-t in his greatest care."

The re in some compound words appears to have lost all force, thus recompose is used as simply equal to compose.

3. stand with, be agreeable to. Cf. Formtilaries of Faith, p. xxxi., "It standeth zvith the very due order of charity, a Christian man to pray for the souls of the departed."

8. his decease, i. e. the king's death.

his houshold, i. e. the prince's household.

10. was began, we should now say had begun.

11. riuers, plunderers. The root is the same as that of the last syllable of bereave, and is connected with rob. The more common orthography is reive. Cf. Berners' Froissart, il. cap. 23, "By reason therof there is nother Englyshe, nor Frenche, nor robbers, nor reivers that doth them any hurt to the value of one penny."

12. ejicheason, cause, reason. Cf. Spenser, Shepherd's Calendar, May, 1. 147,

"Thou raylest on right without reason,

And blamest hem much for small encheasony 14. refraine, used as an active rh = to restrain hold in check. Cf. Berners' Froissart, ii. cap. 100, "But fynally he refreyned his displeasure by the good means of the queen."

15. 7z r j- = outrages. The first e is only kept because the writer would have spelt the word out as oute.

20. z r=others. This form for a plural is common in the older English. Cf, Bp Pilkington's Works,". 7, "Phinees. punished that wickedness M hich other winked at."

22.-r=nearest. Cf. More, Utopia (Pitt Press Series), 123. 28, "They know this to be the next way to break love between man and wyfe."

23. drifte, i. e. scheme, plan, that at which she was driving.

24. of youth, in youth, i. e. during the king's youth. Cf. Shaks. Love's Laboia-'s Lost, I. i. 43,

"And not be seen to wink all the day."

28. bca7'ing- himself their fauor. ILimsclf'v= here the dative, and the sense is "bearing their favour towards himself," "favourably inclined towards himself." Halle has or to " beare toward hymselfe any favoure."

brake, disclosed. Cf. Shaks. Macbeth, i, 7. 48, ' What beast was't then That made you break this enterprise to me?"

29. by mouth. The modern expression is by 7vord of mouth.

33. sequestred, separated, withdrawn. Cf. Sir Thos. More's Works, p. 1046, "Him hath God the Father specially ji? j-r and severed and set aside out of the number of al creatures."

in wrt;;' = almost. Cf. 106. 18 and note there. The speaker here means that not only was the prince kept away from them but they were almost prevented from approaching him in any way.

P. 13, line I. ought, owed. Cf. Shaks. i Ben. IV. iii. 3. 152, "You oiight him a thousand pound."

4. vnmetely, unfit (an adjective). Cf. Sir Thos. More's Works, p. 1316, "Sainte Peter havynge our Savyour in suche estimacion and honoure as it well became hym to have, thoughte it in hys mynde mj-vietely that his Lorde and Mayster shoulde weshe his feete."

5. as who say, i. e. as one may say. Cf. 113. 26, 121. 23.

8. from, away from, apart from. Cf. Shaks. Winter's Tale, IV. 2. 43, "He is seldomr w the house of a most homely shepherd."

9. wel proued, i. e. those who have given full proof of what they are.

10. euil xvillers, i. e. those who wish us evil. Well-willers is found Shaks. Merry Wives, i. I. 72, 'Be ruled by your well ivillers."' Cf. Ps. cxxix. 5 (Pr. Bk.), "As many as have evil will 2X Sion."

II. namely which is, which is especially. For namely in this sense cf. More's Utopia (Pitt Press Series), 159. 5, "thankynge him for so many benefites. but namely that he hath chaunced into that publyque weal."

lighte of beliefe, quick in belief. Cf. Shaks. Lear, III. 4. 95, "False of heart, light of ear," i. e. easily credulous.

14. bende, band, company. Here used of the queen's relations who were in great favour with Edward IV. Cf below, 15. 19.

stodc with, i. e. stood with = w.?, consistent with. Cf. Shaks. Coriola-nus, II. 3. 91, "If it may stand with the tune of your voices that I may be consul."

20. holden better place, i. e. been of more influence. Cf below, line 32, and see Shaks. Merchant, I. i. 174, "To hold a x'w? place with one of them," i. e. to have as good a chance of success as any of them.

21. betrapped, entrapped. Cf. Mirrour for Magistrates, p. 307, "How they conspire another to betrap."' 22. confusion. The word here is used as in Isaiah xxiv. 10, xxxiv. IT in the sense of destruction. Cf. Halle, Hen y IV. fol. 146, "Kynge Rycharde, perceivyng them armed, knewe well that they came to his confusion."'' Cf also 17. 2.

24. our Lord, the reference is to God and to His Grace.

27. wjZjz knowledge. The noun is not very common, but cf. Fabyan, Chronicle, c. 117, "When Constantyne had wyttynge he assembled a great hoste of Brytons."

might abuse the name of his commaundement, i. e. might make a wrong use of the plea of the prince's command: might pretend they were bidden by the prince, and on that pretence do anything they wished.

29. vndoing, ruin, destruction. Cf. Holland, Pliny, b. xxxiii. c. 11, "Their rich plate set their enemies teeth on water, who for the love and desire thereof, practised by all cunning means their utter undoing."' prouision. In the literal sense of Lat. ;- z'rt!";' = foresight. Cf. Shaks. Tefnpest, i. 2. 28, "with sxich. provision in mine art."

31. attonemente, i. e. at onemerit=setting at one, bringing into accord. Cf. Bp Hall, Satires, in. 7,

"such discord betwixt agreeing parts, Which never can be set at onement more."

32. hadde fnore place, was more regarded, i. e. they only professed to be in accord, out of regard to the pleasure of the dying king.

P. 14, line I. of, i. e. out of Cf. Milton's Par. I ost, ix. 563, "How camest thou speakable mute? " and 712, "I brute human, ye?" human Gods."

2. houerly, of only an hour's duration or formed in an hour. Ilalle has "an onely kindenesse."

"Corruption bare such sway in most matters that learning and truth might skant bee admitted to shewe it selfe."

4. stomackes, minds, tempers. See above, p. 5, 1. 6.

6. suche othe7', similar ones.

8. ethe, easy. Cf. Spenser, Shepherd's Calendar, September, 1. 17, "Ech thing imparted (i. e. shared with some one else) is more eath to beare."

15. af? ioue, remove. Cf. Speed, History of Gi Britain, anno 1230, "The King of Connaught and his Irish had invaded the King's people with a purpose and hope utterly to expel and amove our nation from among them."

16. vnder the name of, i. e. on pretence that they were. Cf. Shaks. Taming of the Shrew, iv. 3. 12,

"He does it tinder iiame perfect love." 19. him, i. e. the king.

21. hi n, i. e. the Duke of Gloucester, to whom also the his in line 24 refers.

24. doubtuotcs, doubtful, uncertain. More frequently spelt dotibtottse. See More, Works, p. 457, "Either the Scripture is plaine and easy to perceive or doiibtoiise and hard to understand."

25. 2? ya(: =appearance. Cf. Shaks. Tempest, I. 2. 104,

"Executing the outward izr of royalty."

27. brought in the i? iynd, i-o x i. X. o the opinion. Cf. Shaks. As You Like It, ill. 3. 91,

"I am not in the mind but 1 were better to be married of him."

wer nede, i. e. was necessary.

28. jeopardoiis, dangerous. Cf. Sir Thos. More, Utopia, p. 68, 1. 2, "The forefrontes of frontiers of the ii corners, what with fordes and shelves, and what with rockes, be Vitxyejeoperdotis and daungerous."

the king to come vp strotig, i. e. for the king to come to London with a strong force.

30. stiidyed 7';? = regarded, turned their thoughts unto. Cf. Shaks. Antony and Cleopatra, v. 2. 10, "Bids thee study or what fair demands thou meanest to have him grant thee."

33. attvixte, betwixt, between. Cf. Chaucer, I or? i. of the Rose,

"Sir mirth her by the finger had Daunsing, and she him also, Great love was atwixt hem two."

P. 15, line 3. enpugncd, fought against, was fighting against, was opposing. Cf. Shaks. Merchant, IV. i. 197,

"The Venetian law cannot impugn you." 8. fall on a ro; v=break out into an uproar. Roar in this sense is now obsolete. "We use uproar. But cf. Fox, Actes, p. 656, King Edwd. IV., "He perceiving his enemies dayly to increase upon him and all the countries about to be in a rore making fires and singing songs."

11. in thewyght = n the blame. It is now more frequently spelt wiie. Cf. Spenser, F. Q. vi. 3. 16,

"He passed forth with her in fair array-Fearless who aught did think or aught did say, Sith his own thought he knew most dear from w."

19. hende. See above, p. 13, 1. 14.

23. sober, moderate, limited.

28. The blank for the number of miles was left to be filled up in a revision of the work for which Sir Thomas never found time. Stratford is about eleven miles south of Northampton.

29. 07; ere, before. Cf Latimer, Sermons, p. 255, "The great man was gone forth about such affairs as behoved him, or I came."

31. incontinente, immediately. Cf. Shaks. J ichard II. V. 6. 48,

"Put on sullen black incontineiit."' 33. lodged, i. e. gone away to his lodging.

P. 16, line 6. to horsebackivard, i. e. toward horseback, about to mount on horseback. For this separation of the two parts of the preposition, cf. 2 Cor. iii. 4, "Such trust have we through Christ to Godward."

12. beest(m'ed=i z. ct. Cf. 2 Kings v. 24, "he took them from their hand and bestowed theia in the house."

16. for as micche as, c. This was the language in which the duke's adherents excused their proceedings.

19. bare. in hande. The phrase signifies "to be always going to do something and never performing it," hence "to illude with false pretences." Cf. Shaks. Cy? fibelinc, v. 5. 43,

"Your daughter, whom she bo7-e in hand to love With such integrity, she did confess Was as a scorpion to her sight."

22. gone. A remnant of the Old English infinitive ending in an or en, hence goen or goie for a time continued to be the infinitive form. The older English had both gangan and gan as infinitives.

24. for notighte, for no reason. Cf. of noughte, 7. 23, above.

26. sithe, since. Cf. Shaks. 3 Henry VI. i. 3. 41, ' Thou hast one son; for his sake pity me, Lest in revenge thereof, sith God is just. He be as miserably slain as I."

27. m = get.

keepe himselfe close, i. e. hide and lie in concealment. Cf i Chron. xii. I, "While David yet kept himself close because of Saul."

30. snretie. "Uppon the suretie of his own conscience" means "because he was secure and confident in his mind about his own innocence."

P. 17, line I. sette distaiince, make an estrangement. Distant ior estranged in? natijter is still in common use. For a like phrase cf below, p. 68. 26.

Troihis, i. i. 16, "He that will have a cake out of the wheat must needs tarry the grinding."'" 6. putte him in wardc i. e. placed him under a guard, in confinement, in prison. Cf. Gen. xlii. 17, Hq put them all together iito ivard three days."

8. Stonye Stratforde is in Buckinghamshire on the banks of the Ouse, and on the opposite side of that river is Old Stratford in the county of Northampton.

11. streighte, narrow; strait is now the more common spelling. The them in the previous line means the duke and his company.

12. ado7ijie, down. Cf. Spenser, F. Q. i. 8. 3,

"Then took that Squire an home of bugle small Which honge adowne his side in twisted gold And tasselles gay."

14. yomen. According to Spelman (see Wedgwood's Glossary, s. V.) connected with Germ. gazi = a district, country, place, village, and so Frisian gaemon = i ager.

15. rowmes, places; here = the order of marching, cf. St Matt, xxiii. 6, "They. love the uppermost rooms at feasts, and the chief seats in the synagogue."

16. sallied, saluted. The influence of the French forms such as saltier, c. prevailed largely in Elizabethan times, and modified many preterites as in the text. Cf. Spenser, F. Q. iv. 6. 25,

"Full glad of so good end, to them drew nere And her salezud with semely bel-accoyle" (i. e. with kindly greeting).

19. by and by, immediately. Cf. St Mark vi. 25, "I will that thou give me by and by in a charger the head of John the Baptist."

(3, with, against. Cf. Shaks. Tzvelfth Night, iii. 4. 248, "I am sure no man hath any quarrel to me."

30. sailing that somniewhat, (! i: c. =only that they were obliged to say somethuig.

P. 18, line 5. Both here and in line 21, Halle adds to the other names " and Sir Richard Hawte."

10. lyked better them, pleased them better. Cf. Gascoigne, Steele Glas, p. 83, "But if my Glasse do like my lovely lorde."

11. booted not, was of no use. Cf. Lyly's Euphiies, p, 95, "Whether your deserts or my desire have wrought this chaunge, it will boote you lyttle to know."

19. iwe, use. We have still the verb to inure. Cf. Puttenham, p. 55, The Arte of English Poesie, "Mo and more excellent examples may be fained in one day by a good wit, then many ages through man's frailtie are able to put in 7; v."

24. Fo? nfrait. Pontefract in Yorkshire. The orthography in the text shews that the present pronunciation of the name as "Pomfret" is of old standing.

28. vppezvarde. Just as we still speak of going up to London.

31. in the sorest ivisc, i. e. in the most painful manner.

p. 19, line r. wot, know. Cf. Lovers Labour's Lost, i. i. 91, "Those that walk and xvot not what they are."

I. fright. The original iz. flight, but this is probably a misprint. ram = reign. Cf. 38. 7. Halle prints " reign."

6. Palyce of Westtninster. Commenced at the time of the building of the Abbey by Edward the Confessor. The Chamber of St Edward, or the Painted Chamber, was the kernel of the palace, and the memory of the royal residence still remains in the names " Old Palace Yard " and "New Palace Yard." See Stanley, Memorials of West? fiinster Abbey, pp.?3 seqq.

8. Sainctiiarye. The right of sanctuary'at Westminster professed to be founded on charters of King Lucius and on the special consecration by St Peter. The right of asylum rendered the whole Cathedral precinct a " Cave of Adullam." Its privileges ceased in 1566. For a full account of the Sanctuary, see Stanley, ut supra, pp. 363 370. Halle adds to this sentence "and she and all her chyldren and compaignie were reges-tred for Sanctuarye persons."

9. the abbottcs place, i. e. the lodging, or house, belonging to the Abbot of Westminster.

II. the Lorde Chainnbei'layn, i. e. Lord Hastings, see 8. 33. archbishoppe of Ynrke. This was Thomas Scott, who was also surnamed Rotherham. He was translated from Lincoln to York and held the archbishopric from 1480 to 1501. Halle gives the name " Dr Rotherham" and also adds this "his place" was "called Yorke place." 13. The his in this line refers to the Lord Chancellor, as does "-his reste" in line 15. ' His master," in 15, means the Lord Chamberlain.

15. forbeare, spare, let alone. Cf. Shaks. 2 Henry LV. IV. 5. no,
"What! canst thou not foj'bear me half an hour?"

16. letted, forbore. Cf. Shaks. Litcrcce, 10,
"Collatine unwisely did not let To praise."

17. hard, heard. Cf. Sir Thos. More, Utopia (Pitt Press Series), II. 7, "Onelye to write playnelie the matter as I hard it spoken."

24. by and by. See above, p. 17, 1. 19.

27. weap07ied, armed. Cf. Bp Pilkington, Works, p. 436, "These braggers, like thieves, will set on no man that they see zvcaponed."' thegreate Seale, v i c is in the special keeping of the Lord Chancellor.

31. fardelles, bundles. Cf. 0., Discourse of English Poetrie, p. 17, "Infinite 77? i'of printed pamphlets."

trusses, packages. Cf. Spenser, Shepherd's Calendar, May, 1. 239,
"All as a poore pedler he did wend Bearing a trusse of trifles at his backe."

P. 20, line 2. nexte, nearest. Cf. on 12. 22.

to bringe in the nexte waye to bring things in by the nearest way.

drezve to them that holpe to carrye a zvronge zvaye = took part with (sided with) those who were helping to carry things in a wrong way. There were thieves about who made their harvest out of the general confusion.

Halle's words here are: " and some carried more than they were com-maunded to another place."

4. alowe, low down, in a low position. Cf. Turberville, Fall of Pride,
"Not him that bears his sails alozoe Nor him that keeps the shore."

risju's, rushes, with which the floor was strewn. Cf. Chaucer, Romaiint of the Rose,

"The stalke was as rishe right,"

i. e. as upright or straight as a reed.

7. as shee tooke it for, i. e. as she thought, imagined it to be.

9. woo worthe him. Worth is the imperative of the Old English verb that is akin to German werden =. o become, so this phrase = may woe become (or befal) to him.

17. behoofe, advantage, benefit. Cf. Shaks. 2 Henry VI. iv. 7. 83,

"This tongue hath parley'd unto foreign kings For your behoof."

18. betooke, presented to her, committed to her. Cf. Bp Pilking-ton, Works, p. 19, "Kings and princes keep their seal signet and ring most surely, either themselves, or betake it to some trusty friend to keep."

28. flockinele, in a flock. Cf. Chaucer, Clerkes Tale, 1. 86,

"Oonly that point his peple bar so soore "Wx-ax. flokniecle on a day they to hym wente."

harneis, armour. Cf. Bp Pilkington, Works, p. 231, "Golias trusted in his harjiess and strength, but David in God's name overthrew him."

29. demeanojire, behaviour, conduct. Cf. Shaks. Couiedy of Errors,

"Fashion your demeanour to my looks."

32. by and by. See above, p. 17, 1. 19. In the next line Halle supplies the word " London" omitted in the text.

P. 21, line 2. ouermuch lightnesse, too great readiness, fickleness. For overmuch see Chaucer, The Court of Love, 385, "But still beware of overmuch resort For that peraventure spilleth all thy sport."

6. cicstomable, usual. Cf. Sir Thos. More, Workes, p. 389, "Marke wel and remembre that we speke here of beliefe and faith, not of workes and deedes, lest, after hys customable fashion, letting the beliefe go by, he answere us with rayling upon niannes maners, and so leade the reader more than a mile from the matter."

17. indiferentelyc, impartially, without distinction. Cf. Foi'mji-laries of Faith, p. 119, "Insomuch, that whereas in the time of the apostles it was lawful indifferently to all bishops (certain of them assembling themselves together) to constitute and consecrate other bishops; the said fathers restrained the said power." See also Prayer-Book, Litany, "truly and indijfcrenily minister justice."

RICH. ro 20. to farref007-th =. oo far forth, i. e. he begged them not to go too far in judging of the matter, not to make too sm-e about it. 22. yrritijigc, irritating.

25. oute of joynt.". vixy, at cross purposes, into discord. Cf. Shaks. Hamlet, l. 5. 188, "The time is out of joint."'" 26. in frame, into order, into proper fashion. Cf. Shaks. Hamlet, III. 1. 321, "Put your discourse z (? j;; y '(7w." PA' o'"" out of frame'"" = disordered, is found Shaks. Love's Labour''s Lost, ill. 193.

27. a fielde, i. e. a pitched battle, an engagement in the field of battle. Cf. Shaks. i Hen. LV. v. 5. 16, "Plow goes theM.?"

28. egall, see above, p. 5, 1. 26.

P. 22, line 8. demeane, rule, manage. Cf. Chaucer, LLoiise of Fame, b. ii. 449,

"Lo is it not a great mischaunce To let a foole have governaunce Of things that he cannot dejjiaiiie?"' 9. colotcrahle, specious, plausible. Colour is still used for pretext.

Cf. Bacon's Henry VIL. (Pitt Press Series), 191. 23, 27, "They did vex men upon scarce colourable titles. nay, contrary to all law and colour, they maintained the King ought to have the half of men's lands and rents."

15. zzj = these.

20. taue=. o have. There are other forms of crar is in this History, as tone, tother, but none where the letter is absorbed from the latter of the two words.

22. almoise, charity, almesse. The word is still pronounced aee -in many parts of England. Cf. Grindal, Works, p. 15S, "A strong chest or box for the aimose of the poor."

25. Sha. Halle spells the name "Shawe."

27. For violette Halle has " murraye."

28. Harncsey, Hornsey, the small village on tlie north of London. Halle has " Harnesay Parke."

32. hare him, behaved. Cf. Shaks. Te)7ipcst, I. 2. 425,

"Some good instruction give, How I may bear 7ne here."

P. 23, line 3. chose, chosen. Cf. Shaks. J. desar, 11. i. 3(4, "O, what a time have you chose out to wear a kerchief!"

6. betake7i, see above, hetookc, p. 20, 1. is.

II. Halle has "Dr John Russell." This prelate was now made Lord Chancellor, and was also Chancellor of the University of Oxford.

15. 7'0'W7nes, places, offices. Cf. Archbp Grindal, Re7? iai7is, p. 292,

"Those men that sue for bishoprics do in that declare themselves vmmeet for the r vv."

17. all, although. Cf. Shaks. Richard LLL. IV. 4. 225, "Whose hand soever lanced their tender hearts Thy head, all indirectly, gave direction."

24. happelye, see above, p. 9, 1. 23.

25. inconlinente, see above, p. 15, 1. 31.

P. 24, line 3. tidcyon. Here in its radical sense of protection, guardianship, without that idea of teaching to which in modern times the word has become ahnost restricted. Cf. Shaks. Much Ado, I. i. 283, "So I commit you to the tuition of God." See also 98. 11, note.

4. standeth in, consists in. Cf. Lyly, Ejiphiies, p. 104, "As you would have me to shewe the duetie of a childe, so ought you to she we the care of a Parent, for as the one standeth in obedience so the other is grounded upon reson." See also the Prayer-Book, "m knowledge of whom standeth our eternal life."

5. vyande, food. Cf. Sir Thos. More, Works, p. 6, "He was content with meane fare at his table: how be it somewhat yet reteyning of the olde plentie in deintie viande, and silver vessell." For " yll vyande " Halle gives " evill dyete."

10. estate conuenient, i. e. of station suitable to be companions for a prince.

12. consideracion, i. e. over-minute care, regarding too small a matter. I have not found the word so used elsewhere. Halle adds after "consideracion" the word "lighte," which makes a good sense, and I think should be supplied.

17. ricnne. Used of a report = " to be current." Cf. Shaks. ijac. IV. 3. 182, "There ran a rumour."

27. tendereth, has a tender regard for. Cf. Shaks. Richard III. I. I. 32,

"In the devotion of a subject's love, Tendering the precious safety of my prince."

29. credence, trust, belief. Cf. Formida7-ies of Faith, p. 98, "That they ought and must give no less faith and credence'lo the same words of absolution, than they would give unto the very words and voice of God himself."

30. vietelye, see above, p. 6, 1. 8.

31. Halle adds after " Cardynall " " Archebishop of Caunterbury." 33. payne, trouble. We generally use the plural pains in such a phrase. But cf. Shaks. Merchant, 11. 2. 193, " Pray thee take pain To allay with some cold drops of modesty Thy skipping spirit."

P. 25, line 2. ivealthe, see above, p. 6,1. 33.

3. after, i. e. next to. Cf. Shaks. Hen. VI. (pt. 3.) IV. 6. 16, ' After God, thou set'st me free."

5. ceased, used passively, meaning "made to cease," "put an end to." Cf. Bacon, Advanconent of learning, I. 56. 32, "He likewise approached a degree nearer unto Christianity, and became, as Agrippa said unto S. Paul, half a Christian; holding their religion and law in good opinion, and not only ceasing (i. e. stopping) persecution, but giving way to the advancement of Christians."

8. percase, perchance, perhaps. Cf. Archbp Grindal, Works, p. 469, "In these things percase some enlargements shall be, both to set forth her Majesty's dohigs justifiably, and his refusal to obey repre-hensively."

10. adtiertyseniente. See above, p. 8, 1. 29.

26. cease. See above, 1. 5.

28. For " Yorke " Halle reads " Canterburye."

31. deuowre, duty, Fr. devoir. Cf. Chaucer, Knightes Tale, 1. 2598, "Tho were the gates shet and cried was lowde,

Do now youre devoir, yonge knightes proude."

P. 26, line 3. tourne to the greate grudge, i. e. arouse great ill-will among all men. 6. bee, been. 21. hit for ani maner nede, i. e. but whatever need there may be.

26. deuoure. See above, p. 25, 1. 31.

P. 27, line 8. as oiire dishonoiire, i. e. as (she desires) our dishonour.

9. zvealthe. See above, p. 6, 1. 33; p. 25, 1. 2. 18. contente, i. e. we should all be content.

23. =easy. See above, p. 14, 1. 8.

24. but goe to suppose. In such phrases go to is a sort of interjection, in the sense of "come now." Cf. Nash, Pierce Penilesse, p. 21, ' ' Goe too, you are unwise, if you make her not a chief saint in your Calendar." In the text the sense is "But come, suppose she be afraid, c."

25. lette, hinder. Cf. Shaks. Hamlet, I. 5. 85,

"By heaven, I'll make a ghost of him that lets me."

27. oughte weefeare. The sign of the infinitive omitted. Cf. above, on II. 10.

28. caste, exhibit, shew. The idea seems to be of throwing forth so that people may see them. The use is singular.

29. fctte, fetched. Cf. infra, on 39. 20.

32. let. See above, 1. 25.

P. 28, line 4. sore, sorely. so7'e jyiymdcth =seriously thinks upon it. Cf. Romeo and yidiet, I. 4. 19,

"I am too sore enpierced with his shaft To soar with his light feathers."

5. lette, hindrance. Cf. Bp Pilkington, Works, p. 576, "Thou reprovest marriages that they be a let to godliness: but wilt thou know that it hurts not to have wife and children." See above, 26. 28.

6. maistrye, a grand work, an achievement. Cf. Lever, Sermons, P- 75 "So the people in Englande gathered together, they would make maisteryes, and be notable fellows."

10. ensure io promise, assure. Cf. Chaucer, Doctor"s Tale, 12077,

"This juge unto this cherl his tale hath told In secre wise and made him to enstire Pie sholde telle it to no creature."

ir. maugrye, in spite of. The more common spelling is luaiigrt. Fr. inalgre. Cf. Bp Pilkington, Works, p. 205, "Saul and his flatterers banished and pursued poor David, whom his God of a shepherd made a king inaiigre all his foes." Spelt viagry, infra, 32. 21.

14. other lyke, similar ones. Cf. Formularies of Faith p. xxxi., "As concerning the rites and ceremonies of the church. the hallowing of the font, and other like exorcisms and benedictions by the ministers of Christ's church." Halle reads " other of that sorte."

24. taketh, i. e. holdeth, esteemeth. Cf. Shaks. Mcas. f. Alcas. III. 2. 17, "We take him to be a thief."

26. fall fro the crafte, i. e. quit the trade (of a thief). Cf. Shaks. JMuch Ado, I. I. 257, "If ever thou do?, t fall from this faith."

28. 77tannequellers, murderers. Cf. Shaks. 2 Henry IV. I. 2. 58, "Thou art a honey-seed, a man-queller and a woman-queller."

33. draiue hym. We now say, "draw a man."

P. 29, line 3. looke me nowe. The "me" is the ethic dative, as it is called. Cf. Shaks. Othello, I. i. 49, "Whip jne such honest knaves."

5. tother. See above, p. 8, 1. 9.

9. twoo places, i. e. the Sanctuary at Westminster, of which so frequent mention is made in this History, and the Cathedral Church of St Paul's. Down to the time of Henry VHI. all churches and churchyards were looked on as sanctuaries. This accounts for the word spe-cyallye in the text.

II. waye, weigh. Cf. Sir Thos. More, Utopia, p. 162, 1. 13, "Therefore when I consider and zvay in my mind all these commen wealthes, which now a dayes any where do florish, so God helpe me, I can perceave nothing but a certein conspiracy of riche men procu-ringe their owne commodities under the name and title of the commen wealth."

17. mendement, amendment. Cf. Mirroitr for Iagistrates, p. 355,

"Zealous hee was, and would have all things mended, And by that mcndment nothing else he meant, But to be king."

19. vppon the boldenesse, because of the impunity which they find for wrongdoing, so long as they can take refuge in a sanctuary. This certainty of safety makes offenders bold.

23. gooe whistle them. A proverbial expression implying that those who use it are out of the way of punishment. Cf. Shaks. Winter s Tale, IV. 4. 715, "This being done, let the law go whistle." The "them" in the text is superfluous, but somewhat like the ethical case. Cf. above, line 3.

27. reue, rive, plunder. Connected with reave in bereave, and with rob, and the Latin rapio.

33. sith. See above, p. 16, 1. 26. For the beginning of this sentence Halle has " The conclusion is, sithe it is so long agoo," c., which is the sense of the text.

P. 30, line 4. take a payne. See on 24. 33.

a Goddes name=m or of) God's name, for God's sake.

Cf. Shaks. J? zci. II. ii. i. 251, "But what, a God's name., doth become of this?"

6. lette. See above, p. 27, 1. 1. Here hinder us from, c.

12. lawful hvrte, i. e. hurt which by course of law might properly come upon him. Cf. line 20 below.

18. to that regarde, on that account, in that respect, as far as regards that.

21. tuicion, protection, guardianship. There is not necessarily in the word anything of the sense of teaching which in modern times has become attached to it. Cf 24. 3, above.

27. require, request. Cf. Archbp Grindal, Remains

"He requireth her Majesty to pardon him."

29. and reason, i. e. and it is reasonable that it should be so. sithe. See above, 16. 26.

30. maketh hym faine neede, causeth him to pretend that he needs it. This his evil conscience does.

31. babe. In the original it is babes, but I have not found that form of the word as a singular elsewhere, and I incline to think that it is a misprint in the old edition. Halle has " babe." Cf. below, 32. 7.

and if, corruption of aji if. An has the same meaning as if. And if, or an if, is simply a redundant expression. Cf. Shaks. AWs Well That Ends Well, ii. i. 74,

"Yes, but you will my noble grapes, and if My royal fox could reach them."

32. The sense is: If he had come to the discretion and knowledge to ask for sanctuary, if he stood in need of it; having that discretion he would now be right angry with those who keep him there, for he would know that he did not need to be there.

P. 31, line 3. homely, plain-spoken. Cf. Shaks. Romeo and Juliet, II. 3. 55,

"Be plain, good son, and homely in thy drift."

6. party. The original has "part" but Halle reads "party," i. e. the person whose goods have been carried off, and this has been adopted in the text.

18. lyste, wish, desire. Cf. Shaks. Taming of the Shrew, iii. 2. 167, "Now take them up, quoth he, if any list."

25. satimple, exa. mple. The word j3: wt'r is still used of specimen pieces of girls' embroidery and needlework. Cf. Shaks. Cymbeline, I. I. 48,

"Most praised, most loved, a sample to the youngest."

29. erste, before. This is the usual sense of the word, though in form it is a superlative and should = first.

P. 32, line 5. temporall menfie, laymen. We still call the members of the House of Lords who are not bishops temporal peers.

5. For whole Halle reads " wholy."

7. in effecte. See above, p. 12, 1. i. For condescend x. the sense of agree to, cf. Carew, Survey of Cornwall, fol. 88, "All parties willingly cotidescended hereunto and it hath ever sithence been observed accordingly." Other examples are in the notes on 58. 23 and 71. 19.

9. all beste. The old English was aller best ox alihej'best=he i o all. The text seems to be in transition from the old to the modern form.

10. assaye, essay, try. Cf. Bp Coverdale, Works, "Even so the eternal God assayeth all manner of ways with us, which are well grown and old in years, but young and tender in faith."

12. sterrechaiimber. The Star Chamber. This was a room in the palace at Westminster. The name is probably derived from Hebrew Shetar = dl bond. For in this place the bonds and business documents of the Jews, whom the English kings at times found it convenient to protect, were deposited for safety.

21. incontinent. See above, p. 15, I. 31.

magry. See above, on p. 28, 1. ir.

her minde. The original reads his minde" which would make the words refer to the Cardinal, who had indeed objected (26. 2) to any attempt to bring the child away without his mother's consent, but as allusion has just been made to the queen's determination to keep her son with her, it seems better to make the words refer to her.

29. souned, sounded. The influence of the French has given to the older language many duplicate forms in which a final d ox t has been dropped. So we have sahied =?,2 x. ed., 17. 16, on which see note.

31. importable, unendurable. Cf. Spenser, F. Q. ii. 8. 35,

"So both attonse him charge on either syde With hideous strokes and importable powre. That forced him his ground to traverse wide."

P. 33, lines 2, 3. tone. tother. See above, on 8. 8, 9.

4. to require her the deliuerye of him, i. e. to require)'?; her, c.,. Cf. Shaks. Coriolamis, ii. 2. 160, "He will require them (i. e. from them) as if he did contemn what he requested should be in them to give."

8. demeaned =ixe2i. G. d. The verb is most frequent as a reflexive, "to demean oneself." But cf. Spenser, Colin Clones come Home again, 681,

"Cause have I none (quoth he) of cancred will To quite them ill that me demeaned so well."

11. ouer that xn addition to that. For an example cf. 45. 22 note.

12. tenderid, i. e. had in regard, had respect unto, held dear. Cf. Shaks. Romeo, in. i. 7,

"Which name I tender as dearly as my own."

whose both great welthe, i. e. the great welfare of both of whom. Cf. their bothe dishonour, above, line i.

16. estemed no slight, thoughe it se?7ie lyghte, i. e. esteemed no slight matter, though it seem only a light or little thing. Halle has "the lordes estemed not lighte, though it semed lighte," and so ' lordes"" has been adopted in the present text.

18. estraunger, ie. stranger. The noun seems to be in the objective case after endure; i. e. their youth cannot endure any stranger. But the sentence is far from clear. Perhaps the simplest way to get a sense would be to supply is before any estratmger. For the word estraunger cf. Nicolls, Thucydides, fol. 78, "And havinge with them souldyars estrawigers, which Pissuthxes and the Arcadians had sent them."

19. metely (adj.) = meet, fit. See above, on 6. 8. The sentence might be constructed thus: "Nor any estraunger (be) so metely (fitting) c."

20. as either of them for other, i. e. as each of them for the other. 24. require, used here = ask, and not in the stronger sense of demand. Cf. 30. 27.

26. r ww a'z = advantage. The best instance of the use of this word is in the Bastard Faulconbridge's speech in King John, ii. i. 561 seqq.,

"Since kings break faith upon Commodity, Gain, be my lord, for I will worship thee."

as for yet a while = ior a time at all events.

ben. Infinitive of "to be," following the Old English form with a termination afi or en. Cf. gone = gocn above, 16. 22.

27. the tender age consydred. We should now say, "considering the tender age."

28. j rza(adverb) = specially. Cf. Shaks. 6(?;7? z i", 52. 11,

"To make some special instant special blest."

30. newly, i. e. lately. Cf. Shaks. Winter"s Tale, v. 2. 105,

"A piece many years in doing and now newly performed."

P. 34, line I. recidiuacion. A relapse or falling back into the disease. Cf. Bp Hall, St Pauvs Combat, "Wo is mee! the swept house is repossessed with seven devils. This recidivation is desperate." Halle has "resiluacion."

2. i?; ra c'rzrt = tired out beforehand. The word differs nothing in sense from the following verb.

3. foreweried, i. e. tired beforehand, for which cf. Shaks. K. John, ir. 233 (K. John loquitur),

"And let us in, your king; whose laboured spirits Forewearied in this action of swift speed Crave harbourage within your city walls." weaked, i. e. weakened. Cf. Fabyan, Chronicle, c. 223, "But in the ende the Walshe men were so weked and feebled that a fewe knyghtes scomfyted of theym a great boost."

to beare out a new suifet, i. e. to endure and last out a new load of disease. For stirfeit in this sense cf. Anson, Voyages, bk. ii. ch. 2, ' Instead of one reasonable fleshmeal, they were now scarcely satisfied with three, each of them too so prodigious in quantity as would at another time have produced a fever or surfeit."'' 4.- fomiden (p. participle) = w?7c. Cf. houndeii botmd. P. B. Comm. Service, "Let us give as we are most bounden continual thanks." See below, 36. 30.

6. to order him, i. e. to manage all that is connected with him, so as to be the best for his health.

7. more tenderly like to cherishe him, i. e. likely to cherish him more tenderly. Sentences with inverted order of words are frequent in this History.

2. stand with h agreeable to. Cf. above, on 12. 3.

14. appoint your selfe, c. The pronoun is not directly the object of the verb, but the sense is, "If you settle that you yourself will tarry here."

19. to haue the childe bee. An expression more full than in Modern English, where the infinitive bee would generally be omitted.

24. in Wales, i. e. at Ludlow Castle. See 12. 8.

31. miscaried, i. e. died. Cf. Shaks. 2 Hen. IV. iv. r. 129,

"All that by indictment and by dint of sword have since miscarried under Boling-broke."

32. he, i. e. the duke. Though the child's death came by nature, the duke would be suspected of foul play.

suspicion orfrande. It is thus in the original, but I fancy for or we should read of.

33. 7 i; r=whereas. Cf. Shaks. Two Gentlefnen, ill. i. 74, "And 7vhere I thought the remnant of mine age should have been cherished by her childlike duty, I am now resolved. to turn her out."

P. 35, line I. it is all their honours ='. is for the honour of all of them.

2. to suffer him byde. Another instance of the absence of to before an infinitive. See above, on u. 10.

5. jubarde, i. e. jeopard. Chaucer, Canon Yeojuan s Tale, 16. 711, writes the noun yjipai'tie, which More below (line 9) spells Jubardye.

after, i. e. like, in the same manner as. Cf. Shaks. Tempest, II. 2. 76, "He does not talk after the wisest."

9. verely sur. Snr may be = r, but I incline to think that it is = stire, and that the phrase is = in very truth.

12. letted. (? = forborne. forbear.

duresse=)r'?, on, harsh confinement (Lat. dw'us). Durance is a more usual form. But cf. Spenser, F. Q. iv. 8. 19,

"The one right feeble through the evil rate Of food, which in her duresse she had found."

colour=Y Yeiext, reason. Cf. Shaks. JVinter s Tale, iv. 4. 566, "What colour for my visitation shall I hold up before him?"

14. made a countinance, i. e. intimated by a look that he should leave off that mode of argument.

18. vpon the matter examined, i. e. after the matter had been examined.

19. neither was, i. e. there neither was, c.

22. with. The usual preposition after beloved is of in the older English, and by in the more modern.

25. of i. e. off.

31. farder, i. e. farther off, more disinclined. For the form of the word cf. murder and muriher; burden and burthen. Halle has "more further and scrupulous to deliver," c.

P. 36, line 3. malyce here signifies rather wrongdoing than evil disposition. The prince, being so young, could have done nothing to deserve the confinement in a sanctuary.

5. which, i. e. the fetching of him out.

8. ia = happen, chance. Cf. Shaks. Tempest, I. i. 28,

"Make yourself ready for the mischance of the hour, if it so a." 12. plight = con. ion. Cf. Shaks. Merry Wives, il. 2. 172, "I think myself in better plight for a lender than you."

to sende out, i. e. to be sent out; for one to send him out.

16. I trust God as strong, i. e. I trust that God is as strong, c. Halle for " as " reads " is." I have therefore inserted is in the text.

17. but. This word, both here and in line 20 and 37. 3, serves to introduce an opponent's statement in his own words, to which an answer is given in the next sentence. Thus it = But (as he says).

19. glose. Used at first to signify some explanatory note or comment to interpret a word or text of Scripture. It came however soon to signify some specious rather than sound explanation. Cf. Udal, St Luke, cap. 12, "Beware that all your life be voide of all clokyng or counterfeit i7j." Also Spenser, F. Q. iv. 5. 15,

"He much more goodly glosse thereon doth shed To hide his falsehood, than if it were true."

24. his painted processe dratveth, i. e. his counterfeit proceedings tend, at what he is aiming in spite of all his pretences.

For processe w'zy or order of proceeding cf. Shaks. Merchant, IV. I. 274,

"Tell her the process of Antonio's end."

For a; z = counterfeit Shaks. IIe7i. VIII. V. 3. 71,

"Your painted gloss discovers, to men that understand you, words and weakness."

For draw = to tend, to approach, cf Shaks. Ant. and Cleop. ill. 4. 21, "Let your best love draw to that point which seeks best to preserve it."

27. be ye sure. Added ironically = as of course you can understand.

30. but z"= unless. Cf. on 10. 2.

31. hist, i. e. liking. Cf. Chaucer, Cant. Tales, Prol. 192, ' Of prikyng and of huntyng for the hare Was al his hcst. "

P. 37, line 4. and if. Said to be the latter part of even, as if is said to ide taken from the former syllable of that word. But some derive and (often written an) from A. S. U7inan = io give, as 7is said to be from gifan to give. Cf. for the meaning, Shaks. Twelfth Night,

And you love me, let's do it."

6. a gay 7nntter. Spoken in irony, as if she would say, "We are discussing a merry subject," while all the time she feels how serious an affair is in hand. Halle has " a straunge matter."

Cf. Wilson, A7'te of Logike, fol. 15, "This may seem to some a gay saying, whereas indeed it is both foolish and wicked."

11. to, i. e. too. Cf. below, 40. 28, 29, c. hence, i. e. out of this place.

12. Halle adds after "-fro me"'" "yf I stale hym not nor owe you nothyng."

14. he hath nothing by discent holden by knightes sertiice. Knighf s service is a term used in the description of feudal tenure of land from the crown, and implies that the holder of such land, either by himself or another, served the king in war and was an independent person.

The queen's words imply that her second son had not even by inheritance from his father any such tenure, and so was not to be regarded in any wise as an independent person, but as a ward in charge of a guardian.

After " knightes service" Halle adds "but by socage."

22. cure, i. e. care (Lat. cura). Cf. Chaucer, Cant. Tales, Prol. 306, "Of studie toke he moste cure and hede."

27. may take benefyte of it, i. e. may avail himself of its privilege of sanctuary.

P. 38, line 3. had the victorye. After the second battle of St Albans, fought Feb. 17, 1461.

7. rayning, i. e. reigning.

8. to the kindes enemye. There is evidently something wrong here. Neither Halle nor Hardyng's continuator has this passage, which, as the sidenote (p. 37) indicates, comes from More's Latin. We should expect something like, "As this place was sometime to him when unborn."

12. wyll the mother kepe, i. e. willeth the mother to keep, c. Cf. above, on 11. 10.

15. and wej'e, i. e. and who would be.

16. hath no man to doe to exa?? iine. To do rawch to do, or as is more common, much ado; so that the sentence means, "No man hath much trouble in finding out."

19. lesse lande then, c., i. e. even less land than a kingdom, implying that the law would forbid such a thing still more stringently where a kingdom would be the inheritance.

20. can no more, i. e. I can do no more. Cf. vshaks. Hamlet v. 2. 331, " can no more: the King, the King's to blame." Halle has here, "I can sale no more."

22. when he may not come to it, i. e. may he need it, and not be able to obtain its shelter.

26. farder of, i. e. farther off, i. e. more and more disinclined to consent. Cf. on 35. 31.

33. estate, i. e. his position, property and condition. He should be maintained in good estate. Cf. Shaks. Alerch. iii. 2. 239, "His letter there will shew you his estatet

P. 39, line 2. there with fz= therewith.

3. shyfte whoso would, i. e. any one might shifte (i. e. contrive, have recourse to fresh means) who pleased in this business, for he would have no more to do with the matter. For the verb, cf. Shaks. Tenipcst, v. i. 256, "Every man shift (i. e. contrive) for all the rest."

8. pj'ocure her sonne to be delynered, i. e. bring about that her son should be given up.

12. for as much her semed, S: c., i. e. for as much as the Cardinal seemed to her.

18. all thinge vnredy. A sort of case absolute = while all things were unready.

19. 7iothing lesse loking for, i. e. while she looked for (expected) nothing less, c.

20. fet, p. p. of the verb to fetch. In the 1611 edition of the Authorized Version this form is found (as an imperfect) in many places where now fetched is printed, e. g. 2 Sam. ix. 5. Cf. Lyly, Eiiphues, p. 93, "Farreyiv and deere bought is good for Ladyes."

22. it might fortune her fere to bee false, i. e. it might chance that her fear was false and groundless. For the verb cf. Tyndale, Works, p. 41, "Unbelief only damneth

and keepeth out the spirit and provo-keth the flesh. as ii fortuned o Adam and Eve in Paradise."

23. tuell she zvaste, i. e. well she wist, she knew well. Halle has "well she wiste." The original here is " will she waste," which is clearly a misprint.

24. shold nedes = must of necessity.

25. dempte, i. e. deemed.

otier that = rcvoxeo Qr, besides. Cf. 3. i; 33. ir.

30. warely, i. e. warily, carefully.

32. betoke, entrusted, committed, gave in charge. Cf. Fabyan, Chronicle, cap. 68, "And whenne Constantyne had all prepared for his voyage, he betoke the land of Britain unto the said Octavius."

of ti'ust= trust, as a trust. Gave him in charge to them as a trust.

P. 40, line 4. either of both, i. e. either of the two qualities, either wisdom or truth.

ir. experience. The allusion in this sentence and the next is to the death of George, Duke of Clarence, whose brothers had been the contrivers of his death.

17. be, i. e. are. Cf. Latimer, Sermons, p. 23, "Which works be of themselves marvellous good."

19. (?? c= goods, possessions. Cf. i Chron. xxix. 3, "I have of mine own proper t? '. prepared for the holy house." See also 68. i, note.

25. if ye cannot elszuhcj-e, i. e. if ye cannot (keep him safe) elsewhere.

32. ojies, i. e. once. This word is really the genitive case of one and signifies, for one time.

P. 41, line 2. as fast. Halle adds "as the mother." 7. hesayd in that of likelihod as he thought = X x xv he spake in all probability as he thought.

9. the bishoppes palice at Powles, i. e. the palace of the Bishop of London at St Paul's. See Stow's Survey of London 1633, P- 4 2 b. " On the north-west side of this St Paul's churchyard is the Bishop's palace, a large thing for receit, wherein divers kings have been lodged and a great household hath been kept, as appeareth by the Great Hall, which of late years, since the rebatement of Bishops' Livings, hath not been furnished with household meynie and guests as was meant by the builders thereof, and was of old time used."

12. This passage between the asterisks, p. 41 43, is represented in Halle as follows: "When the protectour had both the chyldren in his possession, yea and that they were in a sure place, he then began to thirst to se the ende of his enterprise. And to avoyde all suspicion, he caused all the lordes, whiche he knewe to be faithfull to the kyng, to assemble at Baynardes Castle to commen of the ordre of the coronation whyle he and other of his complices and of his affinitee at Crosbies place contrived the contrary and to make the protectour kyng."

13. opened hiinsef rq e Qdi his intentions. vsee below, lines 23 and 27, and cf. Bp Pilkington, Works, p. 423, "He Avas angry with his servants and said they had betrayed and ; chis counsel."

31. broken vnto the dnke, i. e. disclosed. See above, on 12. 28.

32. their crafte maisters, i. e. the masters of their craft, the men most expert at their business.

P. 42, line 2. who, i. e. and they, the kinsfolk. 5. careful, full of care, troubled by anything. Cf. Pierce Plowfnan's Crede,

"And al they songen o one songe, that sorwe was to heren, They crieden al o cry, a careful note."

II. beck, a movement of the head as a sign of command. Cf. Shaks. I Hen. VI. I. i. 68,

"They have troops of soldiers at their beck.""

15. spialles, spies. Often written espiaucs. Cf. Shaks. i lien. VI. I. 4. 48, "The prince's spials have informed me;" in which passage home of the old editions have espials.

16. traines, devices, contrivances. Cf. hyly, Enphues, 38, "The alluring traines of women's wiles."

23. 7;- = forward, on to the end. Cf. Shaks. Measiire for Measure, Y. I. 255, "to hear this mattery rz," i. e. to the end.

26. voided =Zi oide(. Cf. 2. 24.

29. commodite, advantage, profit. Cf. 8. 27.

P. 43, line i. Erledome of Hertford. This is an error in the original for Hereford. Buckingham claimed the earldom of Hereford, because he was descended from Thomas of Woodstock, Duke of Gloucester, who married Aleanore, daughter of Humphry de Bohun, the last Earl of Hereford. Cf. 87. 5, below.

6. at a point in accord, in agreement.

9. other where, i. e. into some other direction. For this use of where, almost like a noun, cf. Shaks. King Lear, I. i. 264, 'Thou losest here, a better where to find." The construction is "turn the eyes otherwhere from perceiving," c.

ir. thick, i. e. in large numbers. Cf. Shaks. Jul. Cces. I. i. 76,

"I'll about, And drive away the vulgar from the streets, So do you too, where you perceive them thick.""" 12. the lord Cardinall. This was the Archbishop of Canterbury, at this time Thomas Bourchier, Cardinal, and Chancellor of Oxford.

13. the Bishoppe of Ely. Dr John Morton. See 88. 14.

19. adhibit (Lat. adhibere) = called, summoned, admitted, i. e. though very few persons were invited.

23. misgiiicth. The nominative is, of course, the plural word hartes, but the singular expression "of a secret instinct of nature" coming between has drawn the verb into the singular.

24. him s elf = it self, which did not exist in More's day. Halle has here, " as the south wynde sometyme swelleth, c."

27. soinzvhat the dealing self, i. e. in some degree the actions themselves which were done, c. For i = itself, cf. infra, 55. 4.

29. close, kept secret. Cf. Shaks. Ro77ieo, I. 1. 155, "To himself so secret and so close.""" for title and little. We should now say, "for little by little," or, "for by little and little."

30. Crosbics place in Bishops gates strete. The place is still marked and known as Crosby Hall.

32. had the resort, i. e. had all the throng of people resorting to him, was visited and courted of all people. Cf. Shaks. Two Gentlemen, I. 2. 4, "Of all the fair resort of gentlemen,

That every day with parle encounter me. In thy opinion which is worthiest love?"

33. that had the doing, i. e. who were the persons through whom all was done, the executive body.

P. 44, line 2. toitrfie them to no good, i. e. turn to no goodyi r them.

4. which, i. e. the protector.

6. of purpose, i. e. with a design. We now say "c purpose," but cf. Shaks. Hen. VIII. V. 2. 14, "This is of purpose laid, by some that hate me, to quench mine honour."

8. yeke, i. e. eke 'ss."o.

10. lord Stanly. This was Thomas Stanley, made Lord Stanley of Lathom in Lancashire in 1456. After playing a prominent part in the events preceding the accession of Henry VII. he was made Earl of Derby in 1485.

t2. scucrall, i. e. separate. Cf. Earle's JMicrocosmographie, p. 23, "His style is compounded of twenty several mens." Also 2 Kings xv. f, "Azariah was a leper, and dwelt in a several ow."'" 15. while one man is there which is netier thence, i. e. as long as one certain man is among them, who never is absent, c.

17. sozvnde amisse toward; = should have any sound or meaning of mischief toward me.

10. by 'va. reference to, concerning, in respect of Cf. Gascoigne, Steel Glas, p. 71, "I speake not this by English courtiers."

22. Iiefe = de2ir, beloved. Cf. Shaks. 2 Hen. VI. ill. i. 1(4, "Stirred up my liefest liege to be mine enemy."

26. much 7-ule bare. An inverted order for " bare much rule."

27. Lcceter, i. e. Leicester. The orthography of the text shews that our present pronunciation is the same as that of More's time. Halle reads, " in the counties of Lecestre and Northampton."

29. onelye, i. e. alone.

. 2. broken all the datince, i. e. frustrated all tlie schemes, upset all the plans.

33. for, i. e. because of. Cf. Shaks. Alidsumnier Nighfs Dream, V. I. 253, " he dares not come there ? r the candle."

P. 45, line 2. none no. Cf. Shaks. Cymbeline, I. 4. 103, "Your Italy contains none so accomplished a courtier."

4. semblaitnce, outward show, i. e. they appeared to be friendly towards him, Cf. Shaks. Comedy of Errors, v. 358, "These two 1)romios, one in semblance."'" 8. quailed, quelled, overthrown. Cf. Shaks. Antony and Cleopatra, V. 2. 85, "When he meant to q nail and win the orb."

11. assayed= made tnal of. Cf. Shaks. Jlerry IVives, II. i. 26, "That he dares in this manner assay me."

14. of very trtcst, i. e. by reason of his complete trust in him.

16. mocions here means the movings, promptings, suggestions, made to him (Catesby) by Buckingham (see above, line 8), and by Catesby to be set before Lord Hastings.

17. viinishe his credence, diminish his credit. For minish d-minish, cf. lible, 1551, Exod. v. 8, "And the nombre of bricke which they were wont to make in tyme passed, laye unto their charges also, and mynnyshe nothing thereof."

For crede72ce cf. Shaks. All's Well, I. 2. 11, "His love and wisdom may plead for amplest credence."'" 19. to ridde him, to remove him out of the way. (X. Shaks. Rich. II. V. 4. II, "I am the King's friend and will;7 his foe."

21. the only desire, c. The sense is: the desire whereof was the sole enticement, c. Cf. Lyly, Eiiphues, p. 70, "I am brought into a Paradise by the only imagination of women's virtues," where we should say either "by the imagination only," or "by the mere imagination."

22. allectiue (Lat. alliceo io entice) an enticement, inducement. Cf. More, Works, p. 12, "But among all thinges the very deadly pestilence is this: to be conversant day and niglit among them whose life is not only an allective to sin, but over that all set in the expugnation i6o HISTORY OF KING RICHARD III.

of virtue." Halle has here, "the thyng that enduced him to be procurer and c."

25. Halle gives the date " the thirtene daye of June."

29. sjitteltics. These were arrangements of figures to make a Talole decoration, and generally had verses attached to them. Fabyan in his Chronicle (ed. 1516) gives an account of the "sotylties" devised at the coronation banquet of Henry VI.

"(r) A Sotyltie of Seynt Edwarde and Seynt Lowys armyd and upon eyther his cote armour, holdyng atwene them a fygure lyke unto kyng Henry, standyng also in his cote armour, and a Scripture passing from them both sayinge, Beholde ii. parfyght Kynges under one cote armour: and under the fete of the sayd seyntes was wryten this balade.

(2) A Sotyltie of an Emperoure and a Kynge araycd in Mantellys of Garters, whiche figured Sygysmunde the Emperoure and Henry the V. And a fygure lyke unto Kynge Henry the VI. knelynge to-fore theym with this balade takked by hym.

(3) A Sotyltie of our Lady syttynge with her child in her lappe and she holdynge a crowne in her hande. Seynt George and Seynt Denys on eyther syde presentyd to her Kynge Henryes figure berynge in hande this halade as foloweth."

30. the7'fore h. QVQ for, i. e. for that (occasion).

32. codioniiig, communing, speaking in common. See 46. 1.

P. 46, line 2. Halle has, "bene a sleper."

5. Holberne. Ely Place in Holborn still marks the place of ancient residence of the Bishops of Ely in London.

require, i. e. request, not necessarily in our modern sense of demanding. See 30. 27, note.

messe, i. e. a dishful, used of meat and other things. Cf. Gen." xliii. 34, "He took and sent messes unto them."

7. in al the hast. We generally now omit the article, and say "in all haste," but cf. Shaks. Lear, 11, i. 26,

"He's coming hither; now, i' the night, i the haste."'

See also below, 48. 21.

9. sette the lordes fast, engaged them busily.

14. froting, i. e. chafing. In the sense of rubbing, the word is found in Chaucer. Halle has here, " fretyng and gnawyng." The sense of " froting" may be gathered from two examples of its use in Trevisa's translation of Higden's Polychrome on (Rolls Sei'les). In vol. I. p. 163, he says of a language that it is " frotynge and unschape," and Higden's text has " ita stridet incondita" where the sense is what we now call "grating" of sounds. Then, vol. ill. p. 25, he says "they clawede and frotede the oliphauntes in the forhedes" where the Latin has " scalpo " = to scratch.

knawing, i. e. gnaw ing.

19. compasse and yinagine, i. e. bring about and plan. Cf. Shaks. Merry Wives, ill. 3. 212, "The knave bragged of that he could not compass."' Also 2 Hen. VI. I. 2. 19, "When I ijnagine ill against my king."

22. astonied, i. e. astonished. Cf. Dan. iii. 24, "Then Nebuchadnezzar the king was astojtied.

Jj = concerning. Cf. 44. 19, and see below, line 32.

23. clere, clear, innocent. Cf. Shaks. Merry IVwes, III. 3. 123, If you know yourself cear, I am glad of it."

28. sorceres. For he is going to charge her with doing him injury by witchcraft.

30. gretly abashed that fatioiired her, i. e. those who were on her side were greatly downcast.

32. better content, that it was moucd by her, then by any other, i. e. better satisfied that the charge was made about her than about anybody else.

P. 47, line I. made of counsell, i. e. made a portion of the council, taken into counsel, entrusted with the secret. Cf. Shaks. Othello, III. 3. in, "He was of my counsel in my whole course of wooing." See also below, line 17.

5. ware, i. e. aware, conscious. Cf. Shaks. Rojneo, ii. 2. 102, "Thou overheard'st, ere I was luare, my true love's passion."

8. Shoris tvife, i. e. Jane Shore.

10. dotcblet, a man's inner garment. Cf. Shaks. Merry Wives, III. I. 46, "In your doublet and hose this raw rheumatic day."

11. wcrish, apparently = ill-shapen, foul, ugly. Cf. Ascham, Schole77iaster, Bk i, "A countenance not werishe and crabbed, but faire and comely."

12. as it was neiier other =ds it had always been.

20. harjne, i. e. the injury done to his person. But Halle and Hardyng print ar7? i, which is most probably correct.

22. woj'thy. The fuller construction is worthy of But cf. Shaks. Merry Wives, v. 5. 64, "Worthy the owner and the owner it."

24. Halle has "with yf and with and." The and in this sentence = if On this word, cf. 37. 4 note.

33. let flee. We now. y let fly: i. e. let a weapon fly, aimed a blow. Halle has, "let flye." Standley i- vxty.

P. 48, line 4. bcstoxved, placed. Cf. above on 16. 12. For the first part of this sentence, Halle gives "Then was the Archebishop of Yorke and doctour Morton bishopp of Ely and the lorde Stanley taken and divers other, which were bestowed in dyvers chambers."

6. shryue him, i. e. make his confession. (2a(r = quickly.

8. at aduentiire, by chance, the first that came to hand.

15. entred, interred. We have the word spelt entered in i. 24.

18. voided, i. e. avoided. Cf. on 2. 24. that= that which.

21. m al the hast. We now say "in all haste." See 46. 7. requirino- requesting, cf. 46. 5.

24. raced= tore. The word is used by Chaucer, as also the form arace.

27. the bore. The boar, being Richard's coat of arms, gave occasion to the rhyme, RICH.

i62 HISTORY OF KING RICHARD III

"The Cat, the Rat, and Lovel the dog, Ruled all England under the hog," The Cat was Catesby, the Rat, Ratcliffe.

cognisaunce =co? it of arms, by which mailed warriors in old times were known cognitus).

After the word cognisaiince, Halle inserts "he ymagined that it should be he."

28. throughly, i. e. thoroughly. Cf. Matth. iii. 12, "He will throughly purge his floor." The sense is the same as utterly in line 22 above.

31. Ey. We write this interjection i."

32. leneth, i. e. leaneth = giveth heed to.

P. 49, line I. fantasieth, i. e. fancieth. The noun fantasy was of common use in Elizabethan English, but the verb not so common. The p. p. is alone found in Shaks. Khigyohn, iv. 2. 144, "I find the people strangelyy zaj-zv ." Cf. below, iii. 7, where the word means " took a liking for."

3. plaine, downright, nothing else but. Cf. Shaks. King John, ii. 462, "He speaks; cannon-fire."

7. likely. Here the sense of the expression seems to be "a cause which would probably make him race us," or "give him warrant for doing so." So the word 6t'y=: well-grounded, adequate.

race. On this word see 48. 24.

10. biding, i. e. staying where we are.

nedes cost, of necessity. The simple word needs is common now.

11. leuer. More commonly spelt liefer rather, by prefere ice. Cf. Joy, Exposiciotin of Daniel, "I had liefer hem to Idc converted and live." The positive lief and the superlative liefest are found in Shakespeare, but not the comparative. Cf. also 6. 19 note, where the spelling is the same as here.

22. cwar = impending, hanging over, near at hand. Cf. 3. 5.

25. eneiniotise, i. e. the work of an enemy. Halle has enviouse, which probably is correct.

26. a knight. Here Halle adds, "Sir Thomas Haward sonne to the Lord Haward (which lord Avas one of the priveyest of the lord protectours counsaill and doyng)."

28. Halle omits the words " wyth. auctorite." They would be somewhat of a contradiction to the words quoted from him in the previous note.

33. brake his tale, i. e. interrupted his conversation. merely, i. e. merrily.

P. 50, line 4. tother properly means "the other" or "that other," but so far had this become forgotten in common speech that we have here "that tother."

6. sene a signe, i. e. observed (to be) a sign.

7. I shall rather let anye thinge passe me, i. e. I shall notice such a matter even before anything else.

10. sone after. Here Halle adds "as a man might wel caste a balle."

11. and of their iiieting. We should now say " by their meethig." Cf. Latimer, Rem. p. 240, "That the Scripture of God may be read in Enghsh all his obedient subjects."

18. fere of himselfe, i. e. fear for, on account of, himself.

22. while he was therin, i. e. in the danger and jeopardy.

1". art thott reme77ibred. To be remembred is an old English expression = "to recollect." Cf. Shaks. Taming of Shrew, iv. 3. 96, "If you be re?)iejnbred, I did not bid you mar it."

28. els, i. e. few else, few beside me.

31. but nothing ware, i. e. but was in no degree aware.

P. 51, line 4. After the word suerty, Halle adds "I praye God it prove so (quod Hastynges). Prove (quod he)? Doubtest thou that? Nay, nay, I warraunt the: And so iti nianer displeased he entered into the Towre, where he was not long on lyve, as you have heard."

12. passing, i. e. exceedingly. Cf. Shaks. Othello, I. 3. 160, "'Twas strange, w? ispassing strange."

17. to set some colour vpon, i. e. " to give reason or excuse for it." Cf. Shaks. lvi7it. Tale, iv. 4. 566, "What colour iox my visitation shall I hold up before him? " See also 53. 19 below.

18. se? nbstahncial. Halle has " substancial."

20. harnesed, c. = armed in old ill-looking coats of mail. Halle has "evil-favoured briganders,"

30. next to hande, i. e. nearest, first to hand.

32. required, i. e. requested. Cf. 46. 5.

P. 52, line 2. in al the hast, see on 48. 21. Cf. also 51. 17.

3. herode. Halle has " heralde."

16. sinister procuring, i. e. wrongful contrivances.

21. pict vnto. As we say now '""pict to death."

27. m inakyng, i. e. while or for the purpose of) making. Cf. Shaks. Cor. iv. 6. 131, "cast your caps ; hooting at Coriolanus' exile."

29. politikely, i. e. in accordance with wise policy.

33. curiously, with much care, carefully. Cf. Shaks. Mtich Ado, V. I. 157, "If I do not carve most curiously, say my knife's naught."

so zvel a set hande, i. e. in a hand so well written. This inversion of the order of words is common with the author.

P. 53, line I. processe, used here of a legal document. We still call the officer of a law court who serves the writs, "ar c i'J'-server."

2. prepared before. Here Halle has "prepared and studyed before (and as some men thought by Catesby)."

4. bare writing, i. e. mere writing out; cf. i Cor. xv. 37, ari? grain = nothing but grain.

all had it bene, i. e. although it had but been on paper, i. e. and not so grandly engrossed on parchment.

7. of chaunce. We now say " by chance."

9. He means "Here is a fine grand work of skill, shamefully spoiled by hurrying." Of course he was speaking in irony on the excellent composition done apparently in so short a time.

II. j r Q', i. e. prophetically.

12. the protector sent. Here Halle inserts "Sir Thomas Hawarde."

15. i. e. two or three thousand marks.

16. laide vnto her, for the uianer sake, i. e. laid against her, accused her, for appearance sake.

31. otit of al rr j rwithout any dress but her kirtle (i. e. petticoat with a jacket above).

33. rud, Halle has red. But for the interchange of vowels cf. ruddy.

P. 54, line 7. worshipftiuyfrended. Halle has "well frended." 10. proper. This word is frequently used of the form and outward appearance of persons. Cf. Burton, Anatomy, p. 575, "This Cymon was a fool, a proper man of person, and the governor of Cyprus' son, but a very ass."

17. After ' cha7'nel house f Halle substitutes for the remainder of the sentence: " and this judgement was in the tyme of Kyng Henry the eyght, in the xviii yere of whose reigne she dyed, when she had nothyng but a reveled skynne and bone."

18. ryitiide, i. e. rivelled, shrivelled. Cf. Holland's Plinie, Xiii. 21, "The leaves be somewhat longer and thicker, with long cuts or lines wrinkled and rxv Ztfcthroughout."

19. whoso ivel aduise, i. e. whoso should well look at.

23. rede ivel. Reading and writing were not such common accomplishments in the fifteenth century as they are now.

P. 55, line 3. rather gay then rich, i. e. gifts which rather made a show than were costly.

15. The sense is: " with all those who in those days had business which they wished to set forward."

30. lordes and knightes. Halle gives the names: "the earle Ryvers, and the lorde Richarde the quene's sone, Syr Thomas Vaughan and Sir Richard Haute."

P 56, line 3. secret with hi7? i = z. sharer of his secrets, a confidant.

14. to nigh to the qnene. o:) near akin to her.

After this sentence Halle adds: "In so much as Sir Thomas Vaughan, goyng to his death, sayed: I, wo worthe them that toke the prophecie that G. should destroy King Edwardes children, meaning therby the duke of Clarence, Lord George, which for that suspicion is now dead, but now remaineth Richard G, duke of Gloucester, which now I se is he that shal and will accomplishe the prophecie and destroy Kyng Edwardes children, and all their alyes and frendes, as it appereth by us this day: whom I appele to the high tribunal of God for his wrongful murther and our true innocencye. And then Ratclyffe sayed: You have well apeled, lay downe youre head. Ye, quod syr Thomas, I dye in right; beware you dye not in wrong. And so that good knight was beheaded and the other three, and buryed naked in the monastery at Poumfret."

16. out of the way. This is followed in Halle by: " then the protectour caused it to be proclaymed that the coronacion for divers great and urgent causes should

be deferred tyll the seconde daye of November, for then thought he that whyle men mused, c."

19. jrmcrzj-=strengths, i. e. strongholds, places of security. He would detain them about his person so that there could be no chance of any gathering in the country to oppose his schemes.

30. made of coimsail. Halle has " made a counsail." This corruption a for of) is found in such expressions as " novv-a-days," " out a doors," c. Numerous instances are found in Shaks. AWs Well That Ends Well, where it forms a peculiarity of the dialect.

31. vpon tricst of, i. e. in the hope of.

32. of a proud larf, by reason of a proud heart.

33. shold frame the cite to their appetite, i. e. should mould and fashion the minds of the citizens to agree with what the protector and his friends desired.

P. 57, line I. spiritual men. The clerg)', as distinguished from the laity. We still use the word of the Bishops, calling them j r czpeers as distinguished from the temporal peers.

4. yohn Shaa. Halle has " Raffe Shaa."

5. Penker. Halle gives the name as " Pynkie."

prouincial. The president over an ecclesiastical district or province.

The order of Augustine Friars was introduced into England in the time of Archbishop Anselm. See Stow's Survey, p. 930, who also describes the Church of the Augustine (or Austin) Friars which was in the Broad Street Ward. Ibid. p. 185 b.

TO. had a sermon. This is one of many examples which might be quoted of how Latin influenced More's language. He is here rendering concionem habere = lo hold a discourse.

12. no mans eares. Halle says "no good man's eares."

17. j; r =heeded, cared for. Cf. Shsivs. Lovers Laboin-'s Lost, v. 1. 440, "Your oath once broke, you forced not to forswear." Other examples of this somewhat rare word are Gascoigne's Steel Glas, p. 26, " I little force (care for) the forces you can use."

Webbe, Discotcrse of Engl. Poetry, p. 35,

"Whether it was Master Sp. or what rare Scholar in Pembroke Hall, force not greatly to set down."

Lyly, Enphues, p. 8r, "I force not (care not for) Philautus his fury, so I may have Euphues his friendship."

It is also used impersonally, "it forceth not" = it matters not.

Cf. Grindal, Remains, p. 195, "What we have once been, it forceth not, God respecteth no man's person."

So Pilkington, Works, p. 427, "But h i forceth 7iot, the truth must be spoken, though some do grudge."

21. at S. Mary hospytall. Halle gives "at Sainct Mary Spittle." This hospital was founded by Walter archdeacon of London in 1197 and was in Bishopgate Ward. Stow (p. 175 b) tells of its surrender to Henry VIII. and says, "A part of the large church yard pertaining to this hospital yet remaineth as of old time, with a pulpit crosse therein,

somewhat like to that in Paul's Churchyard." This was no doubt the scene of Penker's sermon.

24. breke the mater. We still say " break the news."

P. 58, line I. ai'zj-2a:(5 flr= disqualified.

2. by the dtike, i. e. in right of the duke (whose son they were going to assert that Edward was not).

7. he letted not, i. e. he did not hinder them from making such a charge, so that it might further his purpose.

10. (Xi'i obliquely, only glanced at.

21. in embassiate m the capacity of an ambassador.

The nobleman here spoken of was Richard Nevill, Earl of Warwick, known for the part he played in the histoiy of this period as " the Kingmaker."

23. vnto Spaine. Halle says "to the French King" and in the following line instead of "the kinges doughter of Spain" has '"Bona, sister to the French quene, then beyng in Fraunce." Which is Shakespeare's version of the story. See Richard III. iii. 7. 180. The story is told by Grafton as follows. "And now being about 23 years of age King Edward is advised by his council to take a wife. for which no place was thought so convenient to match in as France, nor no lady for all personal qualities and many reasons of state so fit as the Lady Bona, daughter to Lewis duke of Savoy, sister to the present queen of France and now residing in the French court. To treat of which marriage the earl of Warwick is immediately despatched into France, to whose proposals the French very XQ2. y condescend. But King Edward. hunting in the meantime in Witchwood Forest, and coming to the manor of Cirafton, happened to be bewitched with the Lady Elizabeth Grey, the young widow of Sir John Grey of Groby, c."

to intrcate. We now say " to treat for."

32. her mother. This was Jacquetta, Duchess of Bedford. She was the relict of John, Duke of Bedford, and a daughter of Peter of Luxemburg, Earl of St Pauls. Her possessions were afterwards seized by Henry VH. and she lived in a mean estate in ihe monastery of Bermondsey till her death.

33. the lord Wodefeld. Halle gives the full title " Sir Richard Wood vile, lorde Rivers." He succeeded as Baron Rivers in 1448, and was made Earl Rivers by Edward IV. in 1466.

P. 59, line 3. Halle gives the full name " Jhon Gray" and in the next line says: "at the laste battaill of Sainct Albones." The date of the battle was 1461.

10. injoint2(re. The phrase is used of such property asy?";jwas held by husband and wife, while both lived, and which was to become the property of the widow after her husband's death.

11. of a good fa uor, a well-favoured, good-looking person.

15. appointed = coxae to a determination, resolved, agreed, settled, cf. Chaucer, Alarchaiint's Tale, 9469,

"He at the last appointed him on one And let all other from his herte gon."

16. ensured her. The more frequent word is "assured." The sense is, plighted himself to her, and received her pledge in return. Thus = affianced her to himself, and obtained her promise to marry him.

26. standing that. This participial construction is absolute and unattached to any previous word. The force is much the same as "seeing that," but it may be explained = since matters stand thus, that the earl, c.

27. z cr = journey. Cf. Chaucer, Prologue, 792,

"That eche of yow to short with oure weye In this viage shal telle tales tweye."

28. his appointmentes deluded=his arrangements treated as child's play and set at nought.

P. 60, line 9. the only widowhed. We should now say "the mere widowhood," "the widowhood alone." For examples of this use of the word, cf. More's Utopia (Pitt Press Series), p. 144, "For every one of them, whatsoever he taketh for the chief God, thinketh it to be the very same nature, to whose only divine might the soveraintie of al thinges is attributed." See also Ascham, Scholemaster, p. 42, "Boldnes to aske doubtes and wil to win praise be wonne and maintened by the onelie wisdome and discretion of the scholemaster." So Spenser, F. Q.

"The onely breath him daunts who hath escaped the stroke;" and the Leycester Correspondence., p. 237, "The only transportatyon will cost a thousand pound."

14. approche priesthode in denes. It was forbidden to priests to marry a widow by a decree of the council of Lyons in 1274.

15. bigamy, here = marrying with a widow. Cf. Shaks. Richard III. III. 7, 189, where the word is used of this same marriage.

20. at apoitite=i A y determined, come to a fixed point. Cf. 43. 6 above.

P. 61, line 2. happelye, i. e. haply, perhaps.

ir. my cosein of Warwik. " Cousin " is a title frequently given by princes to other princes and distinguished noblemen, without the existence of any blood relationship between them. Thus in Shaks. Measure for Aeasure, V. i. 165, the Duke of Vienna says to Lord Angelo " Come, cousin Angelo."

15. gardain, see 37. 15.

18. estraitnge, i. e. strange. For other examples of this influence of French on English forms, cf. escape with scape; escalade with scale; especial with special; so espousals, espy, esquire, establish, estate, estray have each their shorter form.

21. let the bishop hardely lay if in my 7vai. "Hardely" here seems to mean "harshly," "unfavourably," and so the sense of the clause is " let the bishop lay it in my way as an objection."

23. forbidden a prieste, see note on 60. 14.

28. to Godwarde, i. e. toward God. Cf. 2 Cor. iii. 4; i Thess. i. 8.

33. stcre, i. e. assured, affianced to. Cf. Shaks. As You Like It, V. 4. 141, "You and you are stcre together, as the winter to foul weather."

P. 62, line 8. comfort. In the sense of Lat. fortis = s. xong; here encouragement, strengthening.

ensured. Halle has here "assured." See above on 59. 16.

14. After "impediment" Halle continues: "he shortely after at Grafton, beside Stony Stratforde, maried the lady Elizabeth Grey verie prively. and her father was created Erie Rivers, and her sonne created Marques Dorset."

20. highly- Xioxwy. Q. ' i' Antony and Cleopatra, YW. x. 1, "Let me rail so highly. " 26. in sa7tcticary. See the queen's answer, above, pp. 37, 38. 32. vmch what = iox the most part, cf. 6. 21, above.

P. 63, line 7. he, i. e. the Earl of Warwick. The battle of Barnet was fought on Easter-day, 1471. II. z= condition. Not with the bad sense which now generally attaches to the word.

15. lenght, for length. This orthography seems to have been usual. Cf. strenghtis for strengths, 56. 19, above.

16. biiilded his colour ='S, Q. up his pretext.

18. The sense of the sentence is: That invented story pleased them who were satisfied if they only had something to say, as they were sure not to be asked to give more proof than themselves chose to offer.

26. nor were not. An example of the double negative so common in the language of Shakespeare's time. Cf. 66. 30.

P. 64, line I. tyjiie, i. e. the text of his sermon. The word here is probably a corruption of theme.

The text is from the Book of Wisdom, iv. 3. For agejit in the Latin Halle reads dabunt.

8. baste, i. e. bastardy, pronounced "basety."

9. and the troiith hid fro knowlege, i. e. and by the truth being hidden from men's knowledge.

28. secret in the hoiishold, i. e. in the secrets of the family.

30. fauoiirs, i. e. looks, faces, features, cf. 65. 2. The first words of this clause = as being persons who by their looks, c.

31. fro7)i whose vertuous condicions, c., i. e. from whose (the duke of York's) excellent qualities King Edward was far off.

P. 65, line 4. prent, i. e. print, see below, line 30.

5. expresse likenes. The word is from the Latin expi-essus 'por-trayed, moulded, modelled: so the sense is a likeness exactly modelled after another. Cf. Hebrews i. 3, "the expj-ess image of His person." Also Lyly, Euphiies, p. 48, "Another I, in all places the express image of myne owne person." And p. 71, "He created a woman the d'. rr? j image of eternity."

9. to the sermonwarde. Here the warde in toivarde has lost its force. The sense is fully given by "to the sermon."

meting with, i. e. happening at the same moment with (his presence).

15. qziailed = failed. Cf. Bp Pilkingtons Wo-rks, p. 574, "Such practices made the priests something to relent, and at length altogether to qziail."

17. found appears to have the signification of " foundered," ' stuck fast," " stopped." I can find no other instance of the word.

26. patrone. In 64. 33 it wojs, paterae which is probably the correct word.

P. ()(:, line 3. in the vpper story. In the pictures of the Cross at St Paul's (of which there are three in the Pepysian Library of Magdalene College, Cambridge) there is shewn an inner circle of auditors who stand on an elevated platform near the preacher and round the pulpit, while the rest of the audience are placed farther off and on the level of the ground. This platform must be the upper storey. In one of the pictures a new arrival is coming on to the platform, and it seems that as he gained the entrance to it, he would be visible to the whole audience. Hence the arrangement of which More's text tells us.

8. We hear in dialects still "kep" as the past tense of "to keep." And this History is full of colloquial English.

15. Tewesday foloiving this sermon. Here Halle inserts "beyng the xvii. day of June." In 1483 Tuesday fell on the i6th of June. See De Morgan, Book of Almanacs.

17. The sense of the last clause is: perhaps more than knew what the message was which they were bringing (to the people).

19. hiistinges. Halle writes the word " hoystynges." As an explanation ofzz j-'Vz j'Spelman says, "It is the most ancient and high court of the celebrated city of London;" and Fuller, in his Worthies, under London, gives the same.

25. this maner of wyse. An uncommon form, and meaning no more than " this manner."

28. to breake vntoyou. o declare unto you. Cf. above, 57. 24.

P. 67, line I. good, i. e. goods, possessions, cf. 40. 19. 7. eiier more, i. e. always, at all times. Cf. Shaks. Much Ado, ir. I. ir, "like my lady's eldest son, evei'more tattling."

9. grennes. Hall writes " gynnes." Both words are in use. Gin z. snare, is found several times in the O. T. (Job xviii. 9; Ps. cxl. 5; Is. viii. 14). But in some of these places the 1611 edition had griti or grenne which is an Anglo-Saxon word, while gin is derived from ingeniu77i, being the last syllable of the modern engine. For examples of grenne or grin (which is much the older word in our language) cf. Saxon Psalms cxl. 11, "geheald me ') thare gryne, hold me (preserve me) against their snare. Also Vicar's Virgil Aen. IV. 132):

"Young gallants nimbly flock about the gates And in their hands boarspears with iron plates, Their nets gins, grins, troops of Massylian sparks. Kennels of senting hounds with loud-mouth'd barks."

Also Geneva Bible Ps. cxli. 9, "Keepe me from the snare which they have layd for me, and from the grennes of the workers of iniquity." Then in the earlier language of the Ancren Riwle we find " deofles jronen" for "the devil's snares." And in the later language of Cotgrave's Dictionary (1611) is given, "Laqs, a snare, ginne ox grinne. Laqs courant, a noose, grintie or snitle."

10. pilling and polling, i. e. plundering and robbing. The two words are not unfrequently connected by old writers. Cf. Naunton, Fragmenta Regalia, p. 27, "His estate confiscate and that for peeling and pollingy So too Dodsley, Conflict of Conscience, vi. 49 (Avarice loquitur), "Every man did descry ray pilling and polling."'

16. lashedoute = 's,(Vi3. ndtxe. d. The idea is in lax, loose; a state of things where all is let go at random.

fiftenes. The tax so named because it was the fifteenth part of all the personal property of a subject, cf. Shaks. Plcnry VI. (pt. II.),

"A proper jest. that Suffolk should demand a o q. fifteenth P Fiftenes were not a modern invention, for Fabyan's Chronicle under the reign of Henry HI. tells " In this xv yere the Kynge had graunted tyll hym a quindecym ox flftetie of the Temporaltie and a dyme (i. e. a tenth) and an halfe of the Spiritualtie to recover his landes lost in Normandy."

18. hcncuolcnce. A name applied to the forced loans in the reign of Edward IV.

24. hazused, i. e. hauled up, dragged, and so increased. Halle has "haunsed" i. e. enhanced, with the same sense.

zw; r w? to=penalties that were inflicted on the body by punishment or incarceration. Such penalties the king is represented as commuting into fines that he might raise money thereby.

25. misprision. This word, which literally means mistake, en'or, acquired a technical sense in law, and was used to signify contempt of the court, or of a sentence.

29. cruelly behedded. Halle here adds: " (This Burdet was a marchaunt dwellyng in Chepesyde at the signe of the Croune, which now is the signe of the flower de liise, over against Soper Lane. This man merely (= merrily) in the rufillyng tyme of King Edward the IIII his rage (? reigne) saied to his awne sone that he would make him inheritor of the croune, meaning his awne house: but these words kyng Edward made to be mysconstrued and interpreted that Burdet meante the croune of the realme: wherfore within lesse space then iiii houres he was apprehended judged drawen and quartered in Chepesyde.)"

31. Alarkam. Sir John Markham was Chief Justice of the King's Bench from 1462 (May 13) till 1469 (Jan. 23).

33. then. This word depends upon no les which has just preceded, but from the word honour which is expressed, we must supply disgrace or some such word after then. So that the sense would be "With no less honour to Markham, than disgrace to the dishonesty, c."

P. ', line I- what. For examples of zuhat thus used superfluously as introduction to a question, cf. Shaks. Tc? np. i. i. 56, "What, must our mouths be cold?" dlso Hafiilet, I. i. 21, "IVhat, has this thing appeared again?"

Coke. Halle gives the name Syr Thomas Cooke. Fabyan in his Chronicle tells us that Thomas Cooke was mayor in 1462, was made a knight of the Bath in 1464, but under 1467 he says "after the departure of Margaret the kyng's sister to be married to Charlys duke of Burgoyne Syr Thomas Cook late mayre, which before was peched of treason by a servaunt of the lordes Wenlokkes called Hawkyns and at the request of the sayd lady Margarete, uppon suertie, suffered to go at large, than was arrested and sent unto the Towre and his goods seased by the Lord Ryverse, than treasourer of England, and hys wyf put oute of hys howse and commytted to the charge of the mayer in whose place she lay a season after. And after the sayd Syr Thomas had lyen a tyme in y Towre he was brought unto the Guyldhal, and there areygned of the sayde treason and quyt by sondry enquestes and after that commytted unto the Countour in Bradstrete and from thens to the Kynges benche in Southwarke, where he lay within the sayd pryson tyll his frendes agreed wyth Syr Johan Brandon, than kepar of y sayd pryson, to take hym home to hys place where to hys great charge he remayned as prysoner longe after. In whych tyme and season he lost moch good, for bothe hys places in the countre and also in London were under the gydynge of the sayd lordes Ryvers servauntes, and of the servauntes of Syr Johan Fogge, than under treasourer, the whych spoyled and dystroyed moche thynge and over that moche of hys jewelles and plate wyth great substaunce of the marchaundyse as cloth of sylkes and clothes of aras were dyscovered by suche persones as he hadde betaken the sayd goodes to kepe, and came to the treasourers handes, which to the sayd Syr Thomas was a greate enemye."

At last the history tells that on paying to the King a fine of; 8ooo, and 100 marks on each thousand pounds as an additional fine to the queen, he was released after "many good gyftes that he gave unto her counsayll."

13. agreidd, i. e. aggravated, made into mighty grievances.

17. for a pretext of treson, i. e. as a ground on which to accuse him of treason.

19. legcr aquaintaunce. Apparently from the Fr. Icger, hght, slight. Cf. Bacon, Charge against Dudley, "It is weakness and dis-esteem of a man's self to put a man's life upon such ledgier performances."

26. fal at distaimce =: QCo ne estranged, alienated. Cf. Shaks. Macbeth, ill. i. 115, "in such bloody distance,"' i. e. "in such deadly enmity."' 32. what about. We more frequently say now ' ' uihat with this and what with that." Cf. Shaks. Meastwe for Measure, I. 2. 83, "What zvith the war, zuhat with the sweat, whatzvith the gallows, and what zuith poverty, I am custom-shrunk."

garland. For the use of this word victory, and the emblem of victory, cf. Shaks. Cor. I. 9. 60, "Marcius wears this war's garland." So Antony iv. 15. 64, "Withered is. q garland oi. h. e war."

P. 69, line 10. displesure. An offence given, not as now generally, an offence taken. Cf. Bp Pilkington, Works, p. 253, "This is the common practice of the world, that when a man is down, then even those which were his feigned friends afore, will be the first that shall work him displeasure. " In the original there is a not which seems superfluous before out of peryl at the end of this sentence. It has therefore been omitted in the text.

ir. The alhision is to King Edward's murder of his brother Clarence.

18. p'ocioure, i. e. procurator, attorney, deputy. Ci. S) 2l. He7t. VI. (pt. 2) I. I. 3, "I had in charge as proctirator to your excellence," and Halle, Rich. III. anno 3, speaks of "affiances made and taken by proctors and deputies on both parties."

21. The sense is "And although it was so that the realm was in every part annoyed with this and other intolerable actions, yet, c."' Cf. 32. 31.

31. renoumed, Fr. 7r; z;; z;; z=: renowned. These forms from the French were common in More's day. Cf. Utopia 166. 26, "the very famous and renoumed. xz. y2! x Ulysses."'

P. 70, line 2. tvhiche yoiire kynde vryndes, c. The sense of the whole clause appears to be this: "Which kindly feelings of yours, exhibited towards the house of York, since he (Edward) has by no means worthily requited, there is one of that house who now by God's grace shall do so better,: c."

3. acquiied. Halle reads "requited," which is the sense.

7. him that can better tell it. He alludes to Doctor Shaw and his sermon.

21. groiindly, i. e. "to the very ground, to the very bottom." " He made it all clear," cf. Tyndall, Works, p. 39, "The more groundly it is searched, the precioser thynges are found in it."

23. lining his ve y tuife = Yi s true wife still living. So Shaks. Ro7neo iii. i. 115, "This gentleman, my voy friend."

26. vnjnetdy. Cf. 13. 4.

29. that. In the text this word is the demonstrative pronoun. Another that (a conjunction) would be supplied after seme to make the sentence full. So the sense It may well appear that that marriage was not well made, c.

31. acconpling. A participial noun = marriage. The verb is found in Bacon's Heniy VII. (Pitt Press Series), p. 78, "King Charles sent a solemn ambassage, acconpling it with an article in the nature of a request."

P. 71, line 3. heariiige. This word refers to the protector, and is equal to " who bears."' 10. deuohite, i. e. devolved, descended unto. Cf. Fox, Martyrs, p. 329. " The Government was devolnted and brought into the priestes hands."

18. abtisions, i. e. abuses, nearly always accompanied with the notion of deception. Cf. Spenser, F. Q. ii. 11. 11, "Foolish delights and fond abiisions. " So in Dodsley, Lusty ynventtis, ii.). 89, where God is addressed, "Alas his life is to Thy Word's abusion."'" 19. haue condiscended= 2isQ agreed. Cf. Fabyan, Chro7i. an. 1361, "It was condiscendcd by the lords spiritual and temporal that Kyng Henry should contynue and reygne as kynge durynge his natural lyfe." Cf. also notes on 32. 7 and 58. 23, above.

27. The sense is: "to him that shall so well fill the office, as I am bold to say he will do, if he accept it," or zvel before occupy may be a misprint in the original for wil.

30. Veil. The common orthography is Vce. The text is from Ecclesiastes x. 16.

P. 72, line r. of so sadde age, i. e. of such a sober age. Sad is the p. part, of the verb " to set," and so means properly, fixed, firm, stable. Cf. Pilkington, Works, p. 416, "A good builder will not build on the sand, but dig to the sad earth." So 73. 10, " a sadde man " = a stedfast trustworthy man.

17. framed, i. e. brought into a proper frame of mind.

24. The sense is, perchance they do not well understand you.

P. 73, line 3. r 7wm = whispering. The word is very frequently spelt "rounding." Cf. Lyly, Etcphiies, p. 71, "Ferardo, rounding Phil-autus in the eare, desired hym to accompanye hym."

4. comen. Here Halle has " common." The meaning is " to commune " or "confer."

9. Halle gives the name as "Thomas Fitzwilliam." On sadde see 72. I.

12. loth was, i. e. was loth, was unwilling.

14. Made a repetition to the commons of that which, c.

17. The sentence is not very clear, but "nothing" seems = in nothing. So the sense would be: "But in nothing did all this make any change in the people." The double negative is not uncommon in the English of this time. Literally the words would run: "In nothing it made no change." Or the words may be taken as two clauses standing absolutely thus: "But all this effecting nothing, no change being ma. l in the people."

18. alway after one, i. e. never changing or varying. Cf. Chaucer, Prologue, 341, "His brede, his ale, was always after one, i. e. always the same and equally good.

30. one or other, i. e. one thing or the other; one way or another.

P. 74, line I. distincke, i. e. distinct. Halle has "base."

3. biishement=-3L party lying in ambush. Cf. Goklyng, Jnstine, fol. 6, "Environing him with a biishiiient of soldiers layd before in the mountains for the same purpose."

and Nashefeldes. Halle gives "and one Nashfield," which is no doubt the right reading. The man was some notorious person among the protector's retainers, whose name was known far and wide. In Hardyng too it stands "and one Nashfielde."

For mo-= belonging cf. Shaks. AWs Well, IV. 2. 42, "It is an honour longing to our house": also Tajning of Shrew, I v. 4. 7, "Such austerity as longeth to a father."

7. gytie, i. e. would allow of.

9. cast back theyr heddes, i. e. turned their heads round and looked back.

23. semhlaunce, i. e. aspect, look. Cf. Shaks. 7? fw, I. 5. 76, "Put off these frowns, an ill-beseeming semblance for a feast."

29. assembling themselves together. Halle adds "at Paules."

30. Baynardes castell. This fortress stood near the bank of the Thames on the north side of the river and gave name to one cf the city Wards. It was burnt down in 1428, afterwards rebuilt by Humphrey, Duke of Gloucester, and at the time of this history it was in the hands of Richard, Duke of Gloucester. The building of Baynard's castle has been long ago pulled down, and its place is now occupied by timber yards, wharfs and private buildings. See Maitland's Hist, of Lo7idon, pp. 878, 879.

32. aprointmente is here in the original, but it is evidently a clerical error for appointmente, which has therefore been printed in the text.

P. 75, line 5. made difficultie, i. e. made a demur, opposed obstacles.

15. to purpose = io propose, and so below in lines 23 and 31.

17. and get not = ZT g:! i. r o. Cf. above, 6. 14.

18. otcer them. Here Halle inserts " with a bishop on every hande of hym."

30. as = z?, though.

P. 76, line 2. arrt'i?; z = permission, as in the common phrase "I beg your pardon,"' which really means "I ask your permission." See 77. 14.

13. 7n that that = rv as much that. This double that is not unlike the style of the time and the book. Cf. above, 2. 13.

15. vnder hys obeysatince, i. e. in obedience to him. Thus the expression = under his rule, though obeysaunce is the reverence paid to the ruler, not the rule which he exercises.

18. That although it were so that, c.

21. tliat so nrache i. e. that he so much.

30. More pain than pleasure for him who would use it in such a way, as unless a man would use it he was not worthy to have it.

P. 77, line 5. dcuor. Fr. devoir = vxy.

8. wsuch persons as before were the occasion of the contrary (i. e. of the bad state of the realm) and who again anew intended so to be.

12. rotmed, cf. 73 3 15. that. Here it seems to be the demonstrative pronoun, "he shewed to the protector that (conclusion) for a final one," c.

16. appointed cf. 59. 15.

17. Both because they had now proceeded so far that there was no safety in going back, as well as because they thought it to be for the general welfare to take these steps were it even so that they had not yet begun to do it.

23. resolnie aunswere. A fixed inflexible answer, which no argument can change.

27. of likelyhoode=m all probability, cf. 41. 7.

33. whoj? t refers to the English people understood in the words " the realm " preceding.

P. 78, line 7. Which of all the titles that might be we consider to be the most valid.

15. established is in the original here but is clearly an error for establish," which is given in the text.

16. And we ask of God to live no longer than while we attend to the securing of its (the realm's) advancement.

-21. as his fantasy e gatie hym, i. e. as his fancy suggested to him.

30. for the manner sake=)y reason of the way of proceeding.

7iot bee a-knowen = not seem cognizant, seem to be ignorant of. For the word, which is not usual, cf. Shaks. Othello III. 3. 319, where Iago having obtained from Emilia the handkerchief says to her: Be not acknoiun on t. I have use for it," meaning "Don't let it be known what has become of it. Keep it a secret." Cf. also Chaucer, Court of Love, 1199,

"Eek Shamefastnes was there, as I took hede, That blushed red, and durst not ben aknozo She lover was, for thereof had she drede,"

i. e. she durst not admit to herself or seem aware that she was in love.

32. billies. The writs from the Papal Court which secure his election.

33. and thoztghe=-Qve. n though. The and here is the word sometimes written an, and mostly =?! Sometimes we find the double form an if ox and if exactly equivalent to if. Cf. Shaks. Tempest, ii. 2. 120,

"These be fine things, an if they be not sprites."

But this same word an sometimes = though. See Shaks. 2 Iden. VI. IV. 7. 112, "He shall die, aji it be but for pleading so well for his life," and More's text here gives an instance oi and (or an) though thou.

P. 79, line 5. soivter (Lat. sutor) = z. shoemaker. 6. can. In its earlier sense of ken to know. "If one should know so little as to shew at an untimely moment, c."

8. tormentors. In the plays the Sultan was always attended by executioners and agents for punishing wrongdoers. For the word cf. Bacon's Hen. VII. (Pitt Press Series), 114. 5, "two butchers or tormentors."' 9. and worthy. An elliptical expression = " and he is worthy of being so treated," "and serve him right."

P. 80, line 6. the saintuary by, i. e. close by, near at hand. For the protector was in Westminster Hall. See 79. 18.

9. a vanitye = 2i mere empty parade and show.

J3. Halle says the "nineteenth day of June," and states that the coronation took place "on the 6th day of July." Also after line 17 there is introduced, in Halle, an account of the coronation.

22. the beste death. More speaks of it thus because it was the best thing for the nation to be rid of this king.

26. ; rz (? = misfortune. Cf. Chapman, Homer, bk. xx.,

"Jove doth decree Fortunes, inforhines to the mortal race."

29. Perken Werbecke. Perkin Warbeck pretended to be Richard, Duke of York, the brother of Edward V. For his whole history cf. Bacon, Henry VII. (Pitt Press Series), pp. 140 seqq., with the notes thereon.

33. so couertly demeaned, i. e. conducted in such an underhand manner. For demean in this active sense, cf. 22. 8.

P. 8r, line 3. Because of the common habit of secret and underhand dealing people held it in their hearts always in suspicion, just as a multitude of good imitations make real jewels doubted of.

18. which he before had intended, i. e. to make himself king.

19. his mindegaiie him, i. e. suggested to him. Cf. Shaks. Corol. IV. 5. 157, "My mind gave me his clothes made a false report of him."

23. z; z j' = natural. Cf. ' "kindly fruits of the earth," Pr. Bk., Litany. The sense is: This act would make him a king of a proper kind, a king such as he ought to be.

27. credence. We say now "credentials," "tokens of trust and which can be trusted to."

30. kneling before otir lady, i. e. Grene found him at his prayers before an image of the Virgin.

31. to dye therfore, i. e. to have to die himself for so doing. 33. yet in his xvay, i. e. still on his road to Gloucester.

P. 82, line 4. zvent, i. e. weened, thought, considered.

6. on your paylet without. Halle gives "in the palet chambre without," alluding to the antechamber where was a small bed for a body-servant.

9. meaning this by sir yames T r , "by" here = concerning. Cf. I Cor. iv. 4, "I know nothing myself," i. e. no wrong concerning myself.

14. sore longed vpwarde, i. e. very much desired to rise, was very ambitious.

18.? zaz; z y= especially; as in many other places of this history.

20. by secrete driftes, i. e. by underhand contrivances. Cf. Dodsley, Old Couple, XII. p. 52, "if my brain fail not, I have found out all your drifts:' 21. Wherefore when this occasion offered, out of very special friendship he embraced the opportunity, c.

P. 83, line I. strange, i. e. reserved, shy of undertaking anything. Cf. Shaks. Romeo, 11. 2. 100,

"But trust me, gentleman, I'll prove more true Than those that have more cunning to be strajige. I should have been more strange, I must confess. But that thou overheard'st, ere I was ware, My true love's passion."

10. tohe himself as kmg i. e. put himself in the position of king, regarded himself as king.

19. a7id see thetii szwe. Halle has "and iiij. other to see them sure," cf. below, line 26.

20. pointes, laces used in fastening the clothes. Cf. Shaks. Hen. IV. (pt. i) II. 4. 238, "Their points being broken, down fell their hose."

21. roiight, the past tense oireck, to heed, to care for.

27. fleshed. Halle has " fleshe bred." The first idea is of a brute fed M'ith flesh and made fierce, and satiated. Then of some one fed with flesh for the first time, and

o initiated. Cf. Sh'aks. Hen. IV. (pt. i) V. 4, 133, "full bravely hast i cvow fleshed hj maiden sword."

31. i- j innocent, harmless. In later English it was written "silly." Cf. Shaks. Zr. VI. (pt. 3) ii. 5. 43, "Shepherds looking on their silly sheep."

P. 84, line 3. smored, smothered, choked to death. The primary sense is " to stifle by smoke," cf. P 'ompt. Paj'v. p. 461, ' ' smore, with smoke,z;; (3." So Sylvester's Du Bartas, ' Some undermines, som other undertook To fire the gates or sviore the towne with smoke."

Also Du Bartas, History of Judith p. 377,

"Some dying vomit blood, and some were S7 iored."''' 19. kynge. Halle adds here, "For he would recompense a detestable murther with a solemyne obsequy."

21. by the occasion of his deathe, i. e. by reason of his death.

22. light. Halle inserts here, "For some saye that Kynge Richard caused the priest to take them up and close them in lead, and to put them in a coffyne full of holes at the endes, with ij. hokes of yron, and so to cast them into a place called the Blacke deepes at the Thames mouth so that they should never rise up nor be sene agayn."

P. 85, line 3. Which thinges on eiiery part ivelpondered, i. e. And if men will well ponder on these things in every part (they will see that) God never gave, c.

9. Sainct Martc7is. Halle adds " le graunde."

10. Dighton. For this sentence Halle has, "John Dighton lyved at Caleys longe after, no less disdayned and haled then poincted at and there dyed in great misery."

14. haryed. The verb "harry" is much more frequently used of the ravaging of a country, or chasing an enemy. Cf. North's Plutarch p. 442,

"The Armenians continually harried them the Parthians out of their skins."

But here it is used of the rough conveyance of the dead body.

17. of the mischiefe that he dyd. The sentence is clearly imperfect. Halle continues it thus: "in three monethes be not comparable," i. e. there is no comparison between the mischief that he underwent in less than three years and the mischief that he inflicted in three months.

RICH.

21. chamberers. Attendants in a chamber, chamberlains. Cf. Berners' Froissart, ii. 61, "nother chatnberer nor varlet entred with them." See below, 86. 10.

23. his body prucily fenced. His body was secretly protected, i. e. he wore a coat of mail under his clothing.

27. a 7iightes Q)ivi."i, i. e. by night.

29. sterte. This, with leape and runne in the next line are past tenses = started, leapt, ran. For the last of the three Halle gives loked =looked.

33. otihaa 'd me3. ns in his external circumstances and surroundings as opposed to his internal agitation of mind.

P. 86, line i. in rest. At this point Halle has a long account of Richard's journey to the north of England, and his triumphal reception in York, as well as a notice of some good laws which he enacted.

5. p)-eiended =stt forth, related, without any of the modern sense of pretence.

7. Kyng Edzuard, i. e. King Edward IV. On the funeral honours paid elsewhere to this king, see i. 23 note.

9. Persal. Halle gives the name here "Persivall," but in another place "Persall."

19. He (Buckingham) would take the same line as he (Gloucester) would, and would wait upon him with a thousand good fellows.

25. sixe C, i. e. six hundred, and below, line 29, CCC 300.

32. lightli, easily, with small provocation. Cf. Mark ix. 39, "No man which shall do a miracle in my name, can lightly speak evil of me."

P. 87, line 5. duke of Herfordes landes, Halle rightly reads "erle" for "duke." On the claim see notes on 43. i. 13. feared =ie2ixed for. An unusual sense.

17. come j-ide. For co? ne thus followed by an infinitive without to intervening. Cf. Shaks. Alerchant of Venice, ii. 7. 43, ' To cotne view fair Portia," also Lear, III. 4. 157, "To co7ne speak with you;" and Othello, III. 4. 50, "To bid Cassio come speak with you," where there are two verbs following bid in this manner.

18. whentpon. Here Halle gives, "Whereupon gorgeously apparelled and sumpteously trapped with burnynge carte naves of golde embrodered he roade before the Kyng through London with an evill will and woorse harte."

19. that notiuithstandi7tg means "and yet in spite of the King's threat."

26. at the daies='3X that time. The article still retaining somewhat of its original force as a demonstrative pronoun.

28. in that grene world, i. e. while all was new and untried. For this figurative use oigreen cf. Shaks. Richard III., 11. 2. 13,

"Yet since it (the compact) is but green, it should be put To no apparent likelihood of breach." 32. a z(??"v w; z z = and men entirely believe. Halle gives "surely" for "utterly." For "utterly" in this sense cf. Bp. Cover- dale's Works, p. 83, "Holy men served God, and knew nothing utterly of the pope's religion," i. e. absolutely nothing.

P. 88, line 3. etiyllcouldbeare, i. e. could ill bear, tolerate.

8. wel knowen. The "was" from the previous clause must be carried on.

10. high behesies, i. e. important orders entrusted to him.

15. waxed, i. e. he waxed.

16. The sense is, Whose (i. e. the bishop's) cleverness abused his (the duke's) pride so that he got free and the duke was destroyed.

23. neuer came home. The conjunction and is here omitted. to the field. Halle adds "at Barnet."

24. the tother, i. e. the king Edward IV., to whom after the death of Henry, Bp. Morton was attached.

29. by the tirant, i. e. the protector Richard.

30. this duke, i. e of Buckingham.

31. in his top. The expression, which I have not found elsewhere, seems to mean "upon him." "Set Buckingham upon attacking Richard."

King Henry, i. e. he who became afterwards King Henry VH.

32. King Edwardes daughter, i. e. Elizabeth, daughter of Edward IV.

P. 89, line I. bothe his masters, i. e. Edward IV,, the father of Elizabeth of York, and Henry VII., her husband, with whom Morton came into great favour, as is stated below.

2. t-ivoo bloodes, i. e. the two families of York and Lancaster.

3. en taeted=unqmete(, disquieted. If en be not a misprint for zm in the original. I have met with one similar instance, Dodsley, Return from Parnassus, IX. 211,

"Where serpents tongues the penmen are to write, Where cats do brawl by day and dogs by night There shall engorged venom be my ink."

In which passage engorged seems to = disgorged.

9. ended them, i. e. he ended them. Cf 88. 15 for a like omission of the pronoun, which is very common in this book.

15. driftes. Cf. on 82. 20.

18. balke. The word is cognate with "belch." To utter a little sound of envy against the glory of the King. Cf. Pilkington, Works, p. 293, "Priests with drunken nowls said matins and belked out with good devotion as they thought."

19. breide. The word means a noise, and is connected with the verb " bray" which now is used only of asses, but formerly was applied to the sound of trumpets, and also to the noises of more noble animals, as elephants and horses. More has the noun again, Works, p. 442, "He bringeth to the matter after his two years musing. only a rashe maliciouse frantike braide. " 10. ethe tofal out, i. e. ready for a quarrel.

23. rather semed him, i. e. rather made himself appear.

i8o HISTORY OF KING RICHARD III 25. host, i. e. boast = to praise. Cf. Shaks. Tempest, iv. 9,

"Do not smile at me that I boast her off." 30. I. e. the son of King Henry VI. and not King Edward IV, 33, ivith a dead ma? i, i. e. on the side of a dead man strive against the living.

P. 90, line 6. he left, i. e. left off, ceased speaking.

22. As being a subject not entirely without danger.

28. bonch, a bump or protuberance. So Richard III. is called hunch backed. Shaks. Richa-'d III. I. 3. 246 and IV. 4. 81, though there is a various reading hicnch backed, in both places.

a great pace. We now say "a a great pace."

33. y= concerning. Cf. above on 82. 9.

P. 91, line 2. and (sometimes written aw) if. What if he call it one? Cf. Dodsley, Every Man, i. p. 142,

"Beware, for and they (his good deeds) be small Before God he hath no help at all."

Also, The Ordinary, Xii. p. 25, ' I'll save your worship that labour, anu (= an it) please you."

5. the bore. In allusion to the coat of arms of the duke of Gloucester. See p. 48. 27.

pyke. For this figurative use of pick =. o find out, discover, cf. Shaks. Mids. N. D., v. 100, "Out of this silence yet I picked a welcome."

18. for the better store. A sentence of much flatter)', implying that in spite of the good store of abilities possessed by the protector, those of Buckingham were of a higher quality.

21. of youre grace. Halle completes the discourse and after that the character of the langiiage differs in toto. The continuation of Har-dyng merely adds after " of youre grace" the words "and there left of agayn," thus shewing a break which Halle has filled up.

P. 92, line 13. Henry, earle of Riche7no7ide. Afterwards King Henry VII.

15. King Edivardes death, i. e. the death of Edward the IVth. during the latter part of whose reign both the earl of Richmond and the earl of Pembroke had been kept in a sort of honourable confinement by Francis duke of Brittany. See Lingard, IV. 96.

16. ivith, i. e. in the custody of.

24. Reynold Breye, i. e. Sir Reginald Bray. He was Steward in the household of the Lady Margaret, King Henry Vllth's mother. He died in 1503. See Bacon's Heti. VII. (Pitt Press Series), 18. 27 and notes.

P. 93, line 5. rested no more, i. e. there remained nothing else to do. 33. Cicile. Cf. p. I. II and note.

P. 94, line 2. mastresse. This orthography shews the connection with master.

13. appoinct. We still use the expression that a man or a house is well "appointed," when all belonging to them is in good order. So here the verb means "to order," "arrange." Cf. 95. 8.

20. In Materials illust. of reign of Hen. VII. (Rolls Series), we find, p. 26, that Hugh Conway was, on 21 Sept. 1485, appointed for life, keeper of the great wardrobe, by King Henry. He was also made a Commissioner of King's mines on 27 Feb. i486. But he afterwards came into disgrace and was removed from his office. See 3 Aug. 1487.

23. Among the. same entries we find a grant, 29 Sept. 1485, to Sir Richard Guldeford, Knt. of the office of master of the ordnance and master of the armoury, and a grant for life of the houses and grounds upon the wharf of the Tower of London, He has to do with the preparations for the Coronation (23 Octr. 1485). He is made guardian of the property of a Minor (14 July, i486) and there are numerous entries of payments made to him.

25. hi w2 r= almost, cf. 12. 33; 106. 18, and for an example 5if4, note.

P. 96, line 2. enfarced, i. e. stuff"ed full. The more common word ' farced. Cf. Jewell, Reply to Harding, p. 233, "The see of Rome, farced Y and set out with lies." The verb is the root oi force-mt2ii = stuffing.

13. and that he might bee asserteined, c. = And that he (the King) might be made certain, assured, c.

25. at one tyme, i. e. at the same time.

Thomas, Marques of Dorcestcr. This was Thomas Grey, Marquis of Dorset, formerly Earl of Huntingdon, and before that Lord Grey of Groby. See above, 8. 31.

29. Edward Courtenay was earl of Devonshire.

P. 97, line 4. disparkle =. o Q."M. Q. x, disperse. Cf. Holland, Am-miamis, p. 422, "Considering a great number of the horsemen were disparcled asunder."

10. embatailed, set in battle array. Cf. Shaks. Merry Wives, i(. 2. 260, "Her defences which now are too strongly embattled against me." So Milton, Tractate on Education (Pitt Press Series), p. 17, "They have solidly united the whole body of their perfeted knowledge like the last embattelling o i z. Roman legion."

21. to bee come, i. e. to get him unto. We feel no difficulty in the corresponding phrase " whither to be gone."

P. 98, line I. helth. In the wider sense q welfare, security.

4. Peter Curtney, bishop of Exeter, received a grant from Henry VII. on II October 1485, of the temporalities of the see of Salisbury forfeited by Thomas, bishop of Salisbury, through rebellion against the king and his royal dignity. See Mat. Illust. of I eign of Hen. VII. Vol. I. p. 81.

7. John Bourshere had been made Lord Berners in 1455 and he seems to have died about this time, for in 1485, 25 Sept. a bailiff is appointed by Henry VII. over the estates during the minority of his son, who is called Lord Berners. Ibid. I. 57.

8. Edzvard Wooduillc, Knt. receives a grant for life (16 Sept. J485), of the office of keeper of the castle and town of Porchester, and of the survey and government of the town of Portsmouth, and the king's place there. The office had been held by John, earl of Salop. Materials, I. 7.

9. Robert Willoughby. A faithful servant of Henry VII. and greatly trusted by him. Mention is constantly made of him in the Materials above quoted, where his name is the first mentioned. He was made Lord Willoughby in 1485.

Giles Daubeney. Afterwards Lord Daubeney. He was made deputy of Calais by Henry VIL

Tho?? ias Harondell. This may be Thomas Arundel, Knt., Lord Matravers, to whom Henry VIL granted on 6 July, i486, an annuity of 300 marks. See Materials, I. 482.

Sir John Cheyne is often mentioned in the Materials, where I. 151, he is called "the King's full trusty Knight," and a grant is made to Cheyne's servant Roger Penne "for faithful true service done to the king in the parts beyond the sea and ever since." Several persons of the name Cheyne are mentioned, and presumably among them are the " two brothers " of our text.

11. William Barkely, Knt. of Bernerston was appointed (17 Sept. 1485) "master and operator of the King's monies, and keeper of the King's exchange within the Tower of London, the kingdom of England and the town of Calais." Materials, I. 7.

Sir William Brandon, who had been "Marshal of the Marshall-sie of the King's Bench," but was "so put in drede of his lyfe by Richard, late in deed and not of right. King of England the iii that he was faine for salvacione of his lyfe to take tuition and priviledge of the seinctuarie of Gloucester and there abode from the second year of the said Richard, unto youre comeing into this realme sovereign lord" was restored to his office by Henry VII. in 1485. Materials I. 125.

12. Sir Richard Edgeco?? ibe is often mentioned in the early notices of Henry VII. On 20 Sept. 1485, he was made one of the Chamberlains of the Exchequer, and on 7 June i486 (in consideration of services as well in parts beyond the sea as in the kingdom of England), he received a grant of the manors of Totnesse, Comeworthy, Huesshe, and Lodeswell.

13. yohn Halwell, Knt. is mentioned as Sheriff of Devon. Materials, I. 549.

Robert not Edward) Pointz is often mentioned in the Materials, and on 25 Sept. 1485 was made Steward of Barton Hundred, c. during the minority of Edward, son of George, late duke of Clarence. This seems most likely to be the person intended in the text.

14. Christopher Urswicke. He was for some time master of King's Hall (now Trinity College) in Cambridge. He was chaplain to Lady Margaret, Henry Vllth's mother, and afterwards employed as ambassador by Henry himself.

24. a bondman. It appears from this that villainage, or servitude to the land, had not yet entirely disappeared.

25. his pardon. It was presumed that if he knew enough to turn informer he must be connected with the movements of Buckingham, and so guilty in the eyes of the party of King Richard. He would therefore be encouraged if it were proclaimed that he should have no punishment.

29. The addition of not which is wanting in the original is clearly-needed here for the sense.

32. in all that he might, i. e. as far as ever he could.

P. 99, line I. to Britain ward. The coasts that looked toward Brittany.

8. or for losyng, i. e. for fear of losing.

hym, i. e. the Duke of Buckingham, who had taken refuge with him. Cf. 97. 23.

9. fiirti-with all. As one word. We now only wze forthwith. 17. behedded. Halle tell us that it was done "upon Allsoules dale."

20. forbode. By this sentence it is implied that the allegiance of Buckingham to the protector had at one time been such that for his sake he would have disregarded all God's prohibitions. He had served him to the uttermost.

23. Bj'itons. Meaning "soldiers of Brittany."

24. of his departure. "Of" is not here = " for," but the construction is "the appointed day of his departure," "the day of his departure which had been appointed."

P. 100, line 3. Poole. On the coast of Dorsetshire.

4. harnessed =tq w Y)' edi with armour. Cf. Bp. Pilkington's Works, p. 30, "David, a young man with a sling and stone, kills Golias so strongly harnessed."'" 10. a land. We still say ashore. Cf. line 20, below.

19. cleane, i. e. utterly, altogether. Cf. Bp Pilkington's Works, p. 308, "The wicked worldlings, that have not God afore their eyes, seek clean contrary ways." See 103. 20.

26. arested=rested. A form unusual because of the other word "arrested." But cf. Grafton's Chronicle R. i. anno 8, "When he had arested hym a litel while he then roade. to Notingham."

29. Charles. This was Charles VHI. who reigned from 1483 to 1498. He was the son of Louis XI. who died in 1483.

30. of libertee, i. e. for liberty. Cf. Shaks. Otiello, ill. 3. 212, ' I humbly do beseech you your pardon." Cf. 102. 11, 107. 7.

P. loi, line 8. sto?? iacke = co. xa. ge. Cf. on 5. 6. 15. Veneti. The town of Vannes in Brittany whence Henry fled afterwards into France.

21. Y ox frame in the sense of "to go on well," "to succeed," cf. Dodsley, Roister Doister, ill. 10,

"Now this year beginneth for o frame."

24. Rhedon, i. e. Redon, on the river Vilaine, some way south west of Rennes in Brittany.

sejit the Marques, i. e. sent the Marquis word, c.

27. rejoysed, i. e. they rejoiced. This omission of the pronoun is common.

32. j'epensed= previously designed or intended. We have the word in " malice; r i-."

P. 102, line 3. tkal The second m is superfluous.

7. did take hym, i. e. did receive, accept, hold him for king.

11. of. Cf. 100. 30, and note, also 107. 8.

30. reputed and taken i. e. regarded and esteemed. Cf. 103. 4.

P. 103, line 12. neither that she shotdd tiot. Another instance of the use of the double negative.

19. borderers. The Englishmen dwelling on the frontier of Scotland.

P. 104, line 8. put theim. Not the ambassadors, but Henry and the lords who were with him.

12. Peter Landose. Landois, the Breton minister, was induced to take the side of Richard by large bribes. See Lingard, IV. 122.

17. desiered hym instantly, i. e. asked him urgently. Cf. Ps. Iv. 18, (Pr. Bk.). Also Latimer, Serm. p. 231, "He prayeth now the third time, He did it so instantly, so fervently that it brought out a bloody sweat."

32. (7 a = came to no result.

P. 105, line 16. few a connsaill. Few of counsel, i. e. took few into his counsel. Cf. i. 8; 85. 27.

18. Penbroucke, i. e. Pembroke.

22. with al that euer thei 7night. With all speed that ever they could.

25. Angeow, i. e. Anjou, and so they were in French territory.

P. 106, line 6. recotiered=xe2ic d. Cf. Shaks. Teinpest, iii. 1, 16, "I swam, 'ere I could recover the shore, five and thirty leagues."

17. in inaner 'vcv some degree, almost. Cf. Shaks. Rich. II, III. I. II, "You have in manner with your sinful hours made a divorce betwixt his queen and him."

1 1. takyng the matter so vnkyndely, i. e. being so much grieved.

P. 107, line 10. ofzuhom, i. e. by whom.

13. to take no care, i. e. not to be over anxious. The king does not mean that Henry is to be less earnest and diligent in his own cause, but only that he is not to let anxiety press too much on him. Cf. Phil. iv. 6.

17. before spoken. The previous mention was in the continuation of Hardyng, not in More's narrative. John, Earl of Oxford, is constantly mentioned among those to whom grants were made at the commencement of Henry VII."s reign. See Materials, pp. 23, 31, c.

19. IIaj? wies. In Andrew Borde's Introdtictiojiof Kjiozvledge (E. E. T. S.), p. I47, we have an account of the " welfavered towne of Calys, the which doth stand commodyously for the welth and succor of all Englande. In the whyche towne is good fare and good cheere, and there is good order and polytike men, greate defence and good ordynaunce for warre. The sayde towne hath anexed to it for defence, Gynes, Hammes and Rysbanke, Newman Bridge, and a blocke-howse at Gravelyng in Flanders."

o. James Blount. In Mat. illus. of Reign of Hen. VII. we find entered-28 Feb. 1486, an indenture between the king and Sir James Blount as to his appointment to be lieutenant of the castle of Hampnes (i. e. Hammes) in the parts of Picardy, and on March 2 of the same year the office was granted to him.

Jhon Forskewe. In the same volume we find, 20 Sept. 1485, that a grant for life was made to John Fortescue knt. of the office of lieutenant of the tower of Ruysbank in the parts of Picardy, with power to appoint officers and soldiers under him for the safe-keeping of the said tower.

P. 108, line 9. knowledge X. O acknowledge. Cf. Bp. Pilkington's Works, p.-237, "But this could not move them to knowledge him to be their Lord and God."

16. bothe more and lesse, i. e. great and small, high and low. Cf. Shaks. Macbeth, V. 4. 12, "Both more and less have given him the revolt." See also Hen. IV. (pt. i), iv. 3. 68 and (pt. 2) i. i. 209.

18. Richard Foxe was King Henry VII."s secretary, then was made bp. of Exeter, Lord Privy Seal, afterwards bp. of Durham and of Winchester. He was a trusted friend of the Lady Margaret, and with Morton, Bray and Daubeney continued to be of great influence through the whole of Heniy VII."s reign.

P. 109, line I. rested nothyng Xio Li x remained (to be done).

6. poiirge hym of his facte, i. e. purge, clear him of what he had already done.

10. menne of grauitee=Y)exsot of weight and influence.

21. al things was pardoned. A not unusual violation of concord in the English of this time. Cf. Shaks. Cymb. ii. 3. 24, "Those springs on chaliced flowers that Vj."

26. To be "in a fool's paradise" is to be beguiled, led away by what is unreal or untrustworthy. Cf. Shaks. Romeo, ii. 4. 176, "If ye should lead her into a fool's paradise, as they say, it were a very gross kind of behaviour."

31. feared, i. e. frightened, deterred. Cf. Pilkington, Works, p. 59, "They that will not be overcome by gentleness must ht feared with authority."

P. no, line 10. dyd gather of this, i. e. concxxadtd from what was said by the king in his complaints.

11. Ere it tvere long after, i. e. before very long.

P. Ill, line I. tozuard, i. e. in connexion with, aiming at. Cf. Shaks. jful. Cces., I. 2. 85, "If it be aught to7ua7-d. q general good."

15. Henry his. A common form for Henry's, from a mistaken idea that the s of the possessive case was a remnant of the pronoun.

32. in a readynesse. We say "in readiness," but the form in the text was anciently the more common. Cf. 2 Cor. x. 6. Also Latimer, Serm., p. 35, "And necessary it is that a kyng have a treasure always in a readiness for that and such other affiiires as be dayly in hys handes."

P. 112, line 2. George Strange. This was George Stanley who in 1482 had been created Lord Strange, in right of his wife who was daughter and heiress of William, Lord Strange.

i86 HISTORY OF KING RICHARD III 6. the land. Here is meant the territory in France at that time held by the English.

12. Calyce, i. e. Calais. There was the strongest English force and Hammes was close by.

17. sorte of menne. Cf. Grindal, Works, p. 44, "Christ ministered this sacrament, not to great and deep philosophers, but to a sort oi ignorant and unlearned fishers." Sort = company.

2 2. to strength. Formerly common where we now use strengthen. Cf. Fabyan, Chronicle c. 156, "His body was viii foot long, and his armes and leggys well lengthed and strengthed after the proporcion of the body."

23. layde harde to their charge that were without. This means " they charged heavily upon their assailants outside."

25. of the backe side, i. e. in the rear.

P. 113, line 6. fooles pat'adice, cf. 109, 25, note. Cf. also Lyly, Etiphiies, p. 69, "Smiling to himself to see how he had brought Philautus into fool'sparadise."'"' 8. sho2ild. to wake. The here is superfluous. But in old times to was not inserted before any infinitive governed by another verb. Thus sho7ild to wake is but an extension of what has been done throughout the whole of the modern language. Cf. ri. 10. stipra and note there.

27. as who say. This seems = as they mean who say. Cf. 13. 5 stipj'a, and infra 121, 23 for a fuller phrase.

31. ficrth, i. e. forward, with the historj'.

P. 114, line 2. Charles the kyng. This was Charles VHI. of France, who began to reign in 1483, being only then thirteen years old.

3. Lewes prynce of Orlyaunce. This was Louis, duke of Orleans, the first noble of the blood royal, and who afterwards became Louis XH.

5. John, i. e. Joan, Jeanne, the sister of Charles VHL and second daughter of Louis XL 25. purchased. In the simple sense of "procured" without anything of the modern idea of obtaining by payment. Cf. Shaks. Winto-'s Tale, iv. 4. 522, ' "Purchase the sight again of dear Sicilia."

28. secrete of their f(? w i' = acquainted with all their plans.

P. 115, line II. Roan, i. e. Rouen. 13. and purposed, i. e. and that he (Richard) purposed. 15. Cicile. See l. 11 and note.

19. i a'= disappointed, frustrated. Cf. Shaks. Hen. VI. (pt. 3), II. I. 118, "With a full intent to dash our late decree."

26. Lorde Harba7't. William Lord Herbert, Earl of Pembroke, and afterwards Earl of Huntingdon.

32. Henry. This was Henry Percy, Earl of Northumberland.

P. 116, line 4. John ap Moj'gan. La the Materials illustrative of the reign of Hen. VJI. we find the office of Clerk of the parliaments granted on 9 Oct. 1485 to John Morgan, and under the same name we find mention of one styled " the kings clerk and councillor." He is mentioned here as a temporal lawyer, because the offices of the law were at this time generally held by the clergy. All the Lord Chancellors before the days of Sir Thomas More himself had been clerics.

5. Also to Ryce ap Thomas are granted 3 Nov. 1485 the offices of constable, lieutenant and steward of the lordship of Brecknock, and three days later the office of Chamberlain of South Wales. Cf. 118. 8.

6. On 19th Sept. 1484 grants were made by Henry VH. to Christopher Savage, son of Sir John Savage (in consideration of true and faithful service as well for the

repressing of our rebels and traitors as otherwise), also to James Savage, another son of Sir John, and to John Savage, the younger, then to Sir John Savage himself, and afterwards to Edward Savage, another of his sons. So that the whole family were high in favour with the new king.

6. his part of course means Henry's part, though ths7i is pronoun immediately preceding.

12. ywov? r=retard. Not ver ' common with an objective case after it. But cf. Shaks. Alids. Night. I. i. 4, "She lingers my desires."

15. calendcs, the first day in any month in the Roman almanac. The word is that from which we derive "calendar." There is clearly some error in the text, for the seventh day after the first could not be the 22nd of the month, but the 8th. Moreover, August 22nd was the day of the battle of Bosworth, between M'hich and the day of Henry's landing some time must have elapsed. It is singular in connexion with these wrong dates, that the rolls of Parliament date the reign of Henry VII. as commencing 21 Aug. 1485, the day before the battle of Bosworth was fought.

21. Harford, i. e. Haverford.

25. make. This use of the verb as = ' effect," ' do," is like its sense in the phrase 'neither meddle nor fuake."' 31. in a 7-edytiesse. Cf. III. 31, and note there, also 117. 21; 118. 12; 122. 18.

32. Gespare the Erie, i. e. Jasper, Earl of Pembroke, who was uncle of Henry VII., and was created duke of Bedford, 27 Oct. 1485.

P. 117, line 3. Ca7-merdine, i. e. Carmarthen.

5. toke himselfe to, i. e. betook himself to, applied himself to. Cf. Shaks. Pericles, ill. 4. 10, 'a vestal livery will I take me to."' 9. was quiet, cf. supra, 109, 20.

30. were. This verb has been drawn into the plural by the word commaujtdementes immediately preceding it.

P. 118, line 10. reii ardcs of them, i. e. rewards received from them.

13. this tidynges. "Tidings" was used indiscriminately as singular or plural in the English of Shakespeare's time. Cf. Macbeth, I- 5- 3i "What is your tiditigs?"" So Rich. II., II. i. 272, "How near the tidings of our comfort j." See below, 120. 25.

27. Aderstone, i. e. Atherston in Warwickshire, 9 miles east of Tamworth.

30. telled, unusual form for told; cf. 120. 17. The son alluded to is Lord Strange; cf. 112. 1.

P. 119, line 2. to be past vpon, i e. to be regarded. Cf. Pilkington, Works, p. 180: "No kind of fruit had prosperously increased all these 3'ears, yet they passed but lightly on it So to p. 529, "To break God's commandment, they passed not of it, so that they might follow their own device."

P. 120, line 13. that was worthy =-i 2i. which, i. e. a matter which was worthy (to be noticed).

18. somies, an error in the original for somie. There was but one son in Richard's hands. See ri2. i.

20. The preparation on the part of King Richard was not so weak as was reported to him by his friends. For slender in this sense cf. below, 123. 5; and Shaks. Tzvo Gentlemen, i. 36,

"Other men, of slender reputation. Put forth their sons to seek preferment out."

P. 121, line 17. Grants were made by King Henry to Simon Digby on 22 Sept. 1485, and to Brian Sandeford on Nov. 30th of the same year.

31. semyng, apparently =aw9, but of this use I find no parallel. Perhaps the sentence is elliptical for " it seeming."

P. 122, line II. towarde the latter daye, i. e. when the end is near, 12. them selfe, i. e. the offences.

25. Northfolke, i. e. Norfolk. This was John Lord Howard who had become duke of Norfolk in right of his wife in 1483.

P. 123, line I. in an ordre. Where we now say "in order." Cf. below 124. II. With an anger = with anger. 14. double to, i. e. twice as much as.

26. "To pay home" is "to pay in full, satisfactorily," cf. Shaks. Tempest, "I willqy thy graces ho? ne" Also lvinter"s Tale, V. 2. 4, "All my services you hziwo. paidhome."'

P. 124, line 6. more freshlier. Double comparatives and superlatives were not unusual in More's day. Cf. Shaks., Tempest, i. 2. 19, more better, and 439 in the same scene more braver.

7. first wardes. As the van was called ih foi'zvard of the host, so all the front would constitute ihefirst-wardes.

9. fcwe. This word is so rarely used with a singular noun as here, that it seems likely for " compaigny" we should read " compaignys."

21. to keep tacke appears to mean "to manage," "to succeed." Can it be =: tact? I don't know the phrase.

22. whiche then vas. This refers to the men, but the singular is used for the plural. Cf. 109. 20; 117. 9.

P. 125, line 20. For xxvii. should be read xxii., and in the following line 1485 for i486. These are signs that the continuation of Hardyng had not been revised, but was left by the author as much in the rough as we have already noticed to have been the case with More's own work.

11. rt=have. This is colloquial English to the present time, and was so in More's day. Cf. Shaks. Hamlet, iv. 5. 64, "So would I a done," and Love's Laboiir"s Lost, v. 2. 17, "She might a been a grandam." Another instance comes in line 23 below.

P. 126, line 6. cannot bee expressed, i. e. the event speaks louder than any words could do, as a warning to deter others.

6. The is is omitted in the original, but clearly by mistake, probably through this being the word just before it.

15. heled, i. e. tended so that they might be healed.

Hardyng's continuator both here and 107, 8 uses itiwiortal in a manner peculiar to himself=the memory of which shall be preserved. There ijiimortal bcnefite 2C! aid which he would never forget, and here the thanks are called immortal because they were not given for the moment only, but to be ever continued.

17. neiier forget. His grants prove that he was as good as his word.

25. carj'iagc in old English meant "baggage" "that which was carried," not "the vehicle in which men rode." Cf. Earle's Mic7'o-cosjhographie, p. 41, "Not load en with any carriage beside."

33. vas buried. Ten years later Henry caused a tomb to be erected over the grave.

P. 127, line 15. The sense is: Which death he would rather suflter by the sword, than he would by shameful flight try and save his life which afterwards might chance to perish by sickness. There is a somewhat similar use of the yvoxd favour in Shaks. Cofu. of Errors, I. i. 150, ' Yet I will favour thee in what I can. Beg thou, or borrow to make up the sum And live, if not, then thou art doomed to die."

6, 18; III, 3 White, William (sheriff), 22, 25 Willoughby (Robert), 98, 9 Winchester (city of), 108, 21 Windsor, i, 24; 3, 24; 48, 15 Wodefeld (Woodville), the lord, 58, 33 Woodville (Edward), 98, 8; io'j, 26

York (city of), 86, 7, 24

York (county of), 96, 27

York, Archbishop of, 19, 11; '20, 5; 21, i; 23, 7; 25, 28; 43, 13

York (Duchess of, mother of Edward IV.), 59' 19; 61, 25

York (Richard, Duke of), i, 9; 4, 24; 34, 15; 58, 2; 64, 18; di, 28; 71, 6; 78, a (interj.), ah, 36, 9 a (v.), have, see notes 125, 22, 23 a (prep.), of, i, 8; 30, 4; 85, 37; 105, 16 abashed y). p.), downcast, 46, 30; 72, 21; 83, 12; 95, 25; 121, 5; 123, 3 abhominable (adj.), abominable, 85, 21 abu2it (adv.), around, standing by, abuse (v.), to turn to a wrong use, to pervert, 88, 16 abusions (n.), abuses, 71, 18 acco? npted (p. p.), accounted, reckoned, III, 19 accoiipliiig (n), union, joining together, 70, 31 acqziited (p. p.), requited, repaid, adhibit (p. p.), invited, summoned, 43. 19 adjoyne (v. trs.), to join, to unite, 115, 26 adoe (n.), ado, trouble, 6, i adowne (adv.), down, 17, 12 advengcd (p. p.), avenged, 93, 15 advenhire (n.), peril, risk, 67, 3 a adventure dx random, by chance, haphazard, 48, 8; 53, 5 advertise (v.), to inform, 86, 14; 92, 28 aduertiscincnte (n.), counsel, instruction, advice, 8, 29; 25, 10 advise (v.), to look upon, 54, 19 advouteresse (n.), adulteress, 58, 6 advowtrie (n.), adultery, 64, 8 afoj-e didw.), forward, 17, 14; before (of time), 110, 9; 120, 8 after (prep.), like as, like unto, after (prep.), next to, 25, 3 r(adv.), afterwards, 10, 4; 57, 20; 58, 30; 121, 14; 127, 16 afyre (adv.), on fire, 14, 7 agayne (prep.), against, 8, 2,; 111, 16 agreueth (v.), aggravateth, makes grievous, 10, 10 agrevid (p. p.), aggravated, made grievous, 68, 13 a-kiiozven (part.), knowing, cognizant of, conscious, 78, 30 al, all (conj.), although, 23, 17; 53. 4; 66, 10; 69, 21 al (adv.), utterly, 74, 22 aland-xd-v.), to land, 100, 10, 20 aZt'j'(n.), allies, 9, 13; 10, is.

allcctive (n.), inducement, enticement, 45, 22 alnoise (n.), alms, a charity, 22, 22 alcft (adv.), to set aloft=io cheer, to raise anybody's spirits, 121, 20 alowe (adv.), in a lowly place, low down, 20, 4 alternate (adj.), changing, varying, 89, 12 aniercenicntcs (n.), punishments in life or limb, 67, 24 amoue (v.), to remove, 14, and cow.), U 37, 4 5 47' 24; 91, 2 2; z?"(conj.), if, 30, 31 (2ir (adv.) quickly, 48, 6 appeased (p. p.), brought to a settlement,-21, 19 appetite (n.), liking, wish, desire, appoinct, appoint (v.), to determine, to settle, to make ready, provide, 34, 14; 94, 13; 95, 8; 100, 23 a(? m? i:(p. p.), prepared, decided, come to a point, 59, 15; 77, 16; 107, 30 aprointincnfe (n.), a misprint in the original for appointmciite, arcstcd (pret.), rested, refreshed, 100, 26 artillary (n.), artillery, not confined as now to great guns, 100, 16 ascertayne," asserteine (v.), to give certain information, to inform, to assure, 96, 13; 113, 22; 117, 25 aslope (adv.), obliquely, indirectly, assaicd, assayed (pret.), made trial of, attempted, 45, 11; 98, 2 assay (v.), to attempt, to try, 98, 2; 110, 20 assemble (n.), assembly, multitude, 14, 22 assc7'teincd (p. p.), certainly informed, made certain, 96, 13 assured (. p.), resolved, 102, 17 astonied as fanned (p. p.), astonished, 46, 22; 106, 17; 114, 24 j- 2uho say = so to say, as if one should say, 13, 5; 113, 26 atchycued. p.), achieved, accomplished, 23, 20 atteinpte (v.), to tempt, 108, 30 attendaimt (adj.), prepared, in attendance, i6, 7 attoncmente (n.), setting at one, reconciliation, 13, 31; 15, 5 atwixte (prep.), betwixt, between, 14' 33 aiicthoritie (n.), authority, 44, 26; 51,.9;

57, 2, 26 aictoritie, auto7-itee (n.), authority, 103, 17; 104, 13 auncient (adj.), old (of persons), 4' 7 autoiwes (n.), authors, devisers, aiiannced. p.), advanced, 4, 28 avoyded (p. p.), put forth, sent away, got rid of, 86, 15; 103, 20 bahle (n), babble, noisy talk, 54,

Wy (v.), to utter forth, to emit, 89, 18 ha7'C (pret.), to bear sore = to be annoyed with, 9, 4 bare (pret.), behaved, 22, 32 baste n.), basety, bastardy, 64, 8 be, bee (i pi. pres. ind.), are, 37, 26; 67, 2 be (3 pi. pres. ind.), are, 10, 12; 27, 11; 29, 15; 40, 17; 73, 31 becons, bekyns (n.), signal-fires, 113, r6, 20 beck (n.), a signal given by a nod, 42, ir bee (p, p.), been, 26, 6; 29, 15 bcedes (n.), (conn, with bid z."iv) prayers, 90, 9 bcestowed., bestowed (p. p.), bestowed, set, placed, 16, 12; 48, 4 beore (adv.), in the front, facing them, 73, 2 begile (v.), to beguile, 51, 11 behestes (n.), commandments, orders what to do, 88, 10 behoofe (n.), possession, enjoyment, 20, 17 ben (inf.), to be, 33, 26 ben (p. p.), been, 46, i; 49, 22 bende (n.), a band, a company, (applied to the body of court-favourites), 13, 14; 15, 19 bene (3 pi. pres.), be, are, 24, 17; benefites (n.), good actions (as oji-posed to evil), 42, hcsctte (p. p.), blocked by guards, watched, ii6, i betaken (p. p.), committed, entrusted, C!,, 6 hetoke (pret.), betook, entrusted, betooke (pret.), gave up to, 20, 18 bctrapped (p. p.), entrapped, 13, i betu (ipret.), beat, 117, 19 bewrapped (pret.), wrapped up, biga?! iy (n.)) used in the text for marriage with a woman who has already had one husband, bloode (n.), family, 20, 11; 89, 2 blowen (p. p.), blown, circulated (of a report), 22, 4 bonch (n,), a bunch, a lump, oo, 28 bondes (n.), bounds, limits, 89, 23 (n.), a boon, a request, 62, 18 boochcrly (adj.), butcherly, 6, 29 boorclye (adj.), burly, large, 2, 28 booted, bated (pret.), profited, availed, 18, 11; 48, 7; 59, 18 bootes (n.), boats, 20, 21 'CAY fe (n.), a table, 47, 27 boi-ne (p. p.) (of the feelings), exhibited, shewn, 70, 2 j- (v.), to extol, talk loudly in favour of, 89, 25 boteles (adj.), bootless, unprofitable, 39, 24 bo2cstiouse (adj.), boisterous, 56, 4 brag v.), to vaunt, to boast, 123, 16 brake (pret.), interrupted, 49, 33 braste (pret.), burst, 74, 26 breake, breke (v.), to disclose, make a communication, 41, 31; 45' 14; 57, 4; 66, 28; 82, 32; 93, 4; 94, 6 brcche (n.), breach, breaking, 37, breide (n.), (connected with bray), a sound, an exclamation, 89, 19 bremiynge. (n.), burning, S, i briginders (n.), brigandines, coats of mail, 51, 20 broken (p- p.)j opened up, revealed, 56, 25 bushment (n.), ambushment, a body of men placed in readiness for any purpose, 74, 3 but (corij.), unless, 9, 26 but if coyi.), unless, except, 10, 2; 36, 30; 54' I 5 58' 6; 75, 5 by (adv.), close by, close at hand, 80, 6 y (prep.) = concerning, of, about, 44, 19; 46, 22, 32; 50, 29; 82, 9; 90, 33 by and by (adv.), soon, immediately, 10, 15; 17, 19; 19, 24; 20, 32; 72, 26; 114, 32; 119, 29; 122, I byde (v.), remain, abide, 35, 2 bye (v.), to buy, 103, 2 byreft (pret.), took away, d, 19 call (v.), to know, 79, 6 care (n.), over-anxiety, 107, 12 careful z., grieved, annoyed at, 42, 5 carriage, carryage (n.), baggage, 22, 16; 126, 25 carriage (n.), the act of carrying, cast (n.), a model, a contrivance, a work of skill, 53, 9 ra.5- (v.), exhibit, shew forth, 27, 28 cease (v.), to put an end to, 25, 26 ceased (p. p.), abated, ended, 25, 5 certaigne (adj.), certain, 103, 22 certes (adv.), verily, 67, 4 chaffed (pret.), chafed, fretted, 127, 8 cha7nberer (n.), a chamberlain, 85, 21; 86, 10 char7iel-house (n.), place for preserving the bones of the dead, 54' 17 dure (n.), mirth, entertamment, chose (p. p.), chosen, 23, 3 clapped (pret.), smote, struck, 47, 26 clapped (pret.), rattled, banged, 47. 28 cleane, dene (adv.), utterly, entirely, 100,

19; 103, 20 cleane made (adj.), well fashioned (of limbs), 2, 26 denes (n.), cleanness, purity, 60, der'e (adj.), clear, innocent, 46, 23 cleved (XQX.), clave, adhered, 117, dose (adj.), to keep dose =. o lie in concealment, to hide oneself away, 16, 27 close (adj.), confined to a cloister, I, 14 close (adj.), kept secret, 43, 29 cognisaimce (n.), coat armour, crest, 48, 27 coherced (p. p.), coerced, compelled, 97, 14 colour (n.), excuse, pretext, reason, el scfpe colourable (adj.), having a shew of reason, specious, 22, 9. co ne apparently pi-et.) = came, 47, 29 cof? ieji, commoji (v.), to commune, to converse, to discuss, 49, 32; 73, 4; 89, 15; 121, 8 comen (adj.), common, ordinaiy, 44, 7; 57, 20; 68, 23; 81, 3; no, 16; III, 17 comen (p. p.), come, 65, 8; 66, 27; 71, 11; 80, 26; 86, 26 comeners, comcns (n.), the commons, the common people, 73, 14, 24; 74, 28 co7noning (pres. part.), communing, 4.5, 32; 46, 9 commodite, commodity, co? n? noditie (n.), advantage, 8, 27; 12, 15; 33, 26; 42, 29; 59, 31 et S(2pe compasse (v.), to contrive, 46, iq compleccion (n.), natural disjoosi-tion, tendency, no, 12 complyces (n.), accomplices, 95, 16; 96, 22 conceyte (n.), idea, notion, imagination, no, 19 condescejided (pret. and p. p.), agreed, 32, 7; 71, 19 condicions (n.), qualities (of a person), 64, 31; 82, 30; cf. ill-conditioned condyng (adj.), condign, well-deserved, 127, 16 confusion (n.), with the strong sense of destruction, 13, 22; 17, 2 conster (v.), to construe, to interpret, 90, 25 contract (p. p.), contracted, formed, 14, 2 contracted (p. p.), engaged to marry, in, 6 convayde (p. p.), communicated, imparted to some one, 6, 30 conveigh (v.), to convey, 106, 29 convenyente (adj.), suitable (of a person), 25, 29 covetise (n.), covetousness, 53, 12 coumpassed (pret.), contrived, planned, 17, 23 coumpinablc (adj.), friendly, kind, 6, 18 counceled (pret.), counselled, took counsel, 121, 14 counsaile (n.), council, counsellors, 24,28 cowitinance (n.), a sign by a look, 35, 14 credence (n.), belief, credit, trust; also a token of trust or credit, 24, 29; 45, 17; 81, 27 cume (v.), to come, 73, 22 cumly (adj.), comely, 72, 29 cunning (adj.), (in a good sense), knowing, intelligent, 70, 12 ctcre (n.), care, 37, 22 curtesly (adv.), courteously, 45, 33 custo7nable (adj.), customary, 21, 6 dager (n.), dagger, 85, 25 dales (n.), days, at the dales, = X. that time, 87, dalay (v.), dally, sport, 114, 20 dashed p. p.), broken down, overthrown, 115, 19 dasill (v.), to dazzle, 123, 21 dealinge (n.), course of action, conduct, 18, 10; 20, 25; 43, 28 debate (n.), contest, quarrel, 11, 20; (?(5; z yr (adj.), affable, courteous, agreeable, 3, 21 decease (v.), to die, i, 22; 4, i; 7'3.

dedticaon (n.), introduction, preamble, 65, 23 defotded (p. p.), defiled, 60, 15 dehided (p. p.), set at nought, overthrown, 59, 28; 62, 21 - w (v.), to think, 6, 33 demeane (v.), to regulate, 22, 8; 80, 33 demeaned (pret.), treated, 33, 8 demeanoiire (n.), behaviour, conduct, 4, 19; 20, 29 dempte (pret. j, deemed, judged, 39 25 depaj-i (v.), to die, 100, 30 (3: r ((p. p.), dead, 7, 18; 12,6; 54, 16 descharging (part.) delivering goods, 19, 33 dcseased (adj.), diseased, sick, 96, 12 despite, dispite (n.), insult, 85, 15; 87, 21 dessimule (v.), to dissemble, 127, II dessolate (adj.), apparently=dissolute, 51, 10 destroide (part.), destroyed, 51, 25 devise (n.), device, 22, 17; 76, 27 devohite (p. p.), descended, come down to, 71, 10 devoure, dcvozure, devor (n.), duty, 25, 31; 26, 26; 77, 5 disceiicion (n.), dissension, discord, 4, 8, et sccpe discharging (part.), relieving of, releasing from, 37, 22 discrccions (n.), considerations, reasons, 21, 18 disgest (v.), to discuss,, 21 dishahled (p. p.), disabled, 58, i disparkle (v.), to disperse, to scatter, 97, 4 dispitiotts, dispiteous (adj.), pitiless, merciless, 6, 18; 85, 3, 8 displesiire (n.), an offence given to another, 69, 10 dissemblyng (part.), dissembling, pretending, 87, 27; 105, 19 dissimuler (n.), a pretender, 6, 16 dissimtdyng (part.), dissembling, pretending, 87, 27; no, 31 dissolved (pret.), of a company, separated, broke up, 74, 22 distaiince (n.), to sette distaunce = to cause estrangement, 17, i; to fal at distance. o be estranged, 68, 26 distincke (adj.), distinct, 74, r divine (v.), to judge, form conclusions, foretell, 7, 10; 24, 24 dooen. T.), done, 102, 10; 109, 7 double to (adj.), twice as much, 123, 14 doublet (n.), a man's under garment, 47, 10 doubtiioiis (adj.), doubtful, 14, 24 draught (n.), a privy, 82, 27 draweth (v.), tendeth, makes for, drives at, 36, 24 dj-eue (v.), to drive, to go driving, 10, 6 drewe (pret.), took part with, went unto, resorted to, 20, 2; 43, 30 drexu aboute (pret.), came close up drifte (n.), meaning, design, intention, plan, scheme, 6, 30; 10, 5; 12, 23; 43,9; 82, 20; 89, 15 duj'csse (n.), prison, 35, 12 dyscomoditie (n.), disadvantage, harm, 79, 32 dyspence (n.), expenditure, 6, 12 eftesooncs, eftsoone, eftsoncs (adv.), presently, soon again, 11, 11; 86, 27; 95, 3 cgall (adj.), equal, 5, 26; lo, 32; 21,

GLOSSARY.

dies (adv.), else, 6, 6 embassiate, ejnbasiatc (n.), an embassy, 58,22; 59, 7; 62, 20 onhatalled (p. p.), set in battle array, 97, 10 cmongcs, emongcst (prep.), among, amongst, 125, 6, 14, 18; 126, I, 20 rzrz aj- z (n.), cause, reason, 12, 12 cncmionse (adj.), inimical, done by an enemy, 49, 25 cnfarced (p. p.), stuffed full, 96, 2 cnfoiirmcd, enformed (p. p.), informed, told, 86, 6; 112, 32 cnpiigncd (pret.), fought against, was fighting against, 15, 3 cnqidetcd (p. p.), disquieted, disturbed, 89, 3 ensue (v.), to happen, to occur, 9, ensure (v.), to assure, promise, 28, ensured (p. p.), made sure, pledged, bound by a promise to marry, 59, 16; 62, 8 intending (part.), intending, 4, 33; 5. 17; 7 7; et sacpe entered (pret. and p. p.), interred, I, 24; 84, 20 enterlaced (p. p.), mixed up with, entier (adj.), entire, complete, 76, 20; zr (v.), to enter on, 91, 28 entreate (v.), to treat of, 4, 20; 5, 25; 81, 7 entreate (v. trs.), to treat, to deal with, to behave towards, 69, 28 entreteigned (p. p.), entertained, treated hospitably, 108, 3 i-;-.: (n.), ear, 51, 16 erste (adj.), first, 7, 27 erste (adv.), before, 31, 29 estates (n.), princes, dignified persons see states), 63, 9 estraunge (adj.), strange, 61, 18 estraunger (n.), stranger, 33, 18 eth, ethe (adj. and adv.), easy, easily, 14, 8; 27, 23; 51, ir; evermore (adv.), always, 67, 7 evyll z. Y.), evilly, ill, 88, 3 express (adj.), moulded, modelled, ey (interj.), ah! 48, 31

eyen (n.), eyes, 74, 27; 85, 23 face (n.), appearance, 14, 25 facte (n.), action, deed, conduct, 109, 6 fain, faine (v.), to pretend, 30, 30; 127, 11 fained (pret. and p. p.), feigned, 63, 13; 68, 13; 87, 15 fall (v.), to fall unto his parte to join his side, 108, 16 fall from (v.), to quit, forsake, 28, 26 fame (n.), rumour, report, 22, 3 fantasieth (v.), fancieth, 49, i fautasied, fancied, took a liking to, III, 8 faiitasye (n.), fancy, inclination, 78, 21 fardclles (n.), bundles, 19, 31 farder (adj.), reluctant, farther away from, farther off, 35, 31, 32; 38, 26 farder, furder. diy.), farther, 51, 15; 113 8 farther (v.), to further, to advance, 58, 8 fasions (n.), fashions, manners, 126, 9 fast 3.1.), closely attached, sted- fast, firm, 45, 12; 88, 19 fastlye (adv.), firmly," fixedly, 21, 10 fant, fante (jx.), fault, 30, 30; 106, 26 fantye (adj.), faulty, 5, 19; 103. 10 favor (n.), expression of face, looks, 59, II; 65, 2, 27 favour (v.), to be well disposed unto, 68, 8; to try and shield, to protect, save, 127, 15 fear (v. t.), to frighten, 109, 30; 126, 7 feared (pret.), was in fear for, 87, feaiihee (n.). fealty, good faith,

T02, 5; 117, 23 fclaivye (n,), fellow, companion, 36, 11 fere (v.), to fear, 35, 11; 38, 13 fci'ther (adv.), farther, 36, i; 38, 17 fct (p. p.)., fetched, 39, 20 7 (p. p.), fetched, 27, 29 Jctiircd (adj.), fashioned (used of limbs), 5, 28 fcive (adj.), small; a fewe couipaigny 'd small body, 124, 9 fielde, fclde (n.), a battle, an engagement in the field, 21, 27; 59 5; 63, 8 fiftenes (n,), fifteenths, the tax so called see notes), 67, 16 flee (v.), let Jlce = Qt fly, 47, 33; 123, 26 fleshed (p. p.), initiated, having had a first taste, 83, 27 flockmele (adv.), in a flock or crowd, 20, 28 fole (n.), fool, 90, 32 y;?!?"(adj.), foolish, 27,28; 28, 12 for- (adv.), because of, by reason of, 44'.3; 81, 3 foi'beai'c (v.), to leave undisturbed, forbere (v.), to forego, give up, 61, forbade (n.), prohibition, forbidding, 99, 20 forced (pret.), heeded, cared for see notes), 57, 17 foregoing (pres. part.), preceding, forelaborid (p. p.), previously tired out, 34, 2 forei)iinded (p. p.), previously intended, 7, 26 forcstudied (pret.), thought about beforehand, anticipated, 51, 12 forteresse (n.), fortress, defence, forethought (pret.), designed beforehand, 7, 2 forezveried (p. p.), previously fati-g ied, 34, 3 forgeate (v.), to forget, 11, 4 forth (adv.), forward, on to the end, 42, 23 fortherlye (adj.), advantageous, such as to fiirtlicr or promote the end desired, 8, 4 fortune (v.), to chance, to happen, 39, 23; III, 2; 127, 16 forzvarde (adv.), to goe forwarde = to make progress, to advance, 9' 30 forwarde (n.), the vanguard, the forepart of an army, 122, 20; 123, 5; 124, 28 foiigjiten (p. p.), fought, 68, 30 found (pret.) (?), stopped, halted see notes), 65, 17 foiinden (p. p.), found, 34, 4; 36, 30; 60, 7; 90, 20 fourth (adv.), forth, 119, 24 frame (n.), order, fashion, propriety, 21, 26; 65, 24 frame (v. trs.), to fashion, to mould, to bring into accord, 56, 33 frauie (v. intr.), to arrange itself, to come about, 101, 21 framed (p. p.), brought into order, fashioned, 72, 17 fro (prep.), from, 67, 15 from (prep.), away from, apart from, 13, 8 froting (pres. part.), rubbing about restlessly, chafing, 46, 14 friistrate (p. p.), frustrated, 59, 28 ful (adv.), fully, 94, 29 furder (adv.), further, 113, 9 furtheffourth, fiu'th (adv.), forth, forward, onward, 6, 30; loi, i; 109, 6; 113, 31; 119' 24 furthzikird:).(.), forward, 101,23 gate (adj.), gay, fine, 96, 7 aine (adv.), again, 11, 9 galatye (n.), a gallery, 75, 18 ga?-dai7ie, gardayne, gardain (n.), a guardian, 37, 15, 21; 38, 11; garland (n.), used in a general sense = prize of victory, 6S, gate (pret.), got, 50, 26; 54, 33 gave (pret.), suggested, inclined, caused him to think, 78, 22; 81, 19 gay (adj.), merry, trifling, witty, clever, showy, 37, 6; 53, 9; 55, Z geat (v.), to get, 16, 27; 31, 15; 32, 11; 78, 14; 79, 30 geld hall n., guildhall, 66, 16 gesse (v.), to guess, 13, 19; 54, 16,? (pret.), gat, 75, 17 gethei' (v.), to gather, 52, 27 geve (v.), to give, 14, 33 gilt (n.), guilt, 6, 13 giltye (adj.), guilty, 80, 11 glose (n.), a specious explanation, goe to (interj.), go p, come now, 27, 24 good (n.), goods, possessions, 40, 19; 67, I, 9 gouernance (n.), selfrestraint, self-control, 2, I grce (v.), to agree, 9, 26

T w (adj.), green, fresh, untried, 87, 28 grennes (n.), gins, snares, 67, 9 grieues (n.), grievances, vexations, II, 26 groiindly (adv.), with good ground, satisfactorily, 70, 21 growen (p. p.), grown, 70, 31 ;7 6' (pret.), felt a grudge, repined, 46, 33 gyve (v.), allow, permit, 74, 7 labilities (n.), abilities, 91, 17 zfl; (adj.), able, 8, 19; 104, 25 halyng Y xt.), dragging, 121, 32; 122, 14 hande (n.), to bear hi haiide = o delude with false information, 16, 20; out of hande, at once, 99, 17 handle (v.), to manage, deal with (a person), 109, 11; 114, 33 liap, happe (v.), to happen, to chance, 9, 18; 21, 27; 36, 8; 51, 2; 68, 8; 79, 9 happed (pret.), chanced, 49, 31; 58, 28 happelye, happely (adv.), haply, perchance, 9, 23; 11, 20; 32, i; 34, 5; 55, 'o; 61, 2 et Sivpe haj'd, harde (pret.), heard, 19, 17; 45, 13; 59' 11; 70, 7; 76, 4; 81, 14; et scepe hardely (adv.), harshly, as an objection (?), 61, 22 harnesed (part.), equipped, accoutred, armed, 51, 20; 100, 4 haj'neys, harneis (n.), armour, 20, 28; 22, 15; 47, 29; 51, 29 hartly, hartelye (adv.), heartily, 62, 17; 72, 8 haiycd), p.), dragged, torn about, 85, 14 hast (v.), to hasten, 49, 28 hasted (pret.), hurried on, 65, 20 have (v.), of a sermon, to deliver, to preach, 57, 10 hawsed (pret.), strained, drawn, dragged, 67, 24 haynous (adj.), heinous, 23, 27 heavynesse (n.), sorrow, i, 23 helcd (p. p.), healed, tended, cured of their wounds, 126, 15 helth (n.), safety, security, 98, I here (v.), to hear, 38, 29; 48, 17 et scepe here (n.), the hair, 85, 15 hcrode (n.), a herald, 52, 3 hcvcly (adv.), heavily, sorrowfully, 48, 8 hcyghnous (adj.), heinous, 29, 9; high (adj.), grand, important, 36, 28; 88, 10 highly (adv.), seriously, indignantly, angrily, 53, 23; 62, 20 hobeit (conj.), howbeit, 43, 27 hoised, hoysedi(x.), hoisted, lifted aloft, 99, 28; 100, 22 hole (adj.), whole, 74, 15 holpe (pret.), helped, 7, 33; 20, 2 holpen (p. p.), helped, 51, 30 homely (adj.), plain spoken, 31, honcste (adj.), honorable, such as would be an honour to accept I03, 13

Jwrsebackwa7-d: id), to hoj'sehack-ward iova. to mount on horseback, i. e. toward horseback, 16, 6 houerly (adj.), created in an hour, 14, 2 houge (adj.), huge, 120, 27 husthiges (n.), the court of the city of London, 66, 19 hythei'waj'de (adv.), up to this time, 26, 13 il (adj.), evi), 44, 33 il-faring 2i.( )), worn-out, 51, 20 immortal (adj.), eternal, never to be forgotten, everlasting, 107, 8; 126, 15 hnportablc (adj.), unendurable, intolerable, 32, 31; 69, 1 impugn (v.), to fight against, to oppose, 9, 28 in (prep,), upon, 58, 3 incontinent, incontincntc, iticonti-nently (adv.), immediately, following at once, 15, 31; 23, 25; 39, 15; 57, 21; 104, 3; et scepe indiffercntelyc (adv.), without partiality, 21, 17 itifect (p. p.), infected, tainted, 10, I inforsed (p. p.), enforced, dwelt upon, 58, 15 infortiinc (n.), misfortune, 19, 3; 80, 26 infoivndcth (v.), imparteth, esta-blisheth, 64, 4 inkelynge (n.), inkling, clue, slight knowledge, 7, 23 instantly (adv.), urgently, 104, 18 intreatc (v.), to treat for, to make proposals for, 58, 23 inward (adj.), (of war) civil, intestine, 69, I jeopardous (adj.), hazardous, 14, 28 Jubarde (v.), to jeopard, put in peril, 35, 5 jiibardy, jubardye, jupardy (n.), jeopardy, peril, 35, 7, 9, 20; 36, 21; 50, 20; 68, 22 judged (p. p.), legally decided, kayes n.), keys, 16, 10 Zy (pret.), kept, 66, 8 kinde (n.), kinship, 4, 10 kindle (v.), to get angry, 38, 27 kindly (adj.), natural, 81, 23 knazving (pres. part.), gnawing, 46, 14 knoiucn (p. p.), known, 51, 27; 64, 30; 67, 17; 88, 8 knowledge (v.), to acknowledge, 108, 8 kyj'tle (n.), a woman's jacket with a petticoat attached, 53, 31 ri (v.), to fail, 6, 30 lapped (pret.), wrapped, 83, 32 lashed oiite (p. p.), squandered, scattered, 67, 16. laugh Jtpon (v.), to laugh at, 50, 3 lazaul (adj.), legitimate (of a son), ay, i y (pret.), was lodging, was living, 19, 7; 74, 31 leape (pret.), leapt, 85, 30 a (conj.), lest. Ill, 14; 113,12; 120, 9; 122, 5; 123, 29 leastzvise (adj.+n.), at the leastwise 'zx. least, 31, 27 lefte (pret.), ceased from, left off, lefte (pret.), ceased, came to an end, legcr (adj.), slight, little, 68, 19 leneth (v.), trusteth, attendeth, in-clineth, 48, 32 lenger (adv.), longer, 21, 15; 38, 30; 48, 29 le iid Yxtt.), leaned, inclined, tended, 45, 18 lese (v.), to lose, 61, 3; 68, 33; St,, 14; 89, 31 lessyd (pret.), lessened, grew less, lest (adj.), least, at the lest wise zx least, at all events, 5, 18; 69, 16 lest, leste (adv.), least, 15, 10; 47, let, lette (v.), to hinder, 27, 25, 32; 30, 6; 61, 8; in, 33 let (v.), to forbear, refrain fi om, 6, let, lette (n.), hindrance, 20, 28; 28, 5 letted (pret. and p. p.), forebore, refrained from, 19, 16; 35, 12; 58,7 letten (p. p.), let, 7, 18 lever (adv.), rather, by preference, 49, II liefe (adj.), dear, 44, 22 (pret.), alighted, 17, 12 lightli (adv.), lightly, on slight provocation, 86, 32 like, lyke (to) (v.) = to be pleasing unto, to please, 18, 10; 76, 5; 77' 4, 21; 93, 24 like, lyke (adj.), likely, 9, 16; 15, 10; 34' 7 likelihod (n.), likeuhood, of likcli- hod=m all probability, 41, 7; 77, 28 likely (adj.), sufficient, adequate, 49' 7 7v;)'(adv.), inallprobabihty, 49, 7 c6Yi (impers. v.), is pleasing unto, 61, 10; 63, 19 z (v.), to like, to wish to do anything, 40, 24; 52, 10; 67, 22, 23 loe (interj.), lo! 22, 15; 40, 6 lokingto (n.), caring for, 33, 29 longing y-i. x'i.), belonging, 74, 4 looke (v.), to expect, 7, 2; 9, 13; II, 22 lust (n.), liking, inclination, 36, 31 lusty (adj.), courageous, spirity, loi, 8 lycence (v.), to permit, give license, 75, 23 lyjiger (v.), to retard, to hinder 116, 12 magcstie, w t-J-Zj(n.), majesty, 13, 7; 6 13; 79' 8 magry, i7iaugrye (prep.), in spite of, 28, II; 32, 21 maistrye (n.), work, achievement, 28, 6 make (v.), to effect, do, influence, 116, 25 malice (n.), wicked deed, 32, i; 36, 3 manncquellers (n.), manslayers, murderers, 28, 28 vianer (n.), in vzanner- almost, 12, 33; 94, 25; 106, 18; 113, 3 marresse (n.), a morass, a marsh, 123, 19, 24 mary (v.), to marry, 42, 32; 58, 20; 59, 15 scepe maryable (adj.), marriageable, of age to marry, 115, 29 masti'esse (n.), mistress, 93, 26; 94, 2 mcane (n.), means, 88, 30; 93, 2; 108, 10 mede (n.), fee, reward, bribe, 99, 7 mendcmcnt xi.), amendment, 29, 17 mcngling (n.), mingling, mixing, 70, 27 111 cues (n.), means, methods, 10, 4 inente (pret.), meant, 75, 20 merely (adv.), merrily, 46, 2; 49, 33; 60, 18; 82, 31; 91, 3 mcry (adj.), merry, 49, 15 mervel x.), marvel, wonder, 52, 20 messe (n.), a dish (of meat or fruit) 46, 5, 8 mete (v.), to meet, 124, 14, 18 mete a.), fii, 127, 11 metely (adj.), meet, fit, 6, 9; 24, 30; 33' 19; 56, 27; 60, 8 metely (adv.), moderately, 84, 11 iiiiddes (n.), midst, 57, 14; 119, 33; 122, 31 minatory (adj.), threatening, 87,11 mind, mynde (v.), to be minded, to intend, 32, 23; 35, 27 minded, (p. p.), intended, 44, 17 minishe (v.), to diminish, 45, 17 minis king in.), Aim. mx'ih. mg, 52, 14 minister (v.), to supply, 4, 19 minister (n.), an agent in any kind of work, 85, miscaned pret.), died, 34, 31 inisgivdh (v.), is in doubt, faileth, .43' 23 mislike (v. impers.), to be displeasing to any one, 6r, 9 misliked (v. a. pret.), disliked, 16, 26; 44, II 7nisprision (n.) z' cztc contempt of the court, 67, 25 7;mi? (n.), lack, want, 54, i mocion (n.), prompting, suggesting, proposal, 45, 16; 76, 32 mockishe (adj.), unreal, pretended, 80, 14 moe, 1710 (adj.), more, 3, 30; 50, 28; 60, i; 66, 17; 68, 10; ct sccpc vioneth (n.), month A. S. inona'S vioreandlesse (used substantively), high and low, great and small, 108, 16 most (adj.), special, chief, 69, 27 viove (v.), to propose, 75, 4; to apply to, 108, 2 miiche (adj.), great in number, muche pai t=2. great part, 22,21 nmche what? id '.), in a great degree, 6, 23; 62, 32 rnw'ther (n.), murder, 109, 31 najjie (n.), pretext, pretence, title, namely (adv.), chiefly, specially, 53.32;,7o T2; 112, 30; namely which zj- = which is especially, 1.3, n natheksse (adv.), nevertheless, 2, 22 et passim ncdes (adv.), of necessity, 7, 6; 9, 29; 39, 24 nedes cost (adv.), of necessity, 49, 10 nere zd.), near, 44, 19 nefe (adv.), nearly, 45, 28 ne?-e (prep.), close to, 50, 9 nere, neere (adv.), never, 10, 14; 30, I nether (adj.), lower, 74, 2 jierv (adj.), of w 7e = afresh, anew.

newly (adv.), lately, 33, 30 next (adj.), nearest, 12, 22; 20, 2;. SI, 30 none (adj.) = no, 45, 2; 50, 26; 62, 14; 90, 27; 91, I nought (adj.), worthless, base, defiled, 53, 24 iionghte (n.), nothing; of nonghte = for no reason, without cause, 7, 24 oheysaiince (n.), rule exercised over another, 76, 15 obteigued (y- p.), obtained, 105, 13 occasions (n.), motives, 81, 6 (adv.), off, 35, 25; 50, 10; 64, 32, et sitpe (?"(prep.), out of, 14, i;

115, 3 of (prep.), for the sake of, out of, through, 49, 27 y (prep.) = by, 85, 14; 96, 10; 120 21 (?'(prep.) = for, 100, 30; to desire of hclp io ask for help, 102, 11; 112, 16; 114, 10 (prep.), on; of the backside = on the backside, 112, 24 "(prep.), concerning, 90, 32 of (prep.) = from; rewards of them = rewards received from them, c. 118, 10 of (prep.), by reason of, co, 11; 82, 22; 97, 19 t" (prep.) = on the part of, 120, 20 onelye (adj.), alone, 44, 29 ones (adv.), once, 40, 32; 44, 16; 50, n onlessc (conj.), unless, 96, 17 open (v.), to reveal, disclose, declare one's intentions, 41, 13, ., 27 or (adv.), ere, before, 15, 29; 62, order (v.), to arrange about, manage, 34, 6 other (adj. y", different, of another fashion, 47, 12 other (pr. sing.), the other, 87, 23 cZ r (adj. pron.), each other, J 21, other (pr.), as a Xv. x'A others, 12, 20; 13, 23; 41, 22; 45, 15; 70, 4; 102, 26 others (poss. sing.) the other's, 40, otheinvere (adv.), in a different direction, 43, 9 ovenmich (adj.), too great, 21, 2; 65, 16 oucrsone (adv.) = too hastily, too soon, 13, 33 over that (adv.), moreover, 3, i; 33 11; 39' 25 ouer this (adv.), moreover, i6, 11 ought (pret.), owed, 13, i oiirselfe (pron. pi.), ourselves, 27, 7 out of (prep.), without, stript of, 53. 31 outward (adv.), outwardly, 85, 33 pageati7ites (n,), shows, spectacles, painted (adj.), counterfeit, 36, 24 palice (n.), palace, 41,9 paradvcnture (adv.), peradven-ture, perchance, 11, 18 parcase, percase (adv.), perchance, 2.5, 8; 72, 24: 79, 5; 81, io pardon, perdon (n.), permission (to do something), or forgiveness (for not doing anything), 75, 25; 76, 2; 77, 14; 96, 12 parfitely (adv.), perfectly, 69, 12 parson, pai'sons (n.), pei"sdn, per-sons, 11, 15; 59, 33; et scbpc parswasio7ts (n.), persuasions, 21, partained (pret.), pertained, belonged, 21, 4 parteners (n.), partners, sharers, 73, 28 partakers (n.), partizans, those who take part with any one, 96, 22 pa7'ties (n.), part5 (i. e. of the country), 73, 25 passing (adv.), beyond, more than, exceeding, 51, 12 past tipon (p. p.), regarded, thought about, 119, 2 patronc (n.), pattern, 65, 26; cf.

payne (n.), pams, 24, 33 pecemele (adv.), piecemeal, piece by piece, 85, 9 pe7'es (n.), equals, 36, 33 ? rrjz' (v.), to understand, 72, 24 perti7ie7's (n.), partners, participators, 73, 5 piked v. pret.), picked, 17, 19 pil (v.), to plunder, 6, 15; 52, 10; 67, 14 pilli7ig (n.), plundering, 67, 10 place (n.), to have hold) place = Xo be more regarded, to have weight, 4, 11; 9, 31; 13, 32 ait (n.), a house, dwelling, 19, 9, 12 place (n.), f a i? place=. o have a result, 104, 32 plai7ie (adj.), downright, out and out, complete, 49, 3 playfelowye (n.), playfellow, 36, 27 plight n.), condition, 36, 12; 63, II poi7ite (n.), ? Zi at a poi7ite, to be resolved, to have made up one's mind, 60, 20 poi77tes (n.), laces with tags, for tying up the hose, 83, 20 politikely (adv.), in accordance with wise policy, 52, 29 polli7ig (n.), robbing, 67, 11 p07-te (n.), carriage, behaviour, 3, 21 p07'ter (n.), the officer in charge of the city gates, 107, 21 possible (adv.), possibly, 59, 21 posies (n.), messengers on horseback, 114, 30 pou7-gc (v.), to purge, to clear, 109, 6 p7-eay, praye, (n.), prey, booty, 23, 21; 102, 32 p7'echers (n.), preachers, 57, 6 p7-eg7iati7it (adj.), expert, clever, ready, 104, 13; 127, 10 pre7itises (n.), apprentices, 74, 5 p7-epe7ised (p. p.), previously intended or thought over, loi, preposcd (pret.), proposed, 23, 26 prese (n.)j press, crowd, 74, 6 prete7tded (p. p.), set forth, related, prevent, prevente (v.), to forestall, anticipate, 5, i; d, 18; 68, 16 prevy (adj.), prevy acquainted with, Informed of, no, 14 p7-ime, priuye (adj.), private, 16, i; 41, 20 processe (n.), proceeding, course of action, 36, 24 processe (n.), (used of a document) compilation, composition, 53, i; 81, io: = a legal warrant, 56, II proctoiire (n.), attorney, agent, representative, 69, 18 procure (v.), to contrive, cause, bring about, care for, 39, 8; 78, procuring (n.), inanagement, contrivance, 52, 16 profecy (n.), prophecy, 53, n prone (adj.), inclined, well disposed, 72, 13 pronosticacion (n.), prognostication, warning, 121, 3 pi'oper (adj.), personally good-looking, 54, 10 protiision (n.), foresight, forethought, 13, 29, 30; 77, 10 providently (adv.), with forethought, 95, 13 piiisant (adj.), puissant, powerful, mighty, 71, 20 puisaiince (n.), a power, a force, an army, 62, 22; 97, 6 purchased (pret.), procured (without any notion of a price to be paid), 114, 24 picrged (p. p.) (of obstacles), cleared away, 62, 5 pttrpose (n.), of purpose ' h a design, 44, 6 p2irpose (v.), to propose, 75, 15, 23, 31 pursevant (n.), pursuivant, a state messenger, an attendant on the heralds, 50, 11, 19 puysaunce (n.), power, forces, 97. 6 pyke (v.), to pick, gather up, find out, 91, 5 qitailed (pret.), failed, came to naught, 65, 15 quailed (p. p.), quelled, ruined, 45.8 quicke (adj.), living, 89, 33 race (v.), to tear, to rend, 49, 7 raced (pret.), tore, rent, 48, 24 rain (n.), reign, 19, 2 raymng pies, part.), reigning, 38, receite (n.), receipt, receiving, 104, 8 receiued (pret.), probably a mistake iox perceived, 8, 20 rechelesse (adj.), reckless, 113, 26 recidivacion (n.), relapse, falling back again into a disease, 34, i reck (v.), to care, 90, 31 rccoijtforting pxt?,. part.), consoling, cheering, 12, i recovered (pret.), gained, reached, 106, 6 redounde (v.), to conduce, 52, 14; 74. 17 rcdrcsse (n.), correction, 24, 26 redyncsse (n.), in a redynesse = n readiness, in, 31; 1x6, 31; 117, 21; 118, 12; 122, 18, 30; 123. 15 refraine (v. a.), to restrain, to check, 12, 14 roncmbraunces (n.), records, memorials, 55, 9 re!)icmbre. tr.), to remind, 67, 27 revienihrcd (p. p.), mentioned, recounted, 55, 30; 59, 7; 71, 4; 74,21 remnant (n.), the rest (of persons), renoiuiicd (adj.), reno'wned, famous, 69, 31 require (v.), to request, wish to have, ask for, 33, 4, 24; 37, 3; 46, 5; 73. 29; 74. 18; 95. I resideiv (n.), the residue, what remains, the conclusion, 29, 33 resolute (adj.), firm, decisive, 39, resort (v.), to have access, be admitted, 75, 14 resort (n.), the throng of visitors, the attendance of courtiers, 43, rested (pret.), remained, 93, 5; 108, 33 reve (v.), to rive, to pkuider, 29, reverente (adj.)) used where we now say reverend 4? 31 riall (adj.), royal, 46, 20 rid, ridde (v.), to rid, to destroy, 45, 19; 81, 22 ridde, ryd (p. p.), destroyed, removed, 56, 16; no, 10 rishes (n.), rushes, 20, 4 rivers (n.), plunderers, 12, 11 roiine (p. p.), run, fled, 125, 25 rore (n.), uproar, 15, 8 '0U7? ie (n.), place, position, 71, 28 rouii, rown (v.), to whisper, 73, 3 19; 77, 12 rought (pret.), recked, cared, 83, 21 rowmes (n.), places, positions, 17, 15;. 23, 15 rowning (n. and part.), whispering, 73, 3 riid wy, redness, 53, 33 riunble (n.), noise, disturbance, 19, 29 riinne (v.), (of a rumour) = to be current, 24, 17; no, 16 rnnne (pret.), ran, 85, 30 lyvilde (adj.), wrinkled, shrivelled, 54, 18 sacre (adj.), sacred, 60, 13 sadde(z.), set, steady, sober, 72, saie (v.), to say, 17, 32 jam?a;; y (n.), sanctuaiy, 34, 17; f scepe salued (pret.), saluted, 17, 16 saue sld.), safe, 37, 22 saiiviple (n.), example, 31, 25 saiiegarde (n.), safeguard, 15, 2; snvely (adv.), safely, 98, 3 saving (n.), keeping, observing, 4S, II saving 2.), only, 17, 30; 45, 7; 70, 5 scacely (adv.), scarcely, 106, 14 scant (adv.), scarcely, hardly, 14, 3; 53, 4; 123, 12 stoutwatche (n.), spies, watchmen, outlookers, outposts, 120, 33 scnipilotise (adj.), scrupulous, troubled with scruples, 57, 3 se (v.), to see, 39, 31; 47, 7; 49, 12 seased pxx.), ceased, 123, 33 jjar(adj.), intimate, confidential, in places of confidence, 64, 28; 82, 2; 85, 20; 87, 26; 114, 28 self pxon.), itself, 43, 28; 55, 4 self, selfe (adj.), same, 7, 14; 10, 24; 48, 19; 50, 6; 55, 26 scly (adj.), innocent, 83, 31 seniblaunce (n.), appearance, pretence, shew, 22, 3; 45, 4; 74, scjnhstanncial (adj.), substantial trustworthy, 51, t8 semyng ptxxt), thinking, 121, 31 sequestred (p. p.), separated, 12, 33 sette by (v.), to esteem, 73, 26; . 119, 10 j- zrra(adj.), separate, 44, 12 shet, shitte (p. p.), shut, 83, 17 shortelye (adv.), shortly, soon, quickly, 22. 1; 48, 2 shote (v.), to shoot, 7, 12 shrctude (adj.), evil, bad, 27, 13; 56, 4 shrift (n.), a confession of sins, 48, shronke (pret.), did shrink, drew back, 47, 33 shryve (v.), to make a confession, 48,6 shulder (n.), shoulder, 127, 3 shyfte (v.), to take new steps, try new means, 39, signe (n.), signal to begin (the battle), 123, 17 signify (v.), to make a sign about, to hint at, 70, 32 sike (adj.), sick, 34, 29 sinister (adj.), wrongful, evil, 52, 16 sins (conj.), since, 38, 10; 74, 14 sircumspectly (adv.), circumspectly, with caution, 39, 31 sithe, sith, syth (adv.), since, 16, scbpe sithen (conj.), since, 11, 9 sitten (p. p.), sat, 46, 17 sleight (adj.), slight, unimportant, slender (adj.), weak, small, inconsiderable, 120, 20; 123, 5 slight (n.?) = a little matter, 33, 16 slipper (adj.), insecure, unstable, 9, 24; 63, 16 smored (p. p.), smothered, 84, 3 sober (adj.), moderate, limited (of numbers), 15, 23 sodain (adj.), sudden, 46, 16 sodainly (adv.), suddenly, 83, 32 so farreforthe, so ferfo7'th (adv.), to such a degree, 3, 23; 44, 9; 67, (et scepe so that (conj.), provided that, 92, 18 sole?? ipnite (n.), solemnization, 45, 27 some (n.), a sum, 70, 5; 106, 31 sojineset (n.), sunset, 116, 17; 120, 2 sorceres (n.), sorceress, witch, 46, 28; 47, 7 sore (adv.), sorely, 28, 4 sorte (n.), company, body, H2, 16; 122, 26 soiined, sowned (pret.), sounded, had a tone of, 32, 29; 58, 3 sowdayne (n.), sultan, 79, 5 sowter (n.), a cobbler, a shoemaker, 79, 5 spare (v.), to spare to do = to refrain from doing, 58, 11; 69, 14 speciall (adv.), especially, 33, 28

RICH.

spede (v. tr.), to promote, set forward, 55, 16 spede (v. intr.), to make haste, 48, 6 spede (n.), success, 7, 30 spiall (n.), spying, watch, 95, 28 spialles (n.), espials, spies, 42, 15 spiritual (adj.), spiritual 7Jien, the clergy, as distinguished from the laity, 57, i spiritualitye (n.), the clergy, 25, spume (v.), (conn, with spur to kick, 90, 4 stably (adv.), firmly, securely, d 10 stale (n.), steady, firm condition, 105, 16 stand (v.), stand with tq be agreeable to, 12, 3; 13, 14; 34, standing (part.), = while it remained, as it was a fact, 59, 26 states (n.), princes, 5, 5, 30; 10, sterre chamber (n.). Star-chamber, i- r (pret.), started, 85, 29 stey (v.), to stop, 112, 10; 114, 25; 120, 23 steye (n.), stoppage, hindrance, 98, 21 steyed (pret.), halted, stopped, 120, 23 stomacke (n.), heart, courage, 5, 6; 14, 4; loi, 8 i-Z ry (n.), storey, a stage, landing, floor of a building, 66, 3 stoutly (adv.), courageously, 42, 24 straunge (adj.), chary, niggardly, slow to give, 2, 16; backward, remiss, 83, i streight (adv.), immediately, 41,21 streighte (adj.), strait, narrow, small, 17, II strength (v.), to strengthen, 112, 21 strenghtis (n.), strongholds, places of security, 56, striken (p. p.), stricken, struck, 48, 14; 97, 32 strived XGi.), strove, 127, 8 stroke (pret.), struck, 124, 6; 124, II studientes (n.), students, 108, 15 stiiffe (n.), baggage of an army or traveller, 22, 10, 11 stiirre (v.), to stir, to bestir themselves, 96, 24 sturre (n.), disturbance, commotion, 117, 4; 119, 8 substaunce (n.), the great part, the chief portion, 2, 5 siiej'ty, surety, siireti, siiretie, suer-tie (n.), security, 11, 30; 13, 8; 16, 30; 35 6; 38, 33; 50, 8; 51, et sccpe stiid p. p.), sued, petitioned, 55, 5 sur (n.), sir, (?) 35, 9 (see notes). sure (adj.), assured, betrothed, 61, sure sid.), secure, safe, 30, 13, 14 sure (adj.), steadfast, faithful, 21, 10 surfet (n.), burden (used of sickness), 34, 4 surmise (v.), to suggest, 58, 13 suspecte (adj.), suspected, 119, 32 suspection (n.), suspicion, the being suspected, 118, 28 sutes (n.), suits, petitions to the

King, 51, I stittelties (n.), i. e. subtleties = designs and figures to adorn a table, or to form part of some great banquet, 45, 29 stittle, stittell (adj.), cunning, 41, 22, 31 tacke (n.), a course, way, direction, 124, 21 take (v.), to hold, to regard, to accept, 28, 24; 78, 7; 83, 10; 102, 7 take (v.), to betake, 117, 5 taken (p. p.), received, wel taken favourably accepted, 56, 26; cf.

taking (n.), the arresting, 47, 2 tallages (n.), tolls, taxes, 67, 11 tariatince (n.), delay, 105, 10; 106, 5 taunting (part), teasing, 54, 25 tave (v.) = to have, 22, 20 tv (pret.), told, 118, 30; 120, 17 tempest! ous (adj.), stormy, full of trouble, 2, 9 tcjuporal men (n.), laymen, 32, 5 tendereth (v.), has a tender regard for, 24, 27 tenderid (pret.), was careful about, regarded, 33, 12 thadvoutry = th advoutry (n.), the adultery, 63, 28 thafore by crasis for the afore, 59, than (adv.), then, 8, 33; 80, 5 et scepe that (pron.), that which, 9, 27; 48, 18; 71, 2; 73, 14; 90, 5; 120, 13; 121, 2 the (pron.), thee, 47, 24 et scepe themself, themselfe (pron.), themselves, 4, 4; 8, 26 et passim then (adv.), than 8, 23 et passim thereby (adv.), in that direction, 105, 28 therefore (pron. + prep.), for that (result or purpose), 8, 11; 45, 30; 67, 10; 70, 10; 81, 32 thereto (adv.), beside that, moreover, 70, 13 there with all (adv.), therewith, 39. 2 thick (adj.), in great numbers, 43, II this (pron.), these, 22, 15 thitherward (adv.), to that place, thorow, thorough (prep.), through, 66, I; 100, 31 thoiight (n.), over-anxiety, annoyance, grief, 82, i; 83, 22; 110, 23 throughly (adv.), thoroughly, 48, 28 to (adv.), too, 7, 12; 40, 28, 29; 51, 13; 54, 8; 75, 20 et sape to (prep.) = with, pick a guarrel to., ? (p. p.), matted together, 85, tone (adj.), the tone = tha. t one, 8, 8; 44, 13; 57, 10 et scrpe too (prep.), to, 8, 28; 100, 31; 106, 24; 108, 20 stspe tormentors, the bodyguard of a despotic prince, executioners, 79, 8; 84, 5; 85, 3 tot her (adj.), the tothcr=: hzt other, toivard (prep, and adj.), friendly with, friendly disposed, well inclined, 7, 22; 58, 26 towarde (prep.), unto, 21, 23 towarde (adj.), near at hand, approaching, imminent, threatening, 3' 5; 49, 22; no, 33 towardcnesse (n.), tractableness, docility, 4, 6 trai7tes (n.), devices, schemes, contrivances, 42, 16 trcasor (n.), treasure, 17, 28 trouth, trout he (n.), truth, fidelity, 39, 6, 8; 40, 3; 88. 30; by viy trouthe xyi ovt. my faith, 7, 18- troweth (v.), thinketh, believeth, 36, 23 ti'ueth (n.), truth, 21, 21; 76, 25 trusses (n.), baggage bound (or trussed) up, 19, 31 tuicyon, tuicion (n.), protection, 24, 3; 30, 21 ty77ie (n.), a theme, a subject of discourse, 64, I under (prep.), inferior to, 5, 27 vtideipropped (p. p.), supported from below, 9, 25 vndersettc (p. p.), propped up, 9, 10 vnmetely (adj.), unmeet, unfit, 13, 4; 70, 26 unsuretie (n.), insecurity, 85, 5 untaken (adj.), without being captured, 39, 22 unthriftes (n.), thriftless persons, 29, 19; 67, 16 unto hym warde (pret. and pron.), towards him, 76, i vntothed (adj.), without teeth, 6, 3 upon (prep.), over, 77, 17 tippcwarde (adv.), upward (used of the journey from the provinces toward London), 18, 28 ure (n.), use, experience, 18, 19 use (v.), to be wont, 55, 20 utterly (adv.), entirely, 48, 22 very (adj.), true, real, 70, 23 viage y.), a journey, 59, 27 vitaile (n.), victuals, especially here, animal food, 45, 30 voice (n.), language, spoken purpose, 22, 2 voide (v.), to depart from, 62, 24 voyded, voided (pret.), avoided, 2, 24; 42, 26; (p. p.) 48, 18 voide (v.), to avoid, 48, 19 vyande (n.), provision, means of life, 24, 5 waies (n.), ways, 88, 19 7uaite (v.), to watch, 100, 5 ivarde (n.), prison, confinement, 17, 6 ware (adj.), aware, conscious, 47, 5;

50,31 warely (adv.), warily, carefully, 39, 30 zuariye (adj.), weirdlike, 5. 31 loaste (pret.), wist, knew, 39, 23 waxen (p. p.), grown, waxed, 12, ix way, waye (v.), to weigh, 29, 11; 73 29 zucaked (p. p.), weakened, 34, 3 wcale (n.), welfare, 72, 7; 73, 28 wealth (n.), prosperity, happiness, 84, 31; 88, 20 wealthIII (adj.), conducive to welfare, profitable, 11, 14 wcaponed (p. p.), furnished with weapons, 19, 27 wedde (v.), to attach, bind, 25, 20 zveder (n.), weather, 100, i weene (v.), to think 24, wd, 7uell, (adv.), entirely, quite, 2, 12; 3, 2 7ael (adv.), very, 15,7 wel n.), weal, welfare, prosperity, 7uel named (p. p.), of a good name and character, 69, 19 2f (n.), welfare, 6, 33 ? c; a (v.), to suppose, 12, 19; 51, 21; 90, 14 went (p. p.), weened, thought, 82, 4 iveitfe aboute (pret.), exerted himself, set himself, 79, 26 7ver (pret. subj.), were, should be, 7veried (p. p.), wearied, 85, 27 werish (adj.), deformed, 47, ir ivhati nio-x.), used as an exclamation and introducing a question.

Almost = Tell me 68, 1 what about (prep.), in regard of, in respect of, 68, 32 zczay r (prep.), in respect of, (),, I 7vhere (conj,), whereas, 34, 33 vhereto (adv.), for what reason, 50, I whole (adj.), all of them, 32, 6 whyther, whither con.), whether, 6. 45 7 7; 7 21 et scepe will (adv.), well (but perhaps a misprint in the first edition), 39, wise (n.), manner, fashion, 18, 31 wist, wyst (prep, of wot) knew, 61, 23 wit (v.), to know, 91, 11 withotd (prep.), outside, 47, 28 tvived (p. p.), married to a wife, 61, 5 worldly (adv.), from a worldly point of view, 60, 27 woo7'ship n.), honour, dignity, 11, I worthy (adv.), deservedly, 79, 9 worthe (v.), to become, to befall, woo 7vorthe him = woe befall him, 20, 9 7C'ot, wote (3 s. pres.), knows, 19, i; 49, 21; 85, 2 wot, wote (i s. pres.), know, 40, 22; 90, 31- uote (i pi. pres.), knovv', 44, 13; 66, 32 woteth (3 sing, pres.), knoweth, 49, 16; 70, 13; 78, 32 7vraste (v.), to wrest, 24,-23 juried- xcl.), twisted, turned aside, 88, 6 wyght (yv, blam. e, 15, 11 zvyttyng n.), knowledge, 13, 27 ye (interj.), yea, 18, 2 yeke (adv.), eke, also, 44, 8 j (pret.), yielded, 125, 11 yies (n.), the eyes, 123, 21 ymagine (v.), to imagine, to plan, 46, 19 yourself (pron.), yourselves, 40, 24 yrked (pret.), annoyed, grieved, was irksome, 8, 16 yrrititige (pr. part.), irritating, provoking, 21, 22 zele (n), zealous, anxious care, 36, 10

Cambridge: printed by c. j. clay, m. a. and son, at the university t-RESS.
CAMBRIDGE UNIVERSITY PRESS.
THE PITT PRESS SERIES.
Many of the books in this list can be had in two volumes Text and Notes separately.
I. GREEK.
Aristophanes. Aves Plutus Ranse. By W. C. Green,
M. A., late Assistant Master at Rugby School. 3. td. each.
Vespae. By C. E. Graves, M. A. Nearly ready.
Aristotle. Outlines of the Philosophy of. By Edwin
Wallace, M. A., LL. D. Third Edition, Enlarged, s. 6(i.
Euripides. Heracleidae. By E. A. Beck, M. A. 3-. 6d.
Hercules Furens. By A. Gray, M. A., and J. T.
Hutchinson, M. A. New Edit. 2s.
Hippolytus. By W. S. Hadley, M. A. 2s.
Iphigeneia in Aulis. By C. E. S. Headlam, M. A. 2s. 6d.
Herodotus, Book V. By E. S. Shuckburgh, M. A. 3.
Book VI. By the same Editor, 4j.

Books VIII., IX. By the same Editor. 4. each.

Book VIII. Oh. 1 90. Book IX. Ch. 1 89. By the same Editor. 2s. 6d. each.

Homer. Odyssey, Book IX. By G. M. Edwards, M. A. 2s. 6d.

Book X. By the same Editor. 2s. 6d. Book XXI. By the same Editor. 2s.

Iliad. Bks. VI., XXII., XXIII. By the same. 2s. each.

Lucian. Somnium Charon Piscator et De Luctu. By W. E.

Heitland, M. A., Fellow of St John's College, Cambridge,- s. 6d.

Menippus and Timon. By E. C. Mackie, B. A. 3. 6d.

Platonis Apologia Socratis. By J. Adam, M. A. 3J. 6d.

Crito. By the same Editor. 2s, 6d.

Euthyphro. By the same Editor. 2s. 6d.

Plutarch. Life of Demosthenes. By Rev. H. A. H olden,

Lives of the Gracchi. By the same Editor. 6s.

Life of Nicias. By the same Editor. 5.

Life of Sulla. By the same Editor. 6s.

Life of Timoleon. By the same Editor. 6s.

Sophocles. Oedipus Tyrannus. School Edition. By R. C.

Jebb, Litt. D., LL. D. 4. 6d.

Thucydides. Book VII. By H. A. Holden, M. A., LL. D. 5.

Xenophon. Agesilaus. By H. Hailstone, M. A. 2s. 6d.

Anabasis. By A. Pretor, M. A. Two vols. ys. 6d.

Books I. III. IV. and V. By the same. 2s. each.

Books II. VI. and VII. By the same. 2s. 6d. each.

Xenophon. Cjnropaedeia. Books I. II. By Rev. H. A. Holden, M. A., LL. D. 2 vols. 6s.

Books III. IV. and V. By the same Editor. 5.

Books VI. VII. VIII. By the same Editor. 5.

London: Cambridge Warehouse, Ave Maria Lane. 10393 II. LATIN.

Beda's Ecclesiastical History, Books III., IV. By J. E. B.

Mayor, M. A., and J. R. Lumby, D. D. Revised Edition. 7J. dd.

Books I. II. In the Press.

Caesar. De Bello Gallico, Comment. I. By A. G. Peskett,

M. A., Fellow of Magdalene College, Cambridge, is. 6d. Comment. II. III. af. Comment. I. II. III. 3J. Comment. IV. and V. is. Sd. Comment. VII. as. Comment. VI. and Comment. VIII. js. 6d. each.

De Bello Civili, Comment. I. By the same Editor, y.

Cicero. De Amicitia. De Senectute. By J. S. Reid, Litt. D.,

Fellow of Gonville and Caius College. 3J. 6d. each.

In Gaium Verrem Actio Prima. By H. Cowie, In Q. Caecilium Divinatio et in C. Verrem Actio.

1? y W. E. Heitland, M. A., and H. Cowie, M. A. 3.

Philippica Secunda. By A. G. Peskett, M. A. y. 6d.

Oratio pro Archia Poeta. By J. S. Reid, Litt. D. 2s.

Pro L. Cornelio Balbo Oratio. By the same. is. 6d.

Oratio pro Tito Annio Milone. By John Smyth

Purton, B. D. 2j. 6d.

Oratio pro L. Murena. By W. E. Heitland, M. A. 3.

Pro Cn. Plancio Oratio, by H. A. Holden, LL. D. a s.6d.

Pro P. Cornelio Sulla. By J. S. Reid, Litt. D.- s. 6d.

Somnium Scipionis. By W. D. Pearman, M. A. 2s.

Horace. Epistles, Book I. By E. S. Shuckburgh, M. A. 2s. 6d. Livy. Book IV. By H. M. Stephenson, M. A. 2s. 6d.

Bookv. By L. Whibley, M. A. 2s. 6d.

Book VI. By H. M. Stephenson, M. A. 2s. 6d.

Book IX. By the same Editor. 2s. 6d.

Book XXI. By M. S. Dims dale, M. A. 2s. 6d.

Book XXII. By the same Editor. 2s. 6d.

Book XXVII. By H. M. Stephenson, M. A. 2s. 6d.

Lucan. Pharsaliae Liber Primus. By W. E. Heitland,

M. A., and C. E. Haskins, M. A. is. 6d.

Lucretius, Book V. By J. D. Duff, M. A. 2s.

Ovidii Nasonis Fastorum Liber VI. By A. Sidgwick, M. A.,

Tutor of Corpus Christi College, Oxford, xs. 6d.

Ovidii Nasonis Metamorphoseon Liber I. By L. D. Dowdall,

Quintus Curtius. A Portion of the History (Alexander in India).

By W. E. Heitland, M. A., and T. E. Raven, B. A. With Two Maps. y. 6d.

Vergili Maronis Aeneidos Libri I. XII. By A. Sidgwick,

M. A. I J. 6d. each.

Bucolica. By the same Editor, is. 6d.

Georgicon Libri I. II. By the same Editor. 2s.

Libri III. IV. By the same Editor. 2s.

The Complete Works. By the same Editor. Two vols.

Vol. I. containing the Introduction and Text. y.6d. Vol. II. The Notes. s.6d.

London: Cambridge Warehouse j Ave Maria Lane.

III. FRENCH.

Comeille. La Suite du Menteur. A Comedy in Five Acts.

By the late G. Masson, B. A. 2J.

Polyeucte. By E. G. W. Braunholtz, M. A., Ph. D. 2j.

De Bonnechose. Lazare Hoche. By C. Colbeck, M. A.

Revised Edition. Four Maps. is.

D'Harleville. Le Vieux C libataire. By G. Masson, B. A. 2s. De Lamartine. Jeanne D'Arc. By Rev. A. C. Clapin,

M. A. New edition revised, by A. R. Ropes, M. A. u. 6d.

De Vigny. La Canne de Jonc. By H. W. Eve, M. A. is. 6d. Erckmann-Chatrian. La Guerre. By Rev. A. C. Clapin,

La Baronne de Stael-Holstein. Le Directoire. (Considerations sur la Revolution Fran aise. Troisieme et quatrieme parties.) Revised and enlarged. By G. Masson, B. A., and G. W. Prothero, M. A. 2j.

Dix Annies d'Exil. Livre II. Ohapitres 1 8.

By the same Editors. New Edition, enlarged, ps.

Lemercier. Fredegonde et Brunehaut. A Tragedy in Five
Acts. By GustAVE Masson, B. A. 2j.
Moli re. Le Bourgeois Gentilhomme, Comddie-Ballet en
Cinq Actes. (1670.) By Rev. A. C. Clapin, M. A. Revised Edition, is. 6d.
L'Ecole des Femmes. By G. Saintsbury, M. A. 2s. 6d.
Les Pr cieuses Ridicules. By E. G. W. Braunholtz,
M. A,, Ph. D. IS. Abridged Edition, is.
Piron. La M6tromanie. A Comedy. By G. Masson, B. A. 2s. Ponsard. Charlotte
Corday. By A. R. Ropes, M. A. 2s. Racine. Les Plaideurs. By E. G. W. Braunholtz,
M. A. 2s.
Abridged Edition, is.
Sainte-Beuve. M. Daru (Causeries du Lundi, Vol. IX.).
By G. Masson, B. A. 2s.
Saintine. Picciola. By Rev. A. C. Clapin, M. A. 2s. Scribe and Legouv. Bataille
de Dames. By Rev. H. A.
Bull, M. A. 2s.
Scribe. Le Verre d'Eau. By C. Colbeck, M. A. 2s. Sedaine. Le Pbilosophe sans le
savoir. By Rev. H. A.
Bull, M. A. aj.
Souvestre. Un PMlosophe sous les Toits. By H. W. Eve,
Thierry. Lettres sur Thistoire de France (XIIL XXIV.).
By G. Masson, B. A., and G. W. Prothero, M. A. 2s. 6d.
R cits des Temps Merovingians I III. By Gustave
Masson, B. A. Univ. Gallic, and A. R. Ropes, M. A. With Map. 3.
Villemain. Lascaris ou Les Grecs du XVe Si cle, Nouvelle
Historique. By G. Masson, B. A. 2s.
Voltaire. Histoire du Siecle de Louis XIV. Chaps. I.
XIIL By G. Masson, B. A., and G. W. Prothero, M. A. 2s. 6d. Part IL Chaps. XIV.
XXIV. 2s. 6d. Part III. Chaps. XXV. to end. 2s. 6d.
Xavier de Maistre. La Jeune Sib rienne. Le L preux de la Cite D'Aoste. By G.
Masson, B. A. is. 6d.
London: Cambridge Warehouse, Ave Maria Lane,
PUBLICATIONS OF IV. GERMAN.
Ballads on German History. By W. Wagner, Ph. D. 2s, Benedix. Doctor Wespe.
Lustspiel in fiinf Aufziigen. By
Karl Hermann Breul, M. A., Ph. D. 3.
Freytag. Der Staat rriedrichs des Grossen. By Wilhelm
Wagner, Ph. D.-is.
German Dactylic Poetry. By Wilhelm Wagner, Ph. D. zs. Goethe's Knabenjahre.
(1749 1761.) By W. Wagner, Ph. D.
New edition revised and enlarged, by J. W. Cartmell, M. A. 2.
Hermann und Dorothea. By Wilhelm Wagner,
Ph. D. New edition revised, by J. W. Cartmell, M. A.- s. 6d.
Gutzkow. Zopf und Schwert. Lustspiel in fiinf Aufziigen.
By H. J. Wolstenholme, B. A. (Lond.). 3J. 6d.

Hauffl Das Bild des Kaisers. By Karl Hermann Breul,
M. A., Ph. D., University Lecturer in German. 3.
Das Wirthshaus im Spessart. By the late A.
SchLOTTMANN, Ph. D. and J. W. Cartmell, M. A. 3J.
Die Karavane. By A. Schlottmann, Ph. D. s.
Immermann. Der Oberhof. A Tale of Westphalian Life, by
Wilhelm Wagner, Ph. D. 3J.
Kohlrausch. Dasjaliri8i3. By Wilhelm Wagner, Ph. D. 2s. Lessing and Gellert.
Selected Fables. By Karl Hermann
Breul, M. A., Ph. D. 3J.
Mendelssohn's Letters. Selections from. By J. Sime, M. A. 3-. Raumer. Der erste
Kreuzzug (1095 1099). By Wilhelm
Wagner, Ph. D. 2s.
Riehl. Culturgeschichtliche Novellen. By H. J. Wolstenholme, B. A. (Lond.). 3J.
6d.
Schiller. Maria Stuart. By Karl Hermann Breul, M. A.
Wilhelm Tell. By the same Editor. 2s.6d. Abridged
Edition, is. 6d.
;- Geschichte des Dreissigjahrigen Kriegs. By the same
Editor. 3J.
Uhland. Ernst, Herzog von Schwaben. By H. J. Wolstenholme, B. A. 3J. 6d.
V. ENGLISH.
Bacon's History of the Reign of King Henry VII. By the Rev. Professor Lumby,
D. D. 3J.
Cowley's Essays. By the Rev. Professor Lumby, D. D. 4. Discourse of the
Commonwealf of thys Realme of Englande.
First printed in 1581, and commonly attributed to W. S. Edited from the MSS. by
the late Elizabeth Lamond. the Press
Milton's Comus and Arcades. By A. W. Verity, M. A."
sometime Scholar of Trinity College 3J
Milton's Ode on the Morning of Christ's Nativity, L'Allegro, II Penseroso and
Lycidas. By the same Editor. 2s. 6d.
Milton's Samson Agonistes. By the same Editor. 2s, 6d. Milton's Paradise Lost.
Books I. II. By the same Editor. 2s.
Bks. III. IV. By the same. Preparing,
Books V. VI. By the same. 2s.
Books XI. XII. By the same. 25.
London: Cambridge Warehouse Ave Maria Lam,
THE CAMBRIDGE UNIVERSITY PRESS,
More's History of King Richard III. B3rj. R. LumBY, D. D. 3.6 More's Utopia.
By Rev. Prof. Lumby, D. D. 3. dd. Sidney, Sir Philip. An Apologie for Poetrie. By
E. S.
Shuckburgh, M. a. The Text is a revision of that of the first edition of 1595. 35.
Thales to Cicero, A Sketch of Ancient Philosophy. By
Joseph B. Mayor, M. A. sj. td.

The Two Noble Kinsmen. By the Rev. Professor Skeat,
Litt. D. 3J. 6a'.
VI. EDUCATIONAL SCIENCE.
Comenius, John Amos, Bishop of the Moravians. His Life and Educational Works, by S. S. Laurie, LL. D., F. R. S. E. 3J. 6d.
Education, Three Lectures on the Practice of. L On Marking, by H. W. Eve, M. A. II. On Stimulus, by A. Sidgwick, M. A. III. On the Teaching of Latin Verse Composition, by E. A. Abbott, D. D. 2s.
Stimulus. A Lecture delivered for the Teachers' Training
Syndicate, May, 1882, by A. Sidgwick, M. A. s.
Locke on Education. By the Rev. R. H. Quick, M. A. 3. dd. Milton's Tractate on Education. A facsimile reprint from the Edition of 1673. By O. Browning, M. A. is.
Modern Languages, Lectures on the Teaching of. By C.
COLBECK, M. A. "2.
Teacher, General Aims of the, and Form Management. Two
Lectures delivered in the University of Cambridge in the Lent Term, 1883, by F. W. Farrar, D. D., and R. B. Poole, B. D. ij. 6rf.
Teaching, Theory and Practice of. By the Rev. E. Thring,
M. A., late Head Master of Uppingham School. New Edition. 4s. d.
British India, a Short History of. By E. S. Carlos, M. A., late Head Master of Exeter Grammar School. s.
Geography, Elementary Commercial. A Sketch of the Commodities and the Countries of the World. By H. R. Mill, D. Sc, F. R. S. E. s.
Geography, an Atlas of Commercial. (A Companion to the above.) By J. G. Bartholomew, F. R. G. S. With an Introduction by Hugh Robert Mill, D. Sc. 3.
VII. MATHEMATICS.
Arithmetic for Schools. By C. Smith, M. A, Master of
Sidney Sussex College, Cambridge. 3. Sd.
Elementary Algebra (with Answers to the Examples). By
W. W. Rouse Ball, M. A. 4. td.
Euclid's Elements of Geometry. Books I. IV. By H. M.
Taylor, M. A. 3;. Books I. and II. i. bd. Books III. and IV. IS. 6d. Books V. and VI. In the Press.
Solutions to the Exercises in Euclid, Books I IV. By
W. W. Taylor, M. A. Nearly ready.
Elements of Statics and Dynamics. By S. L. Loney, MA. 7. 6d. Or in two parts. Fart I. Elements of statics. 4. ed. Fart II. Elements of Dynamics. 35. 6d.
Mechanics and Hydrostatics for Beginners. By S. L. Loney,
M. A. 4-f- 6.
An Elementary Treatise on Plane Trigonometry. By E.
W. HobSON, Scd., and C. M. Jessop, M. A. 4. dd.
Other Volumes are in preparation. London: Cambridge Warehouse Ave Maria Lane.
Wijt mxhxitiqt Mt for cj Dols anil Cciueses
General Editor: J. J. S. PEROWNE, D. D., Bishop of Worcester.

" is difficult to commend too highly this excellent series. Guardian.

"The modesty of the general title of this series has, we believe, led many to misunderstand its character and underrate its value. The books are well suited for study in the upper forms of our best schools, but not the less are they adapted to the wants of all Bible students who are not specialists. We doubt, indeed, whether any of the numerous popular commentaries recently issued in this country will be found tnore serviceable for general use. Academy.

Now Ready. Clotk, Extra Fcaff. Svo. With Maps.

Book of Joshua. By Rev. G. F. Maclear, D. D. 2j. dd.

Book of Judges. By Rev. J. J. Lias, M. A. 3. dd.

First Book of Samuel. Byrev. Prof. Kirkpatrick, D. D. 3.6 .

Second Book of Samuel. By the same Editor. 3-. dd.

First Book of Kings. By Rev. Prof. Lumby, D. D. 3. dd.

Second Book of Kings. By Rev. Prof. Lumby, D. D. y. 6d.

Books of Ezra and Nehemiah. By Rev. Prof. Ryle, B. D. 4. 6d.

Book of Job. By Rev. A. B. Davidson, D. D. 5.?.

Book of Psalms. Book L By Prof. Kirkpatrick, D. D. y. 6d.

Book of Ecclesiastes. By Very Rev. E. H. Plumptre, D. D. 5.

Book of Jeremiah. By Rev. A. W. Streame, B. D. 4. 6d.

Book of Ezekiel. By Rev. A. B. Davidson, D. D. 5.

Book of Hosea. By Rev. T. K. Cheyne, M. A., D. D. y.

Books of Obadiah Jonah. By Archdeacon Perowne. 2s. 6d.

Book of Micah. By Rev. T. K. Cheyne, M. A., D. D. is. 6d.

Haggai, Zechariah Malachi. By Arch. Perowne. y. 6d.

Book of Malachi. By Archdeacon Perowne. is.

Gospel according to St Matthew. By Rev. A. Carr, M. A. 2s. 6d.

Gospel according to St Mark. By Rev. G. F. Maclear,

Gospel according to St Luke. By Arch. Farrar, D. D. 4j. 6d. Gospel according to St John. Byrev. A. PLUMMER, D. D. s.6d. Acts of the Apostles. By Rev. Prof. Lumby, D. D. 4. 6d. Epistle to the Romans. By Rev. H. C. G. Moule, M. A. y. 6d. First Corinthians. By Rev. J. J. Lias, M. A. With Map. 2j.

London: Cambridge Warehouse Ave Maria Lane,

Second Corinthians. By Rev. J. J. Lias, M. A. With Map. is. Epistle to the Galatians. By Rev. E. H. Perowne, D. D. s. 6d. Epistle to the Ephesians. By Rev. H. C. G. Moule, M. A. 2s. dd. Epistle to the Philippians. By the same Editor, is. 6d. Epistles to the Thessalonians. By Rev. G. G. Findlay, B. A. is. Epistle to the Hebrews. By Arch. Farrar, D. D. 3. 6d. General Epistle of St James. By Very Rev. E. H. Plumptre,

Epistles of St Peter and St Jude. By Very Rev. E. H.

Plumptre, D. D. s. 6d.

Epistles of St John. By Rev. A. Plummer, M. A., D. D. 3-. dd. Book of Revelation. By Rev. W. H. Simcox, M. A. 35-.

Preparing. Book of Genesis. By the Bishop of Worcester. Books of Exodus, Numbers and Deuteronomy. By Rev.

C. D. GinSBURG, LL. D.

First and Second Books of Chronicles. By Very Rev. Dean
Spence.

Book of Isaiah. By Prof. W. Robertson Smith, M. A. Epistles to the Colossians
and Philemon. By Rev. H. C. G.

Moule, M. A.

Epistles to Timothy Titus. By Rev. A. E. Humphreys, M. A.

Cl)e Smaller Cambrilige asible for rboolsf

"W can cordially reconifiiend this sehes of text-books.""" Church Review.

"The notes elucidate every possible difficulty zviih scholarly brevity and clearness,
and a perfect knowledge of the subject. ' Saturday Review.

' ' Accurate scholarship is obviously a characteristic of their productions, and the
work of simplifcation and condensation appears to have teen Judiciously and skilfully
performed."' Guardian.

Now ready. Price s. each Volume, with Map. Book of Joshua. By J. S. Black, M.
A. Book of Judges. By J. S. Black, M. A. First and Second Books of Samuel. By Rev.
Prof. Ktrk-

PATRICK, D. D.

First and Second Books of Kings. By Rev. Prof. Lumby, D. D. Gospel according
to St Matthew. By Rev. A. Carr, M. A. Gospel according to St Mark. By Rev. G.
F. Maclear, D. D. Gospel according to St Luke. By Archdeacon Farrar, D. D. Gospel
according to St John. By Rev. A. Plummer, D. D. Acts of the Apostles. By Rev. Prof.
Lumby, D. D.

London: Cambridge Warehouse, Ave Maria Lane.

f)t Camftritrge (Bvttk Cesitament for rftoofe anlj Colleges;, with a Revised Text,
based on the most recent critical authorities, and English Notes.

General Editor: J. J. S. PEROWNE, D. D., Bishop of Worcester.

Gospel according to St Matthew. By Rev. A. Carr, M. A.

With 4 Maps. 4. 6d.

Gospel according to St Mark. By Rev. G. F. Maclear, D. D.

With 3 Maps. 4s. 6d.

Gospel according to St Luke. By Archdeacon Farrar.

With 4 Maps. 6.?.

Gospel according to St John. By Rev. A. Plummer, D. D.

With 4 Maps. ts.

Acts of the Apostles. By Rev. Professor Lumby, D. D.

With 4 Maps. 6s.

First Epistle to the Corinthians. By Rev. J. J. Lias, M. A. 3. Second Epistle to the
Corinthians. By Rev. J. J. Lias, M. A. y. Epistle to the Hebrews. By Archdeacon
Farrar, D. D. 3-. 6d. Epistles of St John. By Rev. A. Plummer, M. A., D. D. 4.

General Editor: Rev. J. A. ROBINSON, B. D., Norrisian Professor of Divinity.

Book of Revelation. By the late Rev. W. H. Simcox, M. A.

Nearly ready.

Eonton: C. J. CLAY and SONS,

CAMBRIDGE WAREHOUSE, AVE MARIA LANE.

(Slasfloto: 263, ARGYLE STREET,

Breinigsville, PA USA
18 July 2010
241984BV00001B/76/P